FOCUS ON
VOCABULARY 1
Bridging Vocabulary

Diane Schmitt
Norbert Schmitt
David Mann

PEARSON
Longman

In honor of your retirements:

*To Paul Meara, thank you for helping
us to understand how the mind
processes vocabulary.*

*To Paul Nation, thank you for guiding
us in how to teach vocabulary effectively.*

Focus on Vocabulary 1: Bridging Vocabulary

Pearson Education, 10 Bank Street, White Plains, NY 10606 USA

Staff credits: The people who made up the *Focus on Vocabulary 1* team, representing editorial, production, design, and manufacturing, are Pietro Alongi, John Brezinsky, Dave Dickey, Oliva Fernandez, Christopher Leonowicz, Maria Pia Marrella, Amy McCormick, Jennifer Stem, and Paula Van Ells.
Development editor: Leigh Stolle
Text composition: Rainbow Graphics
Cover and text design: Maria Pia Marrella
Photo credits: Cover, Jodi Cobb/National Geographic Stock; All photos are from Shutterstock.com except for the following: Page 54, RIA Novosti/Alamy; 83, AP Images/Marcio Jose Sanchez; 136, Image Source/Alamy; 184, (middle left) Pictorial Press Ltd/Alamy, (bottom right) Pictorial Press Ltd/Alamy; 186, Dinodia Images/Alamy; 203, Trinity Mirror/Mirrorpix/Alamy.
Text fonts: Helvetica Neue, New Aster

Library of Congress Cataloging-in-Publication Data

Schmitt, Diane, 1963-
  Focus on vocabulary. 1 : bridging vocabulary / Diane Schmitt, Norbert Schmitt, David Mann. -- 2nd ed.
     p. cm.
  Includes index.
  ISBN 0-13-137619-5 -- ISBN 0-13-137617-9 1. Vocabulary--Problems, exercises, etc. 2. Reading (Higher Education)--Problems, exercises, etc. I. Schmitt, Norbert, 1956- II. Mann, David. III. Title.
PE1449.S343 2011
428.1--dc22
                                                                                          2010036452

ISBN-10: 0-13-137619-5
ISBN-13: 978-0-13-137619-9

Printed in the United States of America
2 3 4 5 6 7 8 9 10—V042—15 14 13 12 11

Contents

To the Teacher

Overview

We know that learners need to have a very large vocabulary in order to be able to function in an English environment. Recent research has shown that learners must know as many as 6,000–7,000 word families to be able to understand spoken discourse in a wide variety of contexts. Furthermore, learners also need to know around 8,000–9,000 word families in order to read a range of authentic texts (e.g. novels and newspapers) (Nation, 2006). Of course, learners can cope to some extent with smaller vocabularies than these, but then unknown words will be a recurring problem.

These figures may seem daunting, but even so, they do not fully reflect the learning that students must do. Each word family includes several individual word forms, including the root form (*reflect*), its inflections (*reflected, reflecting, reflects*), and regular derivations (*reflection, reflective*). Nation (2006) shows that the most frequent 1,000 word families average about six members (types per family), decreasing to about three members per family at the 9,000 frequency level. According to his calculations, a vocabulary of 6,000 word families (enabling listening) entails knowing 28,015 individual word forms, while the 8,000 families (enabling wide reading) entails 34,660 words (Schmitt, 2008). However, it cannot be assumed that knowing one word family member implies knowing (or being able to guess) related members. Schmitt and Zimmerman's (2002) advanced learners of English typically knew only some, but not all, of the noun / verb / adjective / adverb members of word families they studied.

The upshot is that learners must learn a very large number of words to be successful English users. Unfortunately, learners typically fall well short of the size requirements reported here. Laufer (2000) surveyed a number of international teaching contexts and found that some university students knew around 4,000 word families (after 1,800–2,400 hours of instruction). However, the majority of learners she surveyed only knew between 1,000 and 2,000 word families. These learners did know some or all of the most frequent word families in English (often considered the most frequent 2,000) but had woefully inadequate vocabulary sizes compared to the requirements outlined here.

What are teachers to do about this typical deficiency in vocabulary size? Clearly, the long-term goal of 6,000–7,000 or 8,000–9,000 words requires extended study, but in the short term, it makes sense to work towards a more achievable interim objective. For learners who have most of the high-frequency, first 2,000 families in place, the obvious target is the next frequency band, that is, 3,000–4,000.

Focus on Vocabulary 1: Bridging Vocabulary focuses on just this vocabulary. This vocabulary can be considered "bridging vocabulary" as it exists between high-frequency vocabulary (which mainly expresses basic everyday concepts) and the less frequent, extensive vocabulary, which allows the expression of precise, nuanced, and stylistically appropriate communication. After your students have mastered this bridging vocabulary, they should be able to talk about a wider range of topics and use English with more precision. This should put them on the threshold of using English for more academic or formal purposes if they wish. As such, we see this book as a very good foundation for the more academic vocabulary and style found in *Focus on Vocabulary 2: Mastering the Academic Word List*.

In this book, we explicitly teach 504 word families from the 3,000–4,000 frequency band, although the majority of them are from the easier 3,000 band. It would have been possible to include more words in this book, but there is always a compromise between teaching many words in a cursory fashion and teaching fewer words in greater depth. The words in the 3,000–4,000 band are still relatively high frequency vocabulary, and so need to be learned well. Also, it must be remembered that we are teaching *word families*, and so the number of individual words taught will number in the thousands. In order to help students gain a reasonable mastery of these words, we have drawn on the latest vocabulary research to design the most beneficial exercises. The key rationale behind the pedagogy in this book can be summarized in the following points.

- Words must be encountered numerous times to be learned. Nation (1990) reviewed the literature and concluded that it takes from five to sixteen or more repetitions for a word to be learned. In every chapter of *Focus on Vocabulary 1*, each target word appears at least four times, and most appear many more times elsewhere in the book. The Strategy Practice chapters and Unit Tests provide additional recycling opportunities.

- Learning a word entails more than knowing its meaning, spelling, and pronunciation (Schmitt, 2000). In fact, there are a number of other types of word knowledge, including a word's collocations, grammatical characteristics, register, frequency, and associations. In order to use a word with confidence, a learner must have some mastery of all of these types of word knowledge. Some can be taught explicitly (for example, meaning and spelling), while others can only be truly acquired through numerous exposures to a word (for example, frequency and register information). Our extensive recycling can help learners gain intuitions about types of word knowledge that are best learned in context. We have provided exposures to the target vocabulary in both reading passages and in a number of exercise sentences, which model as many different contexts as possible. At the same time, our exercises focus on elements that can be explicitly taught. Every chapter focuses on meaning, the derivative forms of a word (word families), and collocation.

- Students learn best when their attention is focused on the material to be learned (Schmidt, 1990). To make the target words more noticeable, we have placed them in **bold** type in the chapters in which they are the target words. However, to avoid excess clutter, recycled target vocabulary is not boldfaced in subsequent chapters.

- Learners typically do not know all of the members of a word family, even if they know some of these word forms (Schmitt and Zimmerman, 2002). However, a learner must know the correct form of a word (noun, verb, adjective, adverb) for a particular context. Thus, every chapter has a section (Word Families) that deals with the derivative forms of the target words.

- Equally important for the natural use of words is collocation. These word partnerships are actually difficult to teach, but we feel that collocation is so important to the appropriate use of vocabulary that we have included a collocation section in each chapter (Collocation). The exercises explicitly teach a number of collocations for the target words. However, as it is impossible to teach all of the collocations for a word, the tasks are best seen as exercises that help make learners more aware of collocations in general and may help students build their collocation intuitions for individual words more rapidly.

- In order to ensure that the information in this book reflects the actual usage of the target words, we have researched a number of corpora, including the 263 million-word New Longman Corpus. This has allowed us to empirically determine how the target words behave in real contexts. This was particularly useful in identifying the collocations of the words, because intuitions are often unreliable in this area. In addition, the examples and sentence exercises in this book are informed by the patterns and constructions found in the corpus, and so are authentic in nature.

Organization of the Book

The book is divided into seven units, with each unit focusing on a specific subject. Within each unit, there are four chapters—three main chapters plus a Strategy Practice chapter that presents additional information and chances to recycle the target vocabulary.

MAIN CHAPTERS

Each of the three main chapters is organized as follows.

Getting Started provides warm-up questions about the chapter topic. The questions' main purpose is to activate students' prior knowledge about the topic before they read the passage. The questions also usually ask about the students' life or ideas, and so can be used as a more general discussion starter as well.

Assessing Your Vocabulary Knowledge: Target Words presents twenty-four target words and asks students to assess their knowledge of each word both before and after they work through the chapter (Revisiting the Target Words). The assessment test is taken from Schmitt and Zimmerman (2002) and views vocabulary learning as incremental. Thus, even if students do not achieve productive mastery of every word by the time the chapter is finished, the test can show partial improvement (for example, from *no knowledge* to *receptive knowledge*). By avoiding a *no knowledge / full mastery* dichotomy, the test can show smaller degrees of learning. We would expect every student to learn enough about the target words to show some improvement on this test, which should maintain and enhance their motivation.

Reading presents a reading passage that has been graded in difficulty to be suitable for the level of student learning the 3,000–4,000 frequency band of vocabulary. The embedding of the target vocabulary in these texts ensures that it is not introduced in isolation, but in meaningful contexts. There is also a great deal of target vocabulary in these texts that is not specifically focused on in the chapter, and that provides natural recycling in new contexts of words students have already studied.

In addition, the passages are suitable for a wide range of reading-based tasks if you so desire. This integration of reading and vocabulary allows the study of lexis in programs that have a reading focus, and promotes the beneficial concurrent improvement of reading and vocabulary skills. For example, at the end of each passage, we include six questions (Reading Comprehension) that focus on comprehension ranging from literal details to opinions about the issues raised by the text. We also provide the word counts for each main passage to allow you to use the passages for timed-reading purposes. Timed reading of already familiar passages gives students practice in developing fluent reading skills.

Focusing on Vocabulary features the following sections.

- **Word Meaning** features a variety of exercises designed to help students learn the meaning of each of the twenty-four target words. Some of the tasks are deductive in nature, and some are inductive, catering to a range of learning styles.

- **Word Families** provides practice in recognizing and using the various derivative word forms that make up a word's family (*behave, behavior, behavioral*).
- **Collocation** exercises are designed to improve students' intuitions about the collocations a word takes (*human behavior, behavior modification*).

Expanding the Topic provides various reading, discussion, and writing activities that recycle the target words and expand students' word knowledge in new ways.

STRATEGY PRACTICE

The fourth chapter in each unit is a Strategy Practice chapter that gives students another chance to engage with many of the word families they have studied in the unit while at the same time developing vocabulary learning strategies. Each Strategy Practice chapter begins with a Getting Started section and ends with a Focusing on Vocabulary Cards section. The Strategy Practice chapters deal with a variety of topics. For example, in Chapter 4, dictionary use is discussed. In Chapter 8, the focus is on essay writing. The remaining Strategy Practice chapters (12, 16, 20, 24, 28) also have a Learning More about Words section as well as a reading skills section. The Strategy Practice chapters are thus a combination of recycling, focusing on word knowledge types, and developing strategies.

Answer Key and Unit Tests

Focus on Vocabulary 1 is accompanied by an online Student Book Answer Key and Unit Tests. The tests give students additional vocabulary practice and assess their word knowledge.

Focus on Vocabulary 1 draws on our vocabulary research and many years of experience teaching vocabulary. We hope that you enjoy using it in your classes and that it helps your students learn the type of vocabulary they need to use English in more competent ways. Good luck!

References

Laufer, B. (2000). Task effect on instructed vocabulary learning: The hypothesis of involvement. In *Selected Papers from AILA '99 Tokyo* (pp. 47–62). Tokyo: Waseda University Press.

Nation, I.S.P. (1990). *Teaching and learning vocabulary*. New York: Heinle and Heinle.

Nation, I.S.P. (2006). How large a vocabulary is needed for reading and listening? *Canadian Modern Language Review, 63:1*: 59–82.

Schmidt, R. (1990). The role of consciousness in second language learning. *Applied Linguistics, 11*: 129–158.

Schmitt, N. (2000). *Vocabulary in language teaching*. Cambridge, UK: Cambridge University Press.

Schmitt, N. (2008). Instructed second language vocabulary learning. *Language Teaching Research, 12*: 329–363.

Schmitt, N., and Zimmerman, C. B. (2002). Derivative word forms: What do learners know? *TESOL Quarterly, 36*: 145–171.

To the Student

Why Study "Bridging" Vocabulary?

We assume you know the most common words in English. Many of these frequent words are taught in schools and occur regularly in reading materials, so you have probably seen them often. However, they mainly refer to common, everyday topics, and you will probably have trouble finding the right word if you want to talk about other things. The words you will study in *Focus on Vocabulary 1* are beyond this basic vocabulary, at the next level. When you learn the vocabulary at this higher level, you will be able to discuss a much wider range of topics and use English words much more precisely. You can think of the vocabulary at this level as forming a "bridge" between the basic vocabulary you already know and the large vocabulary you would eventually like to learn. Bridging vocabulary is also an important step towards using vocabulary in academic situations, in case you want to continue your education in English.

Knowing a Word

In order to use words effectively in your oral and written work, you must know more than simple word meanings. You must expand your knowledge of a word so that you know which meaning fits a particular context. You must learn which word form to use (for example, a noun or a verb) in a specific sentence. In addition, you must learn how to combine words with other words to form commonly used collocations. Many elements of word knowledge are required in order to choose the best word for a particular situation. Some of these elements of word knowledge include the following.

- **Word Meaning:** Many words in English have more than one meaning. You must be careful to use the right meaning for the right context.
- **Word Families:** Most words are part of a "family" of words with a shared meaning. You need to know how the different family members (for example, noun form, adjective form) are spelled and pronounced.
- **Collocation:** Some words appear together frequently. They are "word partners," or collocations. Knowing these word partners can help you sound more natural.
- **Synonyms:** Synonyms have a similar meaning, but there are often some contexts where one synonym is more appropriate than another one.
- **Frequency:** The frequency of a word can make a difference in how it is used. Generally, higher frequency words are more basic and are used in everyday situations, while lower frequency words are usually restricted to specific situations and tend to be more formal.

Vocabulary Learning Strategies

Focus on Vocabulary 1 will help you learn "bridging vocabulary" words. However, to learn them well, you will need to continue meeting and learning these word families outside of this book. This means you will need to use vocabulary strategies to maximize your learning. Below, we describe a number of these vocabulary learning strategies. Complete the activities to see how the strategies can help you learn the words better.

USING A DICTIONARY

One of the most important reasons to use a dictionary is to discover a word's meaning. However, many words have more than one meaning, and you must be careful to choose the one that matches the context.

Below are three meanings of the word **bolt** from the *Longman Dictionary of American English*. Match the meaning to the following three contexts.

Contexts relating to:	Meanings
_____ **1.** weather	**a.** a screw with a flat head and no point, for fastening things together
_____ **2.** being in a hurry	**b.** lightning that appears as a white line in the sky: **a bolt of lightning**
_____ **3.** mechanical things	**c.** to run away suddenly

GUESSING FROM CONTEXT

Guessing the meaning of a new word from context is a very good way to supplement the learning of vocabulary from a book like this. You can get clues from the surrounding words and the construction of the sentences.

Try this example, which has the target word **mood**.

Have you ever been in such a bad **mood** that nothing made you feel happy? Even hearing your favorite song or seeing your best friend would not cheer you up. Negative feelings like this are normal occasionally, but if they last for a long time, friends may begin to consider you moody and might even start avoiding you altogether.

1. What is the meaning of **mood**?

2. What are the clues that helped you discover this meaning?

3. Did you notice the word **moody** and guess that it is part of the same word family? How could this help you understand the meaning of **mood**?

EXTENSIVE READING

Although you gain a lot of benefits from studying words, you also need to see or hear them in many contexts to understand how to use them appropriately. One of the best ways to gain this wide exposure is to read extensively. The repeated exposure to words in reading will help you remember their spellings and meanings, and will also show the other words they commonly occur with. In other words, by reading widely, you will eventually begin to get a feel for which words collocate with the words you are learning.

Look at the ten examples of *habit* in these sentences. Do you notice any collocation patterns?

1. When dieting, you need to develop sensible eating **habits** and continue to exercise.

2. She had an annoying **habit** of tapping her fingers on the table.

3. John ran his fingers through his hair, a nervous **habit** he had never been able to break.

4. His most annoying **habit** was how he always dominated a conversation.

5. Understand your eating **habits**, and you will be one step closer to changing them.

6. The coach finally was able to cure the player's nervous **habit** of rubbing the ball.

7. Many people find smoking an annoying **habit**.

8. Many Americans have poor eating **habits**, consuming far too many calories per day.

9. Her husband had many annoying **habits**, but she loved him just the same.

10. His nervous **habit** of licking his lips disturbed the others in the meeting.

THESAURUS PLUS DICTIONARY

If you want to expand your vocabulary and use the best word for a particular context, then a thesaurus can help you discover new synonyms. However, you need to confirm with a dictionary that a new synonym is appropriate for the particular context. Most thesauruses will list *elderly, ancient,* and *faded* as synonyms of the word *old*. They have similar meanings, but they are not exactly the same.

Check your dictionary and write the word that best fits each sentence.

ancient	elderly	faded	old

1. Sadly, the _____ man was losing his memory and no longer recognized his friends.

2. The _____ curtain no longer contained the bright colors it had when it was new.

3. She threw her _____ desk out in the garbage.

4. The bones they discovered belonged to _____ dinosaurs that used to live in their area.

USING INTERNET TOOLS

Nowadays, there are many Internet sites that can help your learning. One of the best ones for discovering information about words is the *Lextutor* website (http://www.lextutor.ca). One of the things it can show is how frequent words are. *Lextutor* gives frequency information in 1,000-word bands. For example, "1,000" means that the word occurs in the 1,000 most frequent words in English, and "3,000" means that the word occurs in the band between the 2,001 and 3,000 most frequent words. Frequent words can be used in many situations, as they are not restricted to particular contexts. Less frequent words are likely to be used mainly in particular situations, so you must be careful to only use them in these contexts. For example, *old* occurs about 474 times per million words of English and has many uses. On the other hand, *decrepit* occurs only about once per million words. This is because it is mainly used to describe buildings and machinery that are so old that they are falling apart and no longer of any value.

See if you have a feeling for how frequent the following synonyms are. Rank them from **1** (most frequent) to **4** (least frequent). Then go to the *Lextutor* website and click on the "Vocabprofile" and then the "BNC-20" links to take you to the frequency page. Check and see how frequent the words are.

1. _____ essential   2. _____ excellent
   _____ imperative   _____ exquisite
   _____ necessary   _____ magnificent
   _____ vital   _____ superb

VOCABULARY CARDS—A KEY LEARNING STRATEGY

Focus on Vocabulary 1 will teach you many strategies for learning vocabulary words. Using vocabulary cards is one such strategy. Look at the example of a vocabulary card below. This card was created by a Japanese student who wanted to understand and remember the word *horror*. Study the card and read the directions for creating vocabulary cards of your own.

(Front of card)

Part of speech and pronunciation	Word map
horror (n) ˈhɔrɚ	emotion death horror accident war
Word family -id (adj.) -ibly (adv.) -ify (v.)	**Collocations** horror movie horror struck inspire horror

(Back of card)

First language translation of *horror*	Keyword illustration (*horu* = dig)
きょうふ (in Hiragana) 恐怖 (in Kanji)	
Second language definition intense fear, dread	**Example sentence** The family watched in horror as their house burned.

How to Create and Use Vocabulary Cards

To make your own vocabulary cards for the words in this book, follow these steps.

1. Write the English word in the top left corner of the front of the card. Then write the word's meaning in the top left corner of the back of the card. Include anything that tells the meaning, for example, first language translations or English definitions. With this information, you can start using the card to learn the word. The card on page xiii is for a Japanese student learning the English word *horror*; therefore, it has two Japanese translations, one in Hiragana spelling and one in Kanji spelling.

2. When you review the card, add new information to it in the different sections. This will make you think more deeply about the word and will expand your word knowledge. Include the following kinds of information on your card:
   - an example sentence for the word
   - notes on how to form the other members of the word family
   - a word map with related words
   - a list of collocations
   - any other information you find interesting or important

3. Consider adding a memory picture to the card. This is called the keyword technique. In the sample card, the student drew a picture of someone digging up a skeleton because the English word *horror* sounds like the Japanese word *horu* (meaning "dig"), and a skeleton evokes horror.

4. Keep filling out the different sections until you know the word well. For some words, you may need to complete all of the sections. For other words, you may need less information.

5. Keep your cards in a box or folder. Take some cards out and study them often. They are portable, so you can even take them with you and study them on the way to and from school or work. As you learn a word better, move its card toward the back of your box so you will not study it as often. Put cards for new words toward the front, where you will see them more often.

6. Remember to review each word numerous times. Repetition builds your memory of a word. Even after you "know" a word, go back and review it occasionally to make sure you do not forget it. If you do not review, you will lose all of the benefits of your previous study!

As you study the target words in this book, try making vocabulary cards to help you remember the words. Studying with vocabulary cards will enrich the learning process and add to the knowledge gained by doing the exercises in the book.

About the Authors

- **Diane Schmitt** (*Nottingham Trent University*) began teaching English in Japan and currently lives and teaches in the United Kingdom. She is a senior lecturer in EFL/TESOL at Nottingham Trent University, where she teaches in the EAP program and the MA in ELT program. Her interests revolve around issues related to English for academic purposes, materials development, and second language testing. She is a regular presenter at English teaching conferences, in addition to consulting on vocabulary and testing projects.

- **Norbert Schmitt** (*University of Nottingham*) is a professor of applied linguistics at the University of Nottingham. He has authored or co-authored five books on vocabulary teaching and research, and over seventy journal articles and book chapters on vocabulary topics. He is an active researcher in all aspects of second language vocabulary studies and frequently presents at language teaching conferences, in addition to consulting internationally on vocabulary learning and testing issues.

- **David Mann** (*Nottingham Trent University*) began teaching in Pakistan and then moved to Turkey before returning to teach in the United Kingdom. He currently teaches at Nottingham Trent University where he is a subject coordinator for EAP for business students and deputy program leader for the summer EAP program within the EFL/TESOL department. His interests include materials design and teaching English for specific academic purposes.

AUTHORS' ACKNOWLEDGMENTS

We would like to thank Amy McCormick, Leigh Stolle, Christopher Leonowicz, Marian Wassner, and the rest of the team at Longman who have helped to bring this project to fruition. In particular, we are grateful to Longman for allowing us access to their corpus and for providing the concordancing software. Finally, we would like to thank the following reviewers for their valuable comments on earlier versions of the book: Duane S. Fitzhugh, Northern Virginia Community College; Ray Gonzales, Montgomery College, Maryland; Marlise Horst, Concordia University, Montreal; Craig Machado, Norwalk Community College, Connecticut; Christine Meloni, George Washington University, Washington, D.C.; Margaret Plenert, California State University-Fullerton; Alan Shute, Bunker Hill Community College, Massachusetts; Elaine C.G. Wolin, Instructor, Northern Virginia Community College.

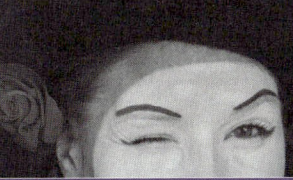

UNIT
1

Happiness

Can We Be Happier?

Getting Started

Discuss the questions with your classmates.

✦ What are the most common things that make people happy?

✦ Do you think it is important to study people's happiness?

✦ When are you happiest?

Assessing Your Vocabulary Knowledge: TARGET WORDS

Look at the words in the box. These are the target words for this chapter. Use the scale to score yourself on each word. After you finish the chapter, score yourself again to check your improvement.

1 I don't know this word.

2 I have seen or heard this word before, but I am not sure of the meaning.

3 I understand this word when I see it or hear it in a sentence, but I don't know how to use it in my own speaking and writing.

4 I know this word and can use it in my own speaking and writing.

TARGET WORDS			
_____assert	_____discipline	_____longing	_____philosophy
_____astonishing	_____esteem	_____manner	_____restaurant
_____boost	_____graft	_____monk	_____review
_____cheerful	_____inherit	_____mystery	_____steak
_____deed	_____instinctively	_____obscure	_____therapy
_____devote	_____intervention	_____pace	_____thrill

KNOWLEDGE CHECK 1

Complete the sentences with words that you have scored as **1**.

1. I am not familiar with the word / term _____.

2. I have no idea what _____ means.

Fill in the first blank with a word that you have scored as **2**. Then complete the sentence.

3. I think _____ could mean _____.

Reading

Why Are You Happy?

1   Are you happy? It is a simple question, one that you can **instinctively** answer with an easy "yes" or "no." However, for some **obscure** reason the question "What *is* happiness?" is more difficult to answer. So too is the question that follows: How do we achieve it?

2   Well, defining happiness is not quite as simple as it might seem. Go into any mall these days and you'll find many people shopping at a frantic **pace**, believing that happiness is the **thrill** of buying a new pair of shoes or the latest high-tech device. Indeed, the idea of happiness has been a topic of much thought and discussion within the fields of **philosophy**, religion, and science for the past 2,500 years. A follower of Confucius, the famous Chinese **philosopher**, would say that happiness is the joy obtained from learning about humanity through social relationships and good **deeds**. Those good **deeds**, however, do not include going to the grocery store because your mother has told you to, or treating yourself to a **steak** at a **restaurant** after a hard day's work. In fact, a Buddhist would say that happiness is the reverse of consumerism, because happiness consists of self-**discipline** and a life without

longing. Another perspective comes from scientists who have demonstrated that 50 percent of happiness is a result of the genes we **inherit** from our parents rather than the jeans we purchase at the mall.

3   So who is right, the shopper, the **philosopher**, the **monk**, or the scientist? Perhaps the answer lies in the field of psychology or, more specifically, positive psychology. In 1998, Martin Seligman, a psychologist at the University of Pennsylvania, gave a speech at the American Psychological Association in which he said that rather than **devoting** attention to unhappiness, psychology needed to change direction and focus instead on people for whom everything was going well. He said psychologists had a reasonably good understanding of depression, but they knew almost nothing about the **mysteries** of a happy life. He argued that if psychologists could isolate what those were, then people might be able to learn how to make themselves more satisfied with and **cheerful** about their lives. This was the beginning of positive psychology.

4   Since then, research on happiness has come up with some **astonishing** facts. If we go back to the mall, shopping can indeed be a source of happiness, but it is significantly less so once your basic needs have been met. The best kind of "retail **therapy**" is to shop for someone else. This is consistent with the Chinese teachings of 2,500 years ago that **assert** that happiness lies in acting within social networks, rather than for our individual benefit only. Again, current research agrees. In 2002, a University of Illinois study found that students with the highest levels of happiness and the fewest signs of depression were those with strong friendship and family networks. Religion facilitates happiness in a similar **manner**. Once again, a **review** of a large number of research studies on the links between religion and happiness has concluded that

there is a positive correlation between religious commitment and higher levels of perceived well-being and self-**esteem**.

5   **Grafting** modern research onto Confucian **philosophy**, we can go back to our original question and say that happiness is a very personal combination of genetics, actions, and beliefs. In the future, it may become a standard practice for therapists to suggest **interventions** that **boost** happiness levels—including thanking people, writing letters to old friends, and hanging out with family. Who knew that learning to feel good could feel so good?

(593 words)

READING COMPREHENSION

Respond to the questions in writing. Base your responses on the reading and your own personal experiences.

1. What does Confucianism say is the source of happiness?

2. How much of our happiness may be the result of our genetic makeup?

3. How did Martin Seligman change the way the field of psychology thinks about human happiness?

4. The passage talks about **grafting** modern research onto Confucian **philosophy**. What does this mean?

5. When was the last time you used shopping to make yourself happy? Did it work?

6. Why do you think strong friendships play such an important role in our happiness?

Focusing on Vocabulary

WORD MEANING

This book presents a variety of strategies for learning and remembering the meanings of target words. Sometimes you will be able to find clues to a word's meaning, or definition, in the sentence in which the word appears. In other cases, the sentence will not contain clear clues to word meaning. You may need to reread the section in which the word appears and think about the ideas presented in the text. If you are still unsure of the correct definition, you may need to look the word up in a dictionary.

A. Match the target words with their definitions. If you are unsure about a word's meaning, try to figure it out from the context by rereading the passage. Then check your dictionary. The first one has been done for you.

Set 1

___g___ **1. instinctively**
_____ **2. philosophy**
_____ **3. deed**
_____ **4. restaurant**
_____ **5. mystery**
_____ **6. manner**
_____ **7. graft**

a. something a person does, especially something that is very good or bad
b. a place where you can buy and eat a meal
c. the way in which something is done or happens
d. an event, situation, etc., that people do not understand or cannot explain because they do not know enough about it
e. to add something very different to something, so that it becomes part of it
f. the study of the nature and meaning of existence, truth, good, and evil
g. occurring because of a natural tendency to behave in a particular way or a natural ability to know something that is not learned

Set 2

_____ **1. pace**
_____ **2. steak**
_____ **3. inherit**
_____ **4. monk**
_____ **5. devote**
_____ **6. therapy**
_____ **7. esteem**

a. the speed at which something happens or is done
b. treatment that helps someone feel better or grow stronger
c. to use all or most of your time and effort in order to do something or help someone
d. to be born with the same character or physical appearance as your parents
e. a feeling of respect for someone, or a good opinion of someone
f. a large, thick piece of good-quality red meat
g. a member of an all-male religious group that lives apart from other people

B. Read each target word and the list below it. One word or phrase in each list is NOT a synonym for the target word. Cross it out. The first one has been done for you.

1. **obscure**

   unclear   vague   ~~precise~~   difficult to understand

2. **thrill**

   boredom   excitement   pleasure   adventure

3. **discipline**

   control   regulation   restraint   indulgence

4. **longing**

   desire   dislike   wish   want

5. **cheerful**

   serious   happy   positive   joyful

6. **astonishing**

   amazing   predictable   surprising   shocking

7. **assert**

   state   declare   claim   deny

8. **review**

   evaluation   assessment   description   proposal

9. **intervention**

   interference   inactivity   treatment   interruption

10. **boost**

    increase   enhance   improve   limit

WORD FAMILIES

Most words belong to a "family" of words with a shared meaning. For example, the words *serious*, *seriousness*, and *seriously* are related to each other—they are word forms in the same family. In the reading "Why Are You Happy?" forms of the word *happy* appear nineteen times. The differences in the spelling indicate parts of speech (verb, noun, adjective, adverb).

Verb	Noun	Adjective	Adverb
X	happiness	happy	happily

Notice the endings for *happiness* and *happily*. These spelling patterns are common at the end of certain noun and adverb forms. However, notice also that there isn't a verb form of the word *happy*. If you aren't sure of the form of a word or if there is a form of the word you don't recognize, you can look the word up in a dictionary.

A. The table contains word families for some of the target words in the reading. Complete the table. An **X** indicates that there is no form or that the form is not common. Sometimes more than one form may be possible. If you are unsure about a form, check your dictionary. The first one has been done for you.

Verb	Noun	Adjective	Adverb
assert	assertion		
		1. 2. **astonishing**	
	1. 2.	1. **cheerful** 2.	
devote			
X		1. 2.	**instinctively**
	longing		
X	**mystery**		
		obscure	
	philosophy		
	thrill	1. 2.	

B. Choose the correct form of the word in **bold** in sentence **a** to complete sentence **b**. Use the word families table you just completed as a guide. The first one has been done for you.

1. a. The United States **asserted** its independence from Great Britain in 1776, but it did not become a reality until the end of the War of Independence in 1783.

   b. The government's _____ assertion _____ that the recession was over did little to reassure the small businesses that were still struggling.

2. a. Happiness experts have discovered some **astonishing** facts.

   b. I was _____ to discover that some people are born with a greater capacity for happiness than others.

3. a. Her **cheerful** personality was appreciated by all her coworkers.

   b. The fans were instantly _____ up by the late goal, which gave their team the win.

4. a. Most parents are very **devoted** to their children.

   b. Her _____ to her studies paid off with high grades.

5. **a.** Flying south in the autumn is an **instinctive** behavior of birds.

 b. Parents often _____ know when their children are lying or telling the truth.

6. **a.** The new clothes, cars, and other things we **long** for don't necessarily make us happier.

 b. She looked _____ at the shoes in the store.

7. **a.** The **mystery** of *Flight 19*, a group of five Navy airplanes that disappeared over the Bermuda Triangle, has never been solved.

 b. A number of musicians have died under _____ circumstances, including Brian Jones from the Rolling Stones and Jim Morrison from the Doors.

8. **a.** The instructions for video games are often so **obscure** that it is much easier to learn to play through trial and error than by reading the instruction manual.

 b. The _____ of many legal documents means that average people often cannot understand them without the help of a lawyer.

9. **a.** **Philosophy** is one of the major subjects studied at university.

 b. He was _____ about the loss of his job and used it as a means of moving into a different career.

10. **a.** She got a real **thrill** when her daughter won the swimming race.

 b. Parachuting over the desert was truly _____.

COLLOCATION

When you look at words in context, you can see patterns in the way they are used. These patterns are not based on rules of grammar, but on traditions of use by native speakers. Certain words tend to occur together, and this is called *collocation*.

> **Example:**
> We say *ice cold*.
> But we do not say *snow cold*.

Sometimes the link between word partners and their meaning is clear and unsurprising—for example, the collocations *bright light* and *heavy load*. Other times, the link may be unexpected—for example, the collocations *bright child* and *heavy heart*. Here are some typical collocation patterns.

> **Example:**
> noun + verb   *birds sing*
> verb + noun   *deliver babies*
> adjective + noun   *specific information*
> verb + adverb   *breathe heavily*
> noun + noun   *bear market*

Because collocations are not based on rules of grammar, the patterns for each word are one of a kind. Therefore, you must build up your knowledge of collocations one at a time. This section introduces a sample of the patterns you need to know in your reading and writing. Apply your growing understanding of collocations to new words and words you already know.

Read the common collocations in the column on the left. Give two examples of things associated with each collocation. The first one has been done for you.

	Example 1	Example 2
1. good **deed**	shopping for neighbor	washing Dad's car
2. inherit property		
3. rare **steak**		
4. leisurely **pace**		
5. physical **therapy**		
6. Buddhist **monk**		
7. rapid **intervention**		

Expanding the Topic

An important part of developing your vocabulary involves forming and supporting opinions about the topic you are studying. Read the statements and indicate whether you agree (**A**) or disagree (**D**). Then discuss your opinions and reasoning with a partner.

_____ **1.** Studying **philosophy** can lead to a happier and more peaceful existence.
_____ **2.** Eating at **restaurants** with your family is a good way to build family ties.
_____ **3.** **Grafting** some fixed relaxation time onto a busy schedule may lead not only to a less hectic lifestyle, but also to a healthier mind and body.
_____ **4.** Strict self-**discipline** is the best road to happiness.
_____ **5.** Writing a diary is the best way to **review** how happy you are.
_____ **6.** Self-**esteem** is dependent on the possessions you have.
_____ **7.** Achieving a calm, relaxed **manner** will **boost** your sense of happiness.
_____ **8.** We should **devote** most of our lives to being happy.

Write a 500-word essay on one of the statements above explaining why you agree or disagree with it.

Revisiting the Target Words

Now that you have completed this chapter, use the scale to describe your knowledge of the target words.

1 I still don't know anything about this word.

2 I am still not sure of the meaning of this word even after studying it.

3 I understand this word when I see it or hear it in a sentence, but I don't know how to use it in my own speaking and writing.

4 I know this word and can use it in my own speaking and writing.

TARGET WORDS

_____assert	_____discipline	_____longing	_____philosophy
_____astonishing	_____esteem	_____manner	_____restaurant
_____boost	_____graft	_____monk	_____review
_____cheerful	_____inherit	_____mystery	_____steak
_____deed	_____instinctively	_____obscure	_____therapy
_____devote	_____intervention	_____pace	_____thrill

KNOWLEDGE CHECK 2

Select examples from the words you now give a score of **3** or **4**, but didn't at the start of the chapter, to complete the sentences.

1. I didn't know that _____ meant _____ before reading this chapter.

2. I wasn't sure that I knew the meaning of _____, but I am now.

3. I now am confident that I know what _____ means, but I would like more practice with how to use it in my speaking and writing.

4. I could next use _____ when I am _____.

Into the Flow

Getting Started

Discuss the questions with your classmates.

✦ What do you normally do in the afternoons or evenings after class? Why do you choose those activities?

✦ Have you ever experienced the feeling of being on a "high"? What kind of activity or situation brought about that feeling?

✦ What kind of activities make you feel excited and challenged at the same time?

Assessing Your Vocabulary Knowledge: TARGET WORDS

Look at the words in the box. These are the target words for this chapter. Use the scale to score yourself on each word. After you finish the chapter, score yourself again to check your improvement.

1 I don't know this word.

2 I have seen or heard this word before, but I am not sure of the meaning.

3 I understand this word when I see it or hear it in a sentence, but I don't know how to use it in my own speaking and writing.

4 I know this word and can use it in my own speaking and writing.

TARGET WORDS			
____absorbed	____explode	____intellectual	____peer
____ache	____feedback	____interval	____strive
____amusement	____fictional	____lung	____tension
____confront	____fiercely	____medal	____thus
____distracted	____fulfillment	____motivation	____trivial
____drift	____gripped	____overcome	____worthwhile

KNOWLEDGE CHECK 1

Fill in the first blank with a word that you have scored as **2**. Then complete the second sentence.

1. I have seen / heard _____. I saw / heard it while I was

   _____.

Fill in the first blanks with words that you have scored as **4**. Then complete the sentences.

2. One meaning of _____ is _____.

3. I last used the word _____ while I was _____.

Reading

Getting into the Flow

1   Do you ever find yourself so completely **gripped** by what you are doing that you lose track of time? All of a sudden you look up at the clock and realize that hours have passed? This could apply to a basketball player **absorbed** in perfecting a shot, or a violinist **fiercely** concentrating on a piece of music. When does this total engagement and loss of time typically occur for you?

2   Contrary to what many believe, these moments in our lives are not passive, receptive, relaxing times. These moments are when the body or mind is voluntarily stretched to its limits in order to accomplish something difficult and **worthwhile**. In turn, we later reflect on these moments as great experiences. It's fair to say then that great experiences don't happen to us; they are something we *make* happen.

3   However, such experiences are not necessarily pleasant at the time they occur. Take Olympic gold **medal**-winning swimmer Michael Phelps as an example. His muscles might have **ached** during his most memorable races, his **lungs** might have felt like they would **explode**, and he might have felt **overcome** with tiredness. Yet these were probably the best moments of his life. He was in control and able to accomplish his goals. Getting control of life is never easy, and it can be painful. But in the long run, great experiences like these add up to a sense of mastery that comes as close to happiness as anything else we can possibly imagine.

4   The loss of self-consciousness that happens when you are completely **absorbed** in an activity—**intellectual**, social, or physical—is described in psychology as a state of *flow*. It is called flow because people regularly describe the experience as similar to **drifting** along with the flow of a river. You don't have to be an Olympic swimmer or star musician to experience flow. In order to achieve flow, you must experience an activity as voluntary and enjoyable, and it must require skill and present an achievable challenge, with the goal being success. You must feel as though you have control and receive immediate **feedback** about your performance with room for growth. **Thus**, you can achieve flow while reading a good book or while fixing your car.

5   A growing body of research supports the notion that by **confronting** and meeting challenges, anyone can create flow in their life. What this means is that we should not aim for a life without stress or **tension** because these pressures actually encourage us to **strive** toward self-**fulfillment**, or the achievement of our hopes and ambitions.

6   Scientists such as Mihaly Csikszentmihalyi (pronounced: me-hay chick-sent-me-hay) study the impact of flow states on human happiness, productivity, and success. In one study, 250 high-flow and low-flow teenagers were asked to report on their feelings and activities at regular **intervals**. The high-flow teenagers generally reported more time spent on hobbies, sports, and homework, and measured higher levels of self-esteem and engagement. Interestingly, however, they self-reported lower levels of fun than the low-flow teenagers. Apparently, high-flow teenagers see their low-flow **peers** as experiencing more fun engaging in low-flow **amusements**, such as video games, TV, and socializing. However, the high-flow teenagers end up having greater long-term happiness as

well as success in school, social relationships, and careers.

7   If flow has such incredible benefits for our happiness, relationships, and success, then why do we usually choose to let ourselves be **distracted** by low-flow, and arguably **trivial**, activities? Why do we often choose our favorite TV program over an engaging **fictional** novel or game of basketball? One hypothesis is that high-flow activities require more initial **motivation** because they require skill and concentration. In other words, high-flow activities are work—but work that pays off!

(618 words)

Adapted from http://pursuit-of-happiness.org/ sciencehappiness.aspx.

READING COMPREHENSION

Respond to the questions in writing. Base your responses on the reading and your own personal experiences.

1. What are some key characteristics of flow?

2. How can someone achieve flow?

3. What are the main differences between high-flow and low-flow activities?

4. What determines whether someone will engage in a high-flow or low-flow activity?

5. What are the most popular high-flow activities among you and your friends? Why do you find them so interesting and exciting? Do you and your friends achieve flow through the same types of activities?

6. The reading focuses on the benefits of high-flow activities, but can you think of any benefits of low-flow activities?

Focusing on Vocabulary

WORD MEANING

Many words have more than one meaning. When you come across an unfamiliar word in your reading, look up the word in your dictionary. If the word has multiple meanings, use context clues—words and phrases around the word—to figure out which meaning fits.

A. Read the target words. Use the paragraph number in parentheses to locate and reread the word in context. Then read the dictionary definitions and choose the one that reflects how the word is used in the reading. The first one has been done for you.

   _a_   **1. gripped** (1)
      a. deeply engaged, interested
      b. strongly affected by something

        2. absorbed (1)
      a. very interested in something, often to the point of not noticing other things happening around you
      b. when light, heat, or energy is taken in and kept, not reflected

        3. fiercely (1)
      a. energetically and with strong feelings
      b. angrily or in a frightening or attacking manner

_____ **4. ache** (3)

    a. to feel a continuous but not very sharp pain in a part of your body

    b. to want to do or have something very much

_____ **5. explode** (3)

    a. to burst into small pieces, making a loud noise and causing damage

    b. to suddenly increase greatly in number, amount, or degree

_____ **6. overcome** (3)

    a. able to successfully control a feeling or problem that would prevent you from achieving something

    b. unable to act or think in the usual way

_____ **7. intellectual** (4)

    a. a person who is well educated and interested in serious ideas

    b. needing serious thought in order to be understood

_____ **8. drift** (4)

    a. to move slowly on water or in the air

    b. to move, change, or do something without any plan or purpose

_____ **9. confront** (5)

    a. to deal with something very difficult or unpleasant in a brave and determined way

    b. to face someone in a threatening way, as though you are going to attack the person

_____ **10. tension** (5)

    a. a nervous feeling that makes it impossible to relax

    b. the difference between the needs or influences of two things, which causes problems

_____ **11. fulfillment** (5)

    a. the feeling of being happy and satisfied with your life because you are doing interesting, useful, or important things

    b. the act of doing something that you promised or agreed to do

_____ **12. motivation** (7)

    a. an eagerness and willingness to do something without needing to be told or forced

    b. the reason why you want to do something

B. Read the target words in the box. Complete each sentence with the target word that matches the meaning of the words in parentheses. You may need to change the form of the word to fit the sentence. The first one has been done for you.

amusement	fictional	medal	thus
distracted	interval	peer	trivial
feedback	lung	strive	~~worthwhile~~

1. Supporters of democracy believe that "life, liberty, and the pursuit of happiness" are not only ____worthwhile____ but also basic human rights.
   (valuable, meaningful)

2. Schoolchildren take standardized tests at preset _____ to find out whether or not they are achieving at the expected level for their age.
   (period, time)

3. Mihaly Csikszentmihalyi has found that teens who spend large amounts of time with _____ instead of doing challenging activities fail to develop their abilities.
   (friend, classmate)

4. When left-handed people try to throw a baseball with their right hand, they may get negative internal _____ highlighting how uncomfortable the action is.
   (response, advice)

5. There are many everyday activities that we do not enjoy but cannot avoid, _____, no one can be in the flow all of the time.
   (therefore, so)

6. It can be very easy to fill your time with _____ tasks and finish the day realizing you haven't done very much at all.
   (not valuable, unimportant)

7. Finishers' _____ and event T-shirts provide extra **motivation** for ordinary runners to participate in road races.
   (award, prize)

8. Everyday _____ such as flying kites and playing video games have the potential to bring about flow if they present the right level of challenge.
   (hobby, activity)

9. In the _____ world of Second Life, an online virtual reality game, residents can create and trade items and services with one another.
   (imaginary, made-up)

10. There are no shortcuts to a fully experienced life; humans must continually _____ to explore, develop, and achieve.
    (make every effort, try hard)

11. Aspects of modern lifestyles such as housing and diet are linked to increases in asthma, a medical condition that affects the small tubes that carry air in and out of the _____.
    (chest, body organ for breathing)

12. For someone who is easily _____, achieving flow is more difficult than for those who can easily concentrate on a task.
    (unfocused, inattentive)

WORD FAMILIES

Most of the target words introduced in this chapter are part of a word family. By learning the other members of a word's family, you can recognize words more quickly when you read or listen, and express yourself more clearly when you write or speak. Spelling patterns can help you identify a word's part of speech.

A. The table contains word families for some of the target words in the reading. An **X** indicates that there is no form or that the form is not common. Study the table. Look for spelling patterns for the noun, adjective, and adverb forms of the words. List the patterns in the space below the table. The first one has been done for you.

Verb	Noun	Adjective	Adverb
absorb	absorption	1. **absorbed** 2. absorbing	**X**
ache	ache	1. aching 2. achy	**X**
confront	confrontation	confrontational	**X**
distract	distraction	1. **distracted** 2. distracting	distractingly
explode	explosion	1. exploded 2. exploding	**X**
X	fierceness	fierce	**fiercely**
fulfill	**fulfillment**	1. fulfilled 2. fulfilling	**X**
intellectualize	intellectual	**intellectual**	intellectually
motivate	**motivation**	1. motivated 2. motivating 3. motivational	**X**
tense	**tension**	tense	tensely

nouns ___+ -tion / -ion_____

adjectives _____

adverbs _____

B. Complete each sentence with the correct form of the word in parentheses. Use the word families table to help you. The first one has been done for you.

1. The girl's total ___absorption___ (**absorbed**) in her book meant that she didn't hear her mother tell her to come to dinner.

2. Even her _____ (**ache**) muscles couldn't take away her joy at achieving a personal best time in the marathon.

3. Instead of _____ (**confront**) her procrastination problem, she kept herself busy working on **trivial** tasks.

4. To achieve flow at work, you need to establish a situation in your job that provides clear goals, useful feedback, and few _____ (**distracted**).

5. For some people, anger is a noisy _____ (**explode**) of feeling resulting from the buildup of **unfulfilled** desires and expectations.

6. The coach led with a _____ (**fiercely**) that inspired his players.

7. A sense of flow can help people achieve more _____ lives. (**fulfillment**)

8. Chess is considered an _____ (**intellectual**) stimulating game.

9. Negative emotions such as fear and anger can actually _____ (**motivation**) people to take action to improve their lives.

10. Although flow comes from doing challenging activities, attempting tasks that are too difficult may leave one feeling _____ (**tension**) and anxious.

COLLOCATION

You develop your knowledge of collocations by seeing and hearing words in many contexts and noticing which words form partnerships with one another. Remember that the words in a collocation can combine with different parts of speech.

Example:
Parents are often eager for their children to participate in activities that will further their *intellectual* development.
adjective + noun

Combine a word from Column A with a word from Column B to form a collocation. Then, on the next page, match the collocation to its definition. The first one has been done for you.

Column A	Column B
fictional	**interval**
constructive	**medal**
brief	transplant
trivial	character
gripping	exercise
worthwhile	**feedback**
bronze	drama
lung	task

1. _____gripping drama_____ exciting and interesting play, movie, or TV show

2. _____ an imaginary person or creature

3. _____ work that is of little value or importance

4. _____ a prize given to the person who comes in third in a competition

5. _____ moving a body organ from one person to another for medical purposes

6. _____ a short period of time between two activities

7. _____ a beneficial or useful activity

8. _____ useful or helpful advice or information

Expanding the Topic

In everyday life we are often required to retell or restate the ideas and words of others. When we do this, we rarely use the exact same words or sentences we hear or read. Instead, we paraphrase—that is, we restate the same idea or information using our own words and sentence structures. To be successful at paraphrasing, you need to develop a large vocabulary and practice using it.

A. Read the original text and match with the paraphrases.

Originals

_____ **1.** Some people find it easy to achieve flow. They are able to focus their attention easily and can experience flow even in difficult situations. Meanwhile, others have to work hard to focus to achieve flow.

_____ **2.** At the end of a long day, people commonly find it "too difficult" to organize themselves to do more demanding activities and instead engage in effortless ones such as watching TV.

_____ **3.** Flow tends to result in personal growth. By engaging in flow, your skills develop, and you require greater and greater challenges to maintain the "high" of flow.

_____ **4.** The feeling of flow is often compared to pleasure, like the feeling of taking a hot bath. However, unlike flow, pleasure neither requires effort nor gives a sense of achievement.

Paraphrases

a. Because flow experiences lead to personal development, we need to keep **confronting** new challenges in order to achieve new flow experiences.

b. The ability to achieve flow differs from person to person. Some people must **strive** to achieve the levels of concentration needed to meet challenges while others can focus their mind on an activity without any difficulty.

c. Taking a hot bath requires no effort; **thus**, flow cannot be achieved through this simply pleasurable activity.

d. Many people are **overcome** by laziness when they finish work or school, so they end the day by watching TV instead of doing something that might bring more personal **fulfillment**.

B. Now you try. Paraphrase the sentences. Use the target word in your paraphrase. You may need to change the form of the target word.

1. Flow is achieved when an experience is so enjoyable that it is like being carried away by a current with everything moving smoothly without effort.

   drift _____

   _____

2. Researchers have interviewed over 10,000 people around the world—women who weave tapestries in the highlands of Borneo, factory workers in the United States, motorcycle riders in Japan—and these people have all said similar things. So flow seems to be an experience that is the same across cultures.

   thus _____

   _____

3. U.S. teenagers experience flow about 13 percent of the time that they spend watching TV, 34 percent of the time they do hobbies, and 44 percent of the time they are involved in sports and games. Yet these same teenagers spend at least four times more of their free hours watching TV than doing hobbies or sports.

   amusement _____

   _____

4. Contrary to what one might expect, Mihaly Csikszentmihalyi found that adolescents from disadvantaged backgrounds have higher levels of enthusiasm and optimism than those from affluent backgrounds.

   peer _____

   _____

Mihaly Csikszentmihalyi and others have carried out a number of research studies investigating the concept of flow. Find an example of a research study on flow and write a 400–500 word summary of the study.

Revisiting the Target Words

Now that you have completed this chapter, use the scale to describe your knowledge of the target words.

1 I still don't know anything about this word.

2 I am still not sure of the meaning of this word even after studying it.

3 I understand this word when I see it or hear it in a sentence, but I don't know how to use it in my own speaking and writing.

4 I know this word and can use it in my own speaking and writing.

TARGET WORDS

____absorbed	____explode	____intellectual	____peer
____ache	____feedback	____interval	____strive
____amusement	____fictional	____lung	____tension
____confront	____fiercely	____medal	____thus
____distracted	____fulfillment	____motivation	____trivial
____drift	____gripped	____overcome	____worthwhile

KNOWLEDGE CHECK 2

Select examples from the words you now give a score of **3** or **4**, but didn't at the start of the chapter, to complete the sentences.

1. I didn't know that _____ meant _____ before reading this chapter.

2. I wasn't sure that I knew the meaning of _____, but I am now.

3. I now am confident that I know what _____ means, but I would like more practice with how to use it in my speaking and writing.

4. I now know that _____ collocates with _____.

Happiness in Bhutan

Getting Started

Discuss the questions with your classmates.

✦ Can money buy happiness?

✦ Is the government responsible for its citizens' happiness?

✦ What can governments do to improve happiness in a country?

Assessing Your Vocabulary Knowledge: TARGET WORDS

Look at the words in the box. These are the target words for this chapter. Use the scale to score yourself on each word. After you finish the chapter, score yourself again to check your improvement.

1 I don't know this word.

2 I have seen or heard this word before, but I am not sure of the meaning.

3 I understand this word when I see it or hear it in a sentence, but I don't know how to use it in my own speaking and writing.

4 I know this word and can use it in my own speaking and writing.

TARGET WORDS			
____ambition	____drugstore	____planet	____relevant
____clinic	____engagement	____pollution	____rural
____conservation	____flourish	____preserve	____spoil
____dictate	____foster	____priority	____tackle
____dispute	____founded	____prosperity	____vastly
____divorce	____outlook	____pursue	____vice

KNOWLEDGE CHECK 1

Check your progress in learning the vocabulary in this chapter.

- First, look at your scores in the table on page 21. Write the number of words for each score (1–4) in the "at the beginning" column. For example, if you scored eight words as **1** ("I don't know this word"), then write **8**.

- At the end of the chapter, score yourself again. Then compare the two sets of scores. For example, if six of the words you originally scored as **1** are now scored higher (**2**, **3**, or **4**), write **6** in the "showing improvement" column. Write **2** in the "no improvement yet" column for words where your knowledge hasn't changed. Are you showing improvement on most of the words in the chapter?

Your score	Number of words …		
	at the beginning:	at the end:	
		showing improvement	no improvement yet
EXAMPLE:	8	6	2
1			
2			
3			
4			

Reading

The passage describes how the government of Bhutan, a small country in Southeast Asia, has officially made the happiness of its citizens the number one **priority**. As you read, pay special attention to the target vocabulary words in **bold**.

Gross National Happiness

1   It is a widely held myth that material **prosperity** makes people happy. In fact, a key factor that **dictates** happiness is social relationships. People who rate themselves as happy tend to have regular and supportive **engagement** with family and friends. They also feel their work is valuable and **relevant**. Likewise, their personal situation is important: whether they are satisfied with themselves, their progress toward their personal goals, and their religious or spiritual life.

2   Med Yones, president of the International Institute of Management, developed a seven-category scale that measures a nation's mental and emotional health. Taken together, the categories can be seen as an overall indication of a country's happiness:

1. Economic satisfaction: income, debt, savings
2. Environmental satisfaction: **pollution**, noise, traffic
3. Physical health: severe illnesses, access to **clinics** and **drugstores**
4. Mental health: positive **outlook**, self-esteem
5. Workplace satisfaction: unemployment, job satisfaction, motivation, workplace complaints
6. Social satisfaction (including family and relationship satisfaction): domestic **disputes**, **divorce** rates, social discrimination, crime rates
7. Political satisfaction: quality of local democracy, individual freedom, foreign conflicts

3   One country, Bhutan, has tried to balance the economic and social aspects of happiness in a unique way. Instead of **pursuing** success solely in terms of economic criteria, such as the Gross National Product (an economic measure), Bhutan has established what's known as Gross National Happiness (GNH) as its central national **ambition**. The idea is to **foster** both material and spiritual development so that they both grow hand-in-hand. Bhutan is committed to building an economy that **preserves** its culture, which is **founded** on Buddhist spiritual values. GNH is realized through four principles: sustainable development of the economy (that is, economic growth that can be continued), **preservation** of cultural values, **conservation** of the natural environment, and effective government.

4   Bhutan's decision to make its citizens' happiness a **priority** seems to have had positive results. Even though it ranks quite low in personal income (124th in the world), it ranks much higher in happiness ratings. A 2005 survey revealed that nearly all Bhutanese reported being either very happy (45 percent) or happy (52 percent), while only 3 percent reported being unhappy. In 2006, *Business Week* magazine ranked Bhutan as the 8th happiest country in the world, and the happiest in Asia. This is far better than many countries with **vastly** greater wealth, such as the United States (23rd), the United Kingdom (41st), France (62nd), and Japan (90th).

5   Furthermore, this happiness appears not to have come at the expense of the environment. The Happy **Planet** Index, a combined measure of human well-being and the environmental

cost of supporting that well-being, ranked Bhutan 17th out of 143 countries. This shows that supporting its happiness does not require **spoiling** its natural resources.

6   So how has Bhutan has been able to **pursue** its unusual GNH? Because it is a small, **rural** country in the Himalayan Mountains, it is able to sustain traditions at the same time it is developing. For example, people entering hospitals with no acute health problems can choose between Western or traditional medicine. However, modern technology, such as TV, video shops, and the Internet, is now becoming more common in the country. This creates challenges for a GNH approach, which has found success by **prioritizing** national identity and culture. On the one hand, such technological exposure might let in outside values and **vices**. For example, it might raise expectations for material goods from outside Bhutan that are not readily available. On the other hand, the Internet and e-mail would undoubtedly offer better communication in a country where mountainous terrain makes travel difficult.

7   It will be interesting to see how Bhutan **tackles** the problems of integrating with the wider world while also **pursuing** its unique "happiness" approach to government. It is certainly a social experiment that we all hope will **flourish** as an example of an alternative vision of what is important in life.

(636 words)

This passage was based on a number of sources, including the Gross National Happiness website: http://www.grossnationalhappiness.com/Default.aspx.

READING COMPREHENSION

Respond to the questions in writing. Base your responses on the reading and your own personal experiences.

1. How does Bhutan rank in world happiness?

2. The passage mentions several things that can make people happy. List these. Then describe which one is most important for your own happiness.

3. What is Gross National Happiness (GNH)?

4. Do you think that the idea of GNH could be used successfully in your home country? Why or why not?

5. Technology such as the Internet can aid communication in a rural country like Bhutan. Can you think of any other advantages?

6. What do you think will happen in the future in Bhutan? Why do you think this?

Focusing on Vocabulary

WORD MEANING

When you encounter an unfamiliar word, use context clues and your previous knowledge to determine the word's meaning. Look at the examples. Suppose that you did not know the exact meaning of the word *flourish* in the following sentences.

Example:
The school created an environment where its students could *flourish*.
(You know schools are places where people develop their skills.)

The effective advertisements helped the new store to *flourish*.
(You know that good advertising can help make businesses successful.)

Clues in both these sentences suggest that *flourish* means "to develop well and be successful."

A. Read the sentences and choose the word or phrase that best matches the meaning of the target word. Use context clues to determine the correct meaning. Check your dictionary if you are not sure of the answer. The first one has been done for you.

1. It is sometimes difficult for people to maintain their **prosperity** once they retire and lose their steady income.

   a. when people have money and everything that is needed for a good life
   b. when people have problems at work
   c. when people have a special interest in something

2. The student wrote about personal debt in America because she thought it was a valuable and **relevant** topic.

   a. directly relating to the subject or problem being discussed
   b. interesting or amusing
   c. concerned with important subjects

3. Coal is a relatively cheap source of energy, but it causes excessive **pollution**.

   a. employment for workers
   b. things that make the environment dirty
   c. profit for companies

4. The United Nations supports a number of health **clinics** in rural parts of Africa where the nearest hospital can be many miles away.

   a. places where marriages are arranged
   b. places where medical treatment is given
   c. places where clothes are made

5. Many doctors believe that having a positive mental **outlook** can lead to better physical health.

   a. general attitude toward life
   b. memory
   c. desire for something

6. The border **disputes** between China and Russia were largely solved by the 1991 Sino-Russian Border Agreement.

    a. industries
    b. disagreements
    c. discussions

7. The **divorce** rate in the United States is very high, with over 40 percent of marriages failing.

    a. legal beginning of a marriage
    b. yearly celebration of the date of a marriage
    c. legal end of a marriage

8. The coach tried to **foster** a positive attitude toward early morning practices.

    a. destroy
    b. design
    c. encourage

9. **Conservation** of our forests and other natural landscapes will allow our children to enjoy them in the future.

    a. protection
    b. sale
    c. admiration

10. The first **priority** of the new government was to increase spending on education. After that, they hoped to make improvements to health care.

    a. difficult problem
    b. idea
    c. important thing

11. Smoking is considered a dangerous **vice** by most doctors.

    a. bad habit or illegal activity
    b. way to remain healthy
    c. type of poisonous food

B. Read the target words and definitions. Then read the sentences. Circle the sentence in which the target word is NOT used correctly. The first one has been done for you.

1. dictate: to control or influence something, or to tell people exactly what they must do

    a. When working in groups, don't let one strong student **dictate** what all of the rest of you should do.
    b. Don't let past actions **dictate** the choices you make in the future.
    c. The children **dictated** their weekly spending money from their parents every Sunday.

2. **engagement:** involvement with something or some activity, usually because it is interesting or important

   a. Novels that have interesting characters and unpredictable plots are more likely to encourage the **engagement** of their readers.
   b. The guitar had poor **engagement** because the strings were very old and weak.
   c. Britain has a long history of **engagement** with the rest of the world.

3. **pursue:** to work hard in order to achieve or get something

   a. It takes a great deal of effort and training to **pursue** the dream of winning an Olympic medal.
   b. Is it right for people to **pursue** their happiness at the expense of others?
   c. The couple **pursued** their friends to hold their wedding in a downtown church.

4. **ambition:** a strong desire to achieve something

   a. The **ambition** to update the document changed its meaning completely.
   b. The president's **ambition** to lower energy use in the country by 10 percent within fifteen years seemed impossible.
   c. A common childhood **ambition** is to become a professional sports star, but very few people fulfill this dream.

5. **preserve:** to make something continue without changing

   a. The company has proposed freezing pay in order to **preserve** jobs.
   b. The movie star avoided reporters' questions about her family in order to **preserve** her family's privacy.
   c. You need to **preserve** a table well in advance if you want to eat at that restaurant on a Saturday night.

6. **founded:** based upon something

   a. The American government is **founded** on the principle of a balance of power between the president, Congress, and the Supreme Court.
   b. Their friendship was **founded** on a shared interest in poetry and literature.
   c. He **founded** the serious illness when he visited his friend in the hospital.

7. **vastly:** very much

   a. The Sahara Desert is **vastly** larger than the deserts of North and South America and Australia.
   b. The director's new movie is **vastly** different from anything he has made before.
   c. The school cafeteria is **vastly** replacing unhealthy foods with more fruit and vegetables.

8. **planet:** a very large round object in space that moves around the sun or another star

   a. The front **planet** on the airplane needed to be replaced because it kept losing air.
   b. Jupiter is the largest **planet**, and Mercury is the smallest.
   c. By 2009, scientists had found over 353 **planets** outside our solar system.

9. **spoil:** to have a bad effect on something, so that it is no longer attractive, enjoyable, useful, etc.

    a. One bad apple in a basket can **spoil** all of the rest if it is not removed.

    b. She found it difficult to **spoil** after her accident, so she couldn't return to work as soon as she had planned.

    c. Don't let a bad experience in the morning **spoil** the rest of your day.

10. **rural:** relating to the country, not the city

    a. In the winter, the days become shorter as the sun becomes more **rural** in the sky.

    b. **Rural** life is often thought to be less stressful than city life.

    c. Farming is the most common job in **rural** areas of the state.

11. **tackle:** to deal with a difficult problem

    a. Many international organizations are trying to **tackle** the issue of poor health around the world.

    b. He decided to **tackle** his weight problem by walking several miles every day.

    c. To avoid sunburn, it is good to **tackle** sun cream on your skin several times a day.

Word Tip

Sometimes American and British English use different words to mean the same thing. In American English, the place where you buy drugs and medicines is called a ***drugstore*** or a *pharmacy*. In Britain, the same store is called a *chemist*.

U.S.: The ***drugstore*** on the corner is a good place to buy cough medicine.

U.K.: *Chemist* shops in England used to sell tea in addition to drugs and medicines.

WORD FAMILIES

A. The table contains word families for some of the target words in the reading. Complete the table. An **X** indicates that there is no form or that the form is not common. Sometimes more than one form may be possible. If you are unsure about a form, check your dictionary.

Verb	Noun	Adjective	Adverb
X	1. **ambition** 2.		
	1. **conservation** 2.	X	X
	1. **divorce** 2.		X
	engagement	1. 2.	
	1. 2. 3. **pollution**		X
preserve	1. 2.		X
	1. 2. **priority**	X	X
	prosperity		
pursue		X	X
X		**relevant**	

When using new words in writing, it is important to select a word with the right meaning and in the right form, or part of speech. When you edit your writing, check to make sure that your words have the meaning you intend and that the words are in the correct form.

Choose the word form based on the function each word performs in the sentence. Does the word stand for a person, place, thing, or event (noun)? Does it describe a noun (adjective), or is it an action or a state (verb)? Or does it describe an action or quality (adverb)? Different word forms may have different spellings. If you do not know the correct spelling of a word form, check your dictionary.

B. Read the sentences. In eight of the sentences, an incorrect form of the target word has been used. If the form of the target word is incorrect, cross it out and write the correct form. If the form is correct, put a checkmark (✔). Use the word families table to help you. The first one has been done for you.

ambitious **1.** She had the ~~ambition~~ goal of entering the Boston Marathon, even though the entry requirement for women aged 18 to 34 was a previous marathon time of three hours, forty minutes.

_____ **2.** The **conserve** of the environment is one of the most important tasks of the twenty-first century.

_____ **3.** In the United States, a very high percentage of all **divorce** people eventually remarry.

_____ **4.** People who **engage** in open-minded discussion are likely to be better informed than those who stick to only one point of view.

_____ **5.** The fines for **pollute** are becoming more expensive as people come to realize the true cost of damage to the environment.

_____ **6.** One goal of the Académie Française is the **preserve** of the French language against Anglicization.

_____ **7.** Busy people should **priority** the tasks they need to do first.

_____ **8.** A steadily rising stock market is often a good indication of a country's economic **prosperous**.

_____ **9.** The police **pursued** the bank robber through five states before he was finally caught.

_____ **10.** The **relevant** of our history to our problems today is often not fully understood.

COLLOCATION

You develop your knowledge of collocations by seeing and hearing words in many contexts and noticing which words combine with one another. Remember that the words in a collocation can combine with different parts of speech, as shown in the examples.

Example:

adjective + noun	_an **optimistic outlook** on the future_
noun + preposition	_a more positive **outlook on** her job_
noun + noun	_a whole new **outlook** on **life**_

In each set of sentences, the target word is paired with different words to form different collocations. Choose the collocation that best fits the last sentence and write it in the blank. You may need to change the form of one word in the collocation to fit the sentence. The first one has been done for you.

1. **a.** One step toward happiness is **tackling the problem** of low self-esteem.
   b. The police were given more money to **tackle crime** in the city.
   c. The governor's priority was to **tackle** high **unemployment** in the car industry.
   d. It will take an international effort to _____ tackle the problem _____ of global warming.

2. **a.** The **budget dispute** between the Senate and the House of Representatives was settled when the president became involved.
   b. The zoos in the cities of Berlin and Neumunster had a **bitter dispute** over a polar bear named Knut.
   c. The **trade dispute** between the United States and China over the sale of American CDs, books, and computer software has been resolved.
   d. The North American Free Trade Agreement was designed to avoid _____ between the countries of Canada, Mexico, and the United States.

3. **a.** In the **vast majority** of cases, people bitten by spiders and snakes do not die.
   b. There is a **vast amount** of information now available on the Internet.
   c. A **vast number** of bird species exist, with some estimates as high as 10,000 different types.
   d. Paintings by famous old artists sell for a _____ of money. For example, a Rembrandt was put on sale for $46 million in 2004.

4. **a.** The National Park Service **dictates policy** on the use of America's fifty-eight national parks.
   b. A judge often must **dictate** the **terms** in a divorce when the husband and wife cannot agree.
   c. The international agreement **dictated** that the **treatment** of prisoners should be safe and fair.
   d. The winner of a war can usually _____ in peace agreement discussions.

5. **a.** **Rural areas** are regularly being absorbed into growing cities.
   b. The **rural population** of America is shrinking: 60 percent of Americans lived in the countryside in 1900, and only 25 percent did so in 1990.
   c. Some young people believe there is little that is interesting to do in **rural communities**.
   d. Over 25 percent of _____ in Costa Rica have been **conserved** as national parks or protected zones.

6. **a.** The local conservation group is worried that the new windmills will **spoil the view** of their valley.
   b. The burned dinner did not **spoil the party**—one of the guests suggested ordering pizza instead.
   c. Slovenia's last-minute goal **spoiled any chance** of Russia going to the World Cup.
   d. A Spanish judge has given the okay to unpopular building plans that threaten to _____ in one of Spain's most beautiful areas.

7. a. The Ryder Cup golf competition was originally created to **foster** good **relations** between Britain and the United States.

  b. The central bank cut interest rates in an attempt to **foster** economic **growth**.

  c. A country's flag and national song are symbols that can help **foster a sense** of unity among citizens of that country.

  d. Joining a club or organization can _____ of belonging for people with few friends.

8. a. The coach was frustrated because his players seemed to **lack the ambition** to improve their overall level of fitness.

  b. For many years, my father has **nursed the ambition** to become a pilot, so for his fiftieth birthday we gave him flying lessons.

  c. The young actress was able to **fulfill her** childhood **ambition** and act in a Broadway play.

  d. In Shakespeare's play, Macbeth is willing to kill King Duncan to _____ to be king.

Expanding the Topic

A. The questionnaire covers the seven categories of mental health and happiness discussed in the reading passage. Rate yourself on a scale from 1 to 4 according to how happy or satisfied you are for each point, with 1 being very unhappy / unsatisfied and 4 being very happy / satisfied.

Economic satisfaction	
• I am **prosperous** enough that I do not have to worry about money for necessities such as food, shelter, and transportation.	1 2 3 4
• I have enough income to **pursue** my hobbies.	1 2 3 4
• My job is secure and will be **relevant** in the future.	1 2 3 4
Environmental satisfaction	
• The place where I live is free of **pollution**.	1 2 3 4
• My government is committed to saving the **planet** from environmental disaster.	1 2 3 4
Physical health	
• I am usually healthy.	1 2 3 4
• I have good access to health **clinics** and **drugstores**.	1 2 3 4
Mental health	
• I have a positive **outlook** on life.	1 2 3 4
• I have enough self-confidence to **tackle** any problems in my life.	1 2 3 4

Workplace satisfaction

- I get along with my coworkers, with few or no **disputes**.   **1 2 3 4**

- I have enough support from my company and coworkers to **flourish** in my job.   **1 2 3 4**

- My company is honest and treats its employees fairly.   **1 2 3 4**

Social satisfaction

- I am fully **engaged** with my community and am involved in clubs and organizations in my city or town.   **1 2 3 4**

- My **priorities** are largely **founded** on spending quality time with family and friends.   **1 2 3 4**

- (If married) My relationship is solid, with little chance of **divorce**.   **1 2 3 4**

Political satisfaction

- I am satisfied with my government's attempts to **foster** international peace and cooperation.   **1 2 3 4**

- The government has been able to keep the level of **vice** to a minimum in my country.   **1 2 3 4**

- My government's **prioritization** of health, education, defense, and international relations issues is about right.   **1 2 3 4**

B. Now average all of your ratings together and write the result.

Average Happiness Rating: _____

Compare your ratings with your classmates. In which areas are you happier, and in which areas are you less happy?

Choose one area in which you are not completely happy and write a 500-word essay about what you and others can do to improve the situation.

Revisiting the Target Words

Now that you have completed this chapter, use the scale to describe your knowledge of the target words.

1 I still don't know anything about this word.

2 I am still not sure of the meaning of this word even after studying it.

3 I understand this word when I see it or hear it in a sentence, but I don't know how to use it in my own speaking and writing.

4 I know this word and can use it in my own speaking and writing.

TARGET WORDS

____ambition	____drugstore	____planet	____relevant
____clinic	____engagement	____pollution	____rural
____conservation	____flourish	____preserve	____spoil
____dictate	____foster	____priority	____tackle
____dispute	____founded	____prosperity	____vastly
____divorce	____outlook	____pursue	____vice

KNOWLEDGE CHECK 2

Go back to the beginning of the chapter and complete the Knowledge Check 1 table.

Strategy Practice

Getting Started

Look at the three images taken from Chapters 1–3. Without looking back at the chapters, how many target words can you remember from each chapter?

Focusing on Skills: DICTIONARY USE

Making good use of your dictionary will help you study and master the target vocabulary presented in this book. In addition to giving you information about a word's meaning, dictionaries also explain pronunciation, grammar, word families, usage, frequency, and other useful information. If you do not have a dictionary, ask your teacher to recommend one. All of the samples and images in this chapter are taken from the CD-ROM that accompanies the *Longman Dictionary of American English (LDAE)*.

UNDERSTANDING DICTIONARY ENTRY STRUCTURE

In order to effectively use your dictionary, it is a good idea to fully understand how dictionary entries are presented and what information is included. The exercises on the next page will help you develop this important skill.

A. Look at the LDAE CD-ROM entry for *fulfillment*. Identify the parts of the entry. Match the descriptions to the entry parts.

Descriptions

a. audio file

b. collocation

c. example sentence

d. part of speech

e. pronunciation in phonetic script

f. word grammar

g. word meaning #1 (most frequent)

h. word meaning #2 (second most frequent)

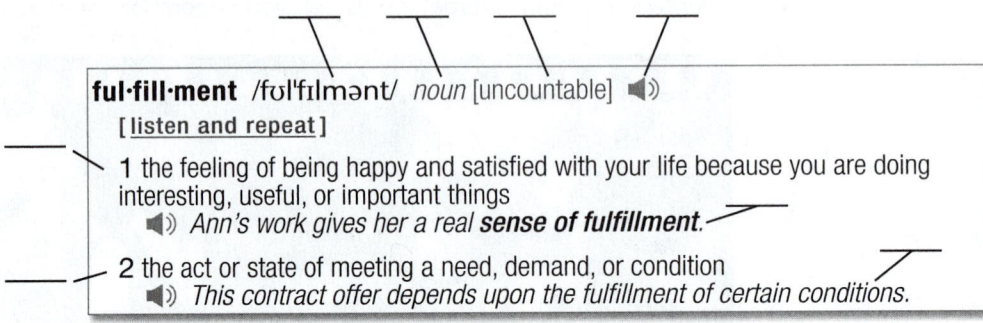

ful·fill·ment /fʊlˈfɪlmənt/ *noun* [uncountable]
[**listen and repeat**]
1 the feeling of being happy and satisfied with your life because you are doing interesting, useful, or important things
　*Ann's work gives her a real **sense of fulfillment**.*
2 the act or state of meeting a need, demand, or condition
　This contract offer depends upon the fulfillment of certain conditions.

B. Now look at the entry for *fulfillment* in your dictionary. What information is provided? Check (✔) the boxes in the table. Compare answers with a partner.

Word information	Longman Dictionary of American English CD-ROM	Your dictionary	Your partner's dictionary
word meaning	✔		
word frequency			
alternative word meanings	✔		
example sentences	✔		
word grammar	✔		
pronunciation in phonetic script	✔		
collocations	✔		
synonyms and / or antonyms			
British / American spellings			
thesaurus entries			
audio files	✔		
part of speech	✔		
other:			

UNDERSTANDING WORD MEANING

When you look up a word, you often find that it has more than one meaning. In many dictionaries, the first meaning is the most common one and therefore likely to be the one you need. However, this is not always the case, so you should read all of the meanings to be sure. To figure out which meaning is correct, think about the context in which you heard or read the word.

A. Match the target words in the box to the correct groups of definitions. Then read the definitions below each target word and choose the one that reflects how the word is used in the reading (Chapters 1–3). Use the chapter number in parentheses to locate and reread the word in context.

> amusement (2)   review (1)   spoil (3)   tackle (3)   vice (3)

1. _____ =
   a. to try to deal with a difficult problem
   b. to force someone to the ground so that the person stops running, as in a game such as rugby or football
   c. to talk to someone in order to deal with a difficult problem
   d. to start fighting someone, especially a criminal

2. _____ =
   a. a careful examination of a situation or process; evaluation, analysis
   b. an article in a newspaper or magazine that gives an opinion about a new book, play, film, etc.
   c. to write opinion pieces for a newspaper or magazine
   d. to report on a series of events or a period of time, mentioning the most important parts
   e. an official show of the army, navy, etc., for a king, president, or officer of high rank to observe

3. _____ =
   a. criminal activities that involve sex or drugs
   b. a bad habit
   c. a bad or immoral quality in a person, or bad or immoral behavior
   d. (usually American English) a tool that holds an object very firmly so that you can work on it

4. _____ =
   a. something that entertains you and makes time pass in an enjoyable way
   b. (British English) a special machine or game that is intended to entertain people, for example, at a fair
   c. the process of getting or providing pleasure and enjoyment

5. _____ =
   a. to have a bad effect on something so that it is no longer attractive, enjoyable, or useful
   b. to let a child do or have whatever he or she wants, often with the result that the child behaves badly
   c. to look after someone in a way that is very kind or too kind
   d. to start to decay
   e. (British English) to mark a ballot paper wrongly so that your vote is not included

B. In most dictionaries, word meanings are listed in order of frequency. Look up the target words from Exercise A in <u>your</u> dictionary and compare definitions with those on page 37. Does your dictionary give the same number of word meanings and are they in the same frequency order? Use the table to record your answers.

Target word	Number of meanings	Same meanings?	Same frequency order?
amusements			
review			
spoil			
tackle			
vice			

C. Compare answers with a partner.

UNDERSTANDING WORD FORMS AND WORD FAMILIES

In addition to word meanings, dictionaries can provide useful information about word forms and word families. This information is particularly useful because it enables you to select the appropriate word form to fit your sentence and therefore improve the overall accuracy of your written work.

Notice in the image below the useful word form and word family information provided in the entries. For example, in the entry for *motivation*, we are told that it is a noun and are given the adjective form *motivational*. In the entry for *motivate*, there's a link to other verb forms.

mo·ti·vate [Ac] *verb* [transitive] ◀))
→ [**verb forms**] [**listen and repeat**]

　　1 to make someone feel determined or eager to do something
　　　◀)) *Praise, rather than criticism, **motivates** children **to** do well.*

　　2 **motivating factor/force** the reason why someone behaves in a particular way
　　　*Money was the **motivating factor behind** their decision.*

mo·ti·vat·ed [Ac] *adjective* ◀))
[**listen and repeat**]

　　1 very eager to do or achieve something
　　　◀)) *an intelligent and **highly motivated** student*

　　2 done for a particular reason
　　　◀)) *The killings were thought to be **racially motivated** (=done because someone hates other races).*

mo·ti·va·tion [Ac] *noun* ◀))
[**listen and repeat**]

　　1 [uncountable] the determination and desire to do something
　　　◀)) *Jack is smart, but he lacks motivation.*
　　　If the task is too difficult, learners lose motivation.

　　2 [countable] the reason why you want to do something
　　　◀)) *a student's **motivation for** learning*
　　　*What was the **motivation behind** his actions?*
→ **—motivational** *adjective*
　　　◀)) *a motivational speech*

mo·tive [Ac] *noun* [countable] ◀))
[**thesaurus**] [**listen and repeat**]

　　the reason that makes someone do something, especially when this reason is kept hidden
　　　◀)) *Police are trying to find out the **motive for** the attack.*
　　　*The people bagan to question the **motives of** their leaders.*

　　➜ ulterior motive at ULTERIOR

THESAURUS

reason, explanation, excuse, rationale, grounds
➜ see Thesaurus box at REASON[1]

A. Use <u>your</u> dictionary to look up the target words. Find the word form / word family information provided. Use the table to record your results. ***Motivation*** has been done for you.

Target word	Word form	What other word forms are listed?	What other word forms are listed as separate entries?	Is a word family table provided?
absorbed				
devote				
longing				
motivation	noun	ADJ = motivational	V = motivate ADJ = motivated N = motive	No
pollution				
therapy				

B. Compare answers with a partner.

UNDERSTANDING COLLOCATIONS

A good dictionary will provide information and examples about words that are found together in patterns called *collocations*. These patterns comprise much of speech and writing. A sound knowledge of collocations not only will improve the overall accuracy of your speaking and writing, but also will help make your utterances and sentences sound more natural to native speakers.

This is the entry for **_engagement_**. Notice that a model sentence or phrase is provided for each meaning sense and that common collocations are highlighted in bold.

en·gage·ment *noun* ◀)
[listen and repeat]

1 [countable] an agreement to marry someone
◀) *Charlene and I have* **broken off** *our* **engagement** *(= decided to end it).*
◀) *an* **engagement ring** *(=a ring that a man gives a woman to show that they are engaged)*

2 [countable] *(formal)* an arrangement to do something or meet someone
◀) *Professor Campbell is in Fort Worth for a* **speaking engagement**.

3 [uncountable] the process of being involved with someone or something
◀) *a strategy of* **engagement** *and cooperation* **with** *China*

4 [countable, uncountable] fighting between people or armies
◀) *military* **rules of engagement** *(=rules that say when you should fight)*

For each of the target words, use your dictionary to find one collocation and model collocation sentence. Write them. Then write a sentence of your own that imitates some of the word order, usage, and phrasing of the model sentence.

1. clinic

collocation = _____

dictionary model sentence =

_____

your sentence =

_____

2. dispute

collocation = _____

dictionary model sentence =

_____

your sentence =

_____

3. fictional

collocation = _____

dictionary model sentence =

_____

your sentence =

_____

4. mystery

> collocation = _____

> dictionary model sentence =

> _____

> your sentence =

> _____

5. rural

> collocation = _____

> dictionary model sentence =

> _____

> your sentence =

> _____

Focusing on Vocabulary Cards: MODEL SENTENCES THAT "TELL" AND "SHOW"

Earlier in this book, you were introduced to the idea of making vocabulary cards and how useful they are as a strategy for learning new vocabulary.

One section of your vocabulary card should be set aside for *model sentences* that use the target word. Good model sentences should include two parts. The first part should "tell" you something about using the target word. The second part should "show" what the word means. Look at the example.

> *trivial (adj)*
>
> *Meaning = not serious, important, or valuable*
>
> *Model sentence = My boss tends to complain about trivial things. Yesterday he complained about the color of the paper clips I had ordered.*

Tell = My boss tends to complain about ***trivial*** things.
Show = Yesterday he complained about the color of the paper clips I had ordered.

Adapted from Kinsella, K. (2009). TESOL presentation.

Although dictionaries provide excellent model sentences, they sometimes fail to provide both "tell" and "show" parts. So it is useful to add your own model sentence as well.

Instructions

Select ten vocabulary cards for target words from Chapters 1–3 that you scored as a **1** or **2**. Check the model sentences you wrote for each word to make sure you have included a "tell" and "show" part for each one. Add model sentences with "tell" and "show" parts where necessary. Compare sentences with a partner.

Mind

What Are You Thinking?

Getting Started

Discuss the questions with your classmates.

✦ What are some key characteristics that make us specifically human?

✦ What do you think the relationship is between thought and language? Can you think about something without having the language to describe it?

✦ What methods might scientists use to study the beginnings of thought?

Assessing Your Vocabulary Knowledge: TARGET WORDS

Look at the words in the box. These are the target words for this chapter. Use the scale to score yourself on each word.

1 I don't know this word.

2 I have seen or heard this word before, but I am not sure of the meaning.

3 I understand this word when I see it or hear it in a sentence, but I don't know how to use it in my own speaking and writing.

4 I know this word and can use it in my own speaking and writing.

TARGET WORDS

____ancient	____commonsense	____multiple	____starvation
____articulation	____deliberate	____origin	____symbolically
____biological	____explore	____possess	____throat
____carved	____indiscriminate	____presence	____tongue
____cave	____intriguing	____primary	____uniquely
____chamber	____jewelry	____rhythm	____verbal

KNOWLEDGE CHECK 1

Complete the sentences with words that you have scored as **1**.

1. I am not familiar with the word / term _____.

2. I have no idea what _____ means.

Fill in the first blank with a word that you have scored as **2**. Then complete the sentence.

3. I think _____ could mean _____.

Reading

The passage looks at the development of human thought. As you read, pay special attention to the target vocabulary words in **bold**.

When Did Humans Begin to Think?

1   Understanding the **origins** of humankind has fascinated scientists for centuries. We know that our ancestors split from those of the chimpanzee (our closest **biological** relative) between 4 million and 8 million years ago. Evidence from fossil bones indicates that these early ancestors spread out from Africa to other parts of the world in **multiple** waves beginning at least 1 million years ago. By about 100,000 years ago, modern humans (*Homo sapiens*) had developed in Africa, and by about 40,000 years ago, they had reached Europe. They also began to have a growing **presence** on other continents.

2   An interesting question in humankind's development is, when did we begin to think critically? In other words, when did we turn from animals focused only on the daily struggle to avoid **starvation** to humans who could think **symbolically** about the world around us? However, answering this question is not easy, as thinking leaves no fossils to discover.

3   A **commonsense** assumption is that higher levels of thought go hand-in-hand with **verbal** language, because higher thinking, such as creative thought, would naturally seek a means of expression. So tracing the development of language could give an approximate idea of when humans began to think critically.

4   Interestingly, we do have some fossil evidence related to speech. Animals whose *larynx* (voice box) is placed high in their **throats** are unable to produce the variety of sounds necessary for speech. Fossil bones tell us that in early humans, the larynx was **originally** high in the **throat**. However, by about 200,000 years ago, it had moved lower in the **throat**. This lowering provided a larger sound **chamber** (the space in the **throat** and the mouth) in which passing air could be controlled by the **tongue**, making the **articulation** of a wide range of sounds and **rhythms** possible. (Most languages use between twenty-five and thirty sounds; English uses more than forty.)

5   So humans were physically able to speak around 200,000 years ago, but when did they actually start doing so? Estimates range from 35,000 to 100,000 years ago. But with no physical evidence of **ancient** language use, we need another approach to determine more precisely when humans began to speak—and to think critically.

6   Professor Richard Klein of Stanford University suggests that art may be the key. After all, no other animal is able to create or appreciate art; it is a **uniquely** human trait. (Although monkeys can put paint on a piece of paper, there is no indication that the result represents any real-world objects or any abstract thinking.) If **ancient** humans had the imagination to create a work of art (which in itself is a means of communication), then it seems highly likely that they would **possess** the **primary** means of communication: language. This suggests that the first works of art can be considered indicators of when language and critical thought began.

7   Until recently, the earliest art was believed to be **cave** paintings, **carved** figures, and **jewelry** found in southwestern Europe and thought to date from about 40,000 years ago. This suggested that humans first became

capable of critical thought about 40,000 years ago. However, this time frame was recently overturned by an exciting discovery in South Africa. Anthropologist Chris Henshilwood spent more than ten years **exploring** a **cave** there. He found many well-made tools, but more **intriguing** were the 8,000 pieces of *ochre*, a soft stone that can be turned into paint. Henshilwood's breakthrough came in 1999 when he found an ochre piece with unmistakable etchings on it. These were not **indiscriminate** knife marks, but lines cut in a careful pattern. In other words, it was a **deliberate** artistic design. Henshilwood had found the oldest piece of art yet, its date of **origin** set at 70,000 years—nearly 30,000 years before the art in Europe.

8   Based on Henshilwood's discovery, it seems that humans began to speak and think critically at least 70,000 years ago. It will be interesting to see if any future archaeological finds push this date back even further into the past.

(667 words)

See the BBC Horizon television program "The Day We Learned To Think" for more on this, available at youtube.com.

READING COMPREHENSION

Respond to the questions in writing. Base your responses on the reading and your own personal experiences.

1. Why is it particularly difficult to investigate early development of thought and language?

2. What is a physical requirement for the ability to speak?

3. How might art, thought, and language be related?

4. When did humans begin to think critically, according to the passage?

5. What do you think pushed humankind to develop thinking and language in the first place? Was it a better chance for survival, or a more social or artistic reason?

6. Think of ways that art represents critical thinking. Give some examples using famous artworks.

Focusing on Vocabulary

WORD MEANING

A. Match the target words with their definitions. If you are unsure about a word's meaning, try to figure it out from the context by rereading the passage. Then check your dictionary.

Set 1

_____ 1. presence
_____ 2. symbolically
_____ 3. tongue
_____ 4. articulation
_____ 5. rhythm
_____ 6. jewelry
_____ 7. indiscriminate

a. the act of making a sound or of speaking words
b. a regular, repeated pattern of sound or movement
c. the existence of someone or something in a particular place
d. the soft part inside your mouth that you can move around and use for eating and speaking
e. an action that is done without thinking about the harm it might cause
f. representing something important
g. small things that you wear for decoration, such as rings or necklaces

Set 2

_____ 1. **origin**
_____ 2. **biological**
_____ 3. **starvation**
_____ 4. **commonsense**
_____ 5. **throat**
_____ 6. **chamber**
_____ 7. **cave**

a. an enclosed space, especially in your body or inside a machine

b. suffering or death caused by lack of food

c. a big hole in the side of a cliff or hill, or under the ground

d. related to the scientific study of living things

e. the area at the back of your mouth and inside your neck

f. the place or situation in which something begins to exist

g. sensible or practical

B. Read each target word and the list below it. One word or phrase in each list is NOT a synonym for the target word. Cross it out.

1. **multiple**

| whole | several | numerous | a lot of |

2. **verbal**

| written | oral | spoken | voiced |

3. **ancient**

| prehistoric | very old | early | advanced |

4. **uniquely**

| individually | distinctively | exclusively | terribly |

5. **possess**

| own | handle | have | belong to |

6. **primary**

| chief | major | final | main |

7. **carved**

| cut | enlarged | scratched | shaped |

8. **explore**

| investigate | escape | inspect | examine |

9. **intriguing**

| fascinating | interesting | wide-ranging | exciting |

10. **deliberate**

| thoughtless | on purpose | planned | intentional |

Word Tip

Commonsense is usually used as an adjective. It can also be written as two words (*common sense*), but then it is usually used as a noun:

> ***common sense:*** to behave in a sensible way and make practical decisions

WORD FAMILIES

A. The table contains word families for some of the target words in the reading. Complete the table. An **X** indicates that there is no form or that the form is not common. Sometimes more than one form may be possible. If you are unsure about a form, check your dictionary.

Verb	Noun	Adjective	Adverb
	articulation	X	X
X	1. 2.	biological	
X	X	deliberate	
explore	1. 2.		X
	X	1. 2. intriguing	
	1. origin 2.		
X	rhythm		
	starvation	1. 2.	X
	1. 2.		symbolically
X			uniquely

B. Choose the correct form of the word in **bold** in sentence **a** to complete sentence **b**. Use the word families table you just completed as a guide.

1. **a.** The child's **articulation** was not very clear, so only his parents could understand what he was asking for.

    b. The teacher carefully _____ every word so that the students could write the words down.

2. **a.** The university was looking for students who had studied a range of subjects in high school—for example, English literature, **biology**, geometry, and world history.

    b. Researchers have found that adults who exercised vigorously over a lifetime appeared _____ younger than people who were not active.

3. a. The firefighters were concerned that the fire had been set **deliberately**.

   b. Our player's _____ attempt to trip the opposing player was considered poor sportsmanship.

4. a. Roald Amundsen, a Norwegian **explorer**, was the first person to reach the South Pole. Amundsen's party arrived on December 14, 1911.

   b. The teenage years are an _____ period in children's lives—a time when they begin to try out many new activities and meet new people.

5. a. The story of the Lost Dutchman Goldmine in Arizona is one of the most **intriguing** legends from the American Southwest.

   b. Thousands of tourists who are _____ by the Northern Lights travel to Alaska, Scandinavia, and Northern Canada hoping to see their amazing display.

6. a. The Academy of Motion Picture Arts and Sciences offers awards for both best **original** screenplay and best adaptation from another source.

   b. The historical basis for the modern-day Santa Claus _____ from a combination of many different stories and traditions from across Europe.

7. a. The normal **rhythm** of the heart is 60 to 100 beats per minute.

   b. Regular practice of comfortable, _____ breathing is important for developing a good swimming style.

8. a. During the 1840s, many Irish **starved** to death because of the failure of the potato crop.

   b. The charity launched an emergency appeal to prevent _____ in the region after life-giving rains failed to arrive for the sixth year in a row.

9. a. Although the queen holds little political power, she is still **symbolically** important as the figurehead of the United Kingdom.

   b. Fast-food hamburgers have come to _____ the exportation of the American consumer culture to the rest of the world.

10. a. Each person's fingerprints are **unique**, with no two being the same.

   b. Hurling is a _____ Irish sport, although Irish emigrants have now carried it to many other countries.

COLLOCATION

Read the common collocations in the column on the left. Give two examples of things associated with each collocation.

	Example 1	Example 2
1. unique opportunity	_____	_____
2. ancient town	_____	_____

3. deliberate
act

_____   _____

4. cheap
jewelry

_____   _____

5. possess an
ability

_____   _____

6. symbolic
value

_____   _____

7. verbal
agreement

_____   _____

8. multiple
users

_____   _____

Expanding the Topic

A. Read the original text and match with the paraphrases on page 51.

Originals

_____ **1.** There is the stereotype that early humans lived a very basic life and were not very intelligent. They lived in holes in rocks and weren't able to communicate, except maybe with a few hand gestures. But is this the way our ancestors really lived?

_____ **2.** In fact, the evidence suggests that early humans were remarkably capable. They had learned how to make stone knives and other cutting instruments to help them hunt and make clothes. They also had art, with some of the best examples being the **cave** paintings in Spain and France. They also cut a variety of artistic patterns into stones, often with a geometric design.

_____ **3.** Early humans also were coming to grips with language. At first, we must just have made sounds which did not mean anything, other than loud sounds perhaps indicating some type of alarm or warning. But eventually humans learned to control the movement of air through the **throat** and mouth by moving the parts of this passage, which made a variety of sounds possible. These sounds then became matched with objects and ideas from the real world. This correspondence of sounds and particular meanings was the foundation of language.

_____ **4.** The use of language provided humans with important advantages over other animals. Language allowed information to be passed from one generation to the next, ensuring that knowledge essential to survival would not be lost. Language also made it possible to work more efficiently as a team, further increasing the chances for success. It also must have helped strengthen group identity, making each family or group stronger and more cohesive. Advantages such as this suggest that language was one of the most important reasons for the survival of early humans.

Paraphrases

a. The ability to use language must have been one of the **primary** reasons why early humans were so successful.

b. Humankind was also moving from making **indiscriminate** sounds toward using language. Early humans learned how to manipulate their **tongues** and other vocal organs to produce a range of sounds that came to be connected **symbolically** with **unique** meanings.

c. Many people have the impression that early humans were crude people, living in **caves** and having no language. But is this true?

d. In fact, humankind was relatively advanced. They made useful tools out of stone, drew beautiful art paintings on cave walls, and **carved** interesting designs into stones.

B. Now you try. Paraphrase the following sentences. Use the target word in your paraphrase. You may need to change the form of the target word.

1. The human throat, larynx, and mouth are well adapted to make the variety of sounds necessary to use language. This open area can be manipulated to change the air flow and the sounds this air makes as it passes.

chamber _____

_____

2. The air passage can be manipulated in a number of ways by the tongue. The area above the larynx can be opened, fully closed, or partially closed, with each position producing a different sound. If partially closed, air goes through the nose, making a "nasal" sound.

throat _____

_____

3. The tongue can make other sounds as well. One of the most distinctive is the "clicking" sounds typical of some languages in southern Africa. These languages belong to the Khoisan language family, which is distinguished by the unusual clicking sounds, which are rare in other language families.

presence _____

_____

4. It is estimated that there are approximately 4,000 to 6,000 languages in the world today. This makes it logical to assume that the development of different languages must have started in very early times.

commonsense _____

_____

Summarize the reading passage in 100 to 150 words. Use paraphrasing to help you meet this reduced word limit.

Revisiting the Target Words

Now that you have completed this chapter, use the scale to describe your knowledge of the target words.

1 I still don't know anything about this word.

2 I am still not sure of the meaning of this word even after studying it.

3 I understand this word when I see it or hear it in a sentence, but I don't know how to use it in my own speaking and writing.

4 I know this word and can use it in my own speaking and writing.

TARGET WORDS

_____ancient	_____commonsense	_____multiple	_____starvation
_____articulation	_____deliberate	_____origin	_____symbolically
_____biological	_____explore	_____possess	_____throat
_____carved	_____indiscriminate	_____presence	_____tongue
_____cave	_____intriguing	_____primary	_____uniquely
_____chamber	_____jewelry	_____rhythm	_____verbal

KNOWLEDGE CHECK 2

Select examples from the words you now give a score of **3** or **4**, but didn't at the start of the chapter, to complete the sentences.

1. I didn't know that _____ meant _____ before reading this chapter.

2. I wasn't sure that I knew the meaning of _____, but I am now.

3. I now am confident that I know what _____ means, but I would like more practice with how to use it in my speaking and writing.

4. I could next use _____ when I am _____.

CHAPTER 6

What Color Is Your Laugh?

Getting Started

Discuss the questions with your classmates.

✦ Do Mondays make you feel blue?

✦ Do you like abstract art? When you look at abstract paintings, what kinds of things do they make you think of?

✦ Color means many different things in different cultures. Think of some examples of color symbolism in your culture.

Assessing Your Vocabulary Knowledge: TARGET WORDS

Look at the words in the box. These are the target words for this chapter. Use the scale to score yourself on each word.

1 I don't know this word.

2 I have seen or heard this word before, but I am not sure of the meaning.

3 I understand this word when I see it or hear it in a sentence, but I don't know how to use it in my own speaking and writing.

4 I know this word and can use it in my own speaking and writing.

TARGET WORDS

____abnormality	____disillusioned	____perception	____rose
____auditory	____flavor	____personality	____seep
____bee	____frequent	____portrayal	____simultaneous
____bolt	____ink	____prominent	____sniff
____bubbly	____inspiration	____refined	____spontaneously
____buzz	____orchestra	____revival	____wobbly

KNOWLEDGE CHECK 1

Fill in the first blank with a word that you have scored as **2**. Then complete the second sentence.

1. I have seen / heard _____. I saw / heard it while I was

_____.

Fill in the first blanks with words that you have scored as **4**. Then complete the sentences.

2. One meaning of _____ is _____.

3. I last used the word _____ while I was _____.

Reading

The passage discusses the remarkable way that some people experience the senses. As you read, pay special attention to the target vocabulary words in **bold**.

Synesthesia

1   When most people read a book, newspaper, or magazine, they see the words as black marks on the page. This is not surprising given that **ink** in most publications is black. However, there is a group of people who do not see the words in front of them as black. Instead they might say that the number *4* is blue or the word *gift* is green. Others might say that the pain from a headache is orange, the **flavor** of sugar round, or a **sniff** of a bouquet of **roses** pink. What's going on here?

2   According to neuroscientists, these people have a condition called *synesthesia*. The word *synesthesia* comes from the Greek words *syn* (meaning *together*) and *aesthesis* (meaning *perception*) and means "joined **perception**." All humans have five senses—touch, vision, hearing, taste, and smell—and typically these are clearly separated from one another. However, for a person with synesthesia the boundaries between the senses are weak. So one sense, for example, sound, may **seep** across to another sense such as sight, so that the *sound* of an **orchestra** playing might be *seen* as green **wobbly** lines. This combination—an **auditory** stimulation accompanied by a visual sensation—is the most common type of synesthesia. Any **simultaneous** combination of two or more senses is considered a form of synesthesia.

3   Neurologist Richard Cytowic became interested in this phenomenon after he found out his neighbor tasted shapes. Cytowic was convinced he should take a deeper look when less than two weeks later he encountered a colleague who saw the sound of his hospital pager as red lightning **bolts**. Cytowic and other scientists believe that synesthesia is not an **abnormality**. In fact, we all may experience synesthesia at birth. It is only when our brain develops that the boundaries between each of our senses become more **refined**. People with synesthesia, on the other hand, retain these indistinct boundaries throughout their lives.

4   Another finding is that the relationships between the different sensory **perceptions** are consistent over time. Someone who hears the **buzz** of a **bee** as purple will always see it as purple. The sensations are also unique to individuals. One person may see the word *table* as yellow and another see it as green.

5   Although anyone can create links between the senses and other ideas or objects through the use of metaphor (for example, heated debate, **bubbly personality**, or loud shirt), this is not the same as synesthesia. Synesthetes experience these relationships **spontaneously** without any conscious thought. One young synesthete blogger reports how **disillusioned** she felt when she saw a famous singer for the first time and he didn't match up to the color she had seen for him when she first heard him sing. Another reports how the sound of paper makes him feel physically sick, so he hates going to restaurants with paper tablecloths and napkins.

6   Thus, while some negative reactions may result from synesthesia, Professor Simon Baron Cohen believes it is more useful to think of it as enriched **perception**, because synesthetes often use their condition as a means to enhance memory or as a source of **inspiration**. The **prominent** Russian artist Wassily Kandinsky's synesthesia may have triggered the creation of

his famous **portrayals** of musical compositions as abstract paintings.

7   Medical science has known about synesthesia for several centuries, but this **revival** of interest has increased our understanding. We now know that it is more **frequent** among women and left-handers and that it appears to run in families. However, estimates of the number of people with synesthesia still vary widely, from 1 in 200 to 1 in 2,000. This may be because many people who have the condition may not realize that it has a name.

(614 words)

READING COMPREHENSION

Respond to the questions in writing. Base your responses on the reading and your own personal experiences.

1. Give a short definition of synesthesia.

2. List some of the possible sensory combinations of synesthesia from the examples in the reading passage.

3. How is synesthesia related to the brain?

4. In what ways might people with synesthesia benefit from this condition?

5. Many or most babies have some degree of synesthesia, but later the boundaries between senses develop. What advantage do you think there is for senses that are clearly separated?

6. The passage relates how metaphors often combine the essence of different senses [feeling blue (depressed), warm colors (colors of fire: red, orange, yellow)]. Can you think of other metaphors that mix senses?

Focusing on Vocabulary

WORD MEANING

A. Read the target words. Use the paragraph number in parentheses to locate and reread the word in context. Then read the dictionary definitions and choose the one that reflects how the word is used in the reading.

_____ **1. ink** (1)
    a. a colored liquid that you use for writing, printing, or drawing
    b. a black liquid in sea creatures such as octopus and squid

_____ **2. flavor** (1)
    a. the quality or feature that makes something have a particular style or character
    b. the particular taste of a food or drink

_____ **3. rose** (1)
    a. a pink color
    b. a flower that often has a pleasant smell

_____ **4. perception** (2)
    a. the way you think about something and your idea of what it is like
    b. the way that you notice things with your senses of sight, hearing, etc.

_____ **5. orchestra** (2)
    a. a large group of musicians playing many different kinds of instruments and led by a conductor
    b. an area of seats in a theater close to and on the same level as the stage

_____ **6. bolt** (3)
    a. the metal bar that you slide across a door or window to lock it
    b. lightning that appears as a white line in the sky

_____ **7. refined** (3)
    a. polite, well educated, or belonging to a high social class
    b. improved in order to make something more effective

_____ **8. buzz** (4)
    a. a continuous, low, humming sound
    b. a lot of activity, noise, and excitement

_____ **9. bee** (4)
    a. a black and yellow flying insect
    b. an occasion when people, usually women, meet in order to do a particular type of work

_____ **10. personality** (5)
    a. someone who is very famous and often appears in the newspapers, on television, etc.
    b. someone's character, especially the way the person behaves toward others

_____ **11. inspiration** (6)
    a. a good idea about what you should do, write, say, etc., especially an idea that you get suddenly
    b. a person, experience, place, etc., that gives you new ideas for how to do something

_____ **12. revival** (7)

    a. when something becomes active or strong again

    b. a new production of a play that has not been performed in a long time

B. Read the target words in the box. Complete each sentence with the target word that matches the meaning of the words in parentheses. You may need to change the form of the word to fit the sentence.

abnormality	disillusioned	prominent	sniff
auditory	frequent	seep	spontaneously
bubbly	portrayal	simultaneous	wobbly

1. Airlines offer _____ flyer miles to their best customers to keep
                    (repeated, regular)
   them loyal.

2. The _____ leg on the chair caused the woman to fall off and hit
           (shaky, unstable)
   her head.

3. The water from the overflowing bathtub began to _____
                                (leak, flow slowly)
   through the floor, then into the ceiling of the apartment below.

4. Scratch and _____ cards in magazines allow perfume
               (smell, breathe in)
   companies to market their product in a way that targets more than one of the
   senses.

5. A phobia (an unreasonable fear of something) is a common type of
   psychological _____.
                (irregularity, imperfection)

6. People with a(n) _____ learning style prefer to learn through
              (hearing, audio)
   listening, and make up perhaps 25 percent of the population.

7. _____ people are usually popular because of their fun-loving
   (cheerful, full-of-life)
   and exciting **personalities**.

8. The corporation had _____ talks with several potential
              (at the same time, all at once)
   buyers in an effort to quickly sell the failing company.

9. Sean Penn won the Academy Award for Best Actor in 2009 for his
   _____ of the San Francisco politician Harvey Milk in the
   (representation, description)
   movie _Milk_.

10. The audience _____ began to cheer when the governor stepped
           (without planning, suddenly)
   onto the stage to speak.

11. As the cost of gasoline goes ever higher, many people are becoming
   _____ with large, inefficient cars.
   (disappointed, depressed)

12. Archbishop Desmond Tutu from South Africa is one of the most
   _____ advocates of peaceful change in politics.
   (famous, well-known)

WORD FAMILIES

A. The table contains word families for some of the target words in the reading. An **X** indicates that there is no form or that the form is not common. Study the table. Look for spelling patterns for the noun, adjective, and adverb forms of the words. List the patterns in the space below the table.

Verb	Noun	Adjective	Adverb
X	**abnormality**	abnormal	abnormally
disillusion	disillusionment	**disillusioned**	**X**
flavor	1. **flavor** 2. flavoring	1. flavored 2. flavorful 3. flavorless	**X**
frequent	frequency	**frequent**	frequently
inspire	**inspiration**	1. inspired 2. inspiring	**X**
orchestrate	1. **orchestra** 2. orchestration	orchestral	**X**
perceive	1. **perception** 2. perceptiveness	1. perceptible 2. perceptive	1. perceptibly 2. perceptively
refine	refinement	**refined**	**X**
seep	seepage	**X**	**X**
X	spontaneity	spontaneous	**spontaneously**

nouns _____

adjectives _____

adverbs _____

B. Complete each sentence with the correct form of the word in parentheses. Use the word families table to help you.

1. Canada suffered from an _____ (**abnormal**) cold and wet summer last year.

2. Many believe the low participation in the election was due to voter _____ (**disillusioned**) with politics.

3. Cinnamon Orange Instant Tea is a _____ (**flavor**) blend of black tea and oils based on an original recipe.

4. The airline has announced that it plans to increase the _____ (**frequent**) of its services to Turkey during peak summer months.

5. Many successful athletes state that they were _____ (**inspiration**) by watching the Olympics when they were young.

6. The indie band has launched a new _____ (**orchestra**)-sounding album. It's unlike anything they have released before.

7. The student's _____ (**perception**) comment showed that she had real insight into the subject.

8. Image editing software allows photographers to _____ (**refined**) the quality of their photos.

9. The _____ (**seep**) from the pipe into the river carried poisonous waste.

10. My New Year's resolution is to leave more room in my life for _____ (**spontaneously**).

COLLOCATION

Combine a word from Column A with a word from Column B to form a collocation. Then match the collocation to its definition.

Column A	Column B
bee	table
indelible	**portrayal**
personality	translation
accurate	sting
prominent	clash
rose	**ink**
simultaneous	citizen
wobbly	garden

1. _____ a garden planted with flowers

2. _____ when two people don't like each other

3. _____ a shaky piece of furniture

4. _____ an insect bite

5. _____ important member of the community

6. _____ realistic representation of a person or event

7. _____ liquid for making permanent marks

8. _____ immediate conversion from one language to another

Expanding the Topic

Most words are related to many other words through meaning links. Take the word *sun* as an example. What related words does it make you think of? Most people would say words such as *moon, shine, light, bright, hot, star,* and *day*. All of these words have some meaning link to *sun* and are called *associations*.

Example:

sun – moon	(The sun and moon are the two main bodies in the sky.)
sun – shine / light	(The sun shines and gives off light.)
sun – bright / hot	(*Bright* and *hot* describe the sun.)
sun – star	(The sun is a star.)
sun – day	(The sun shining causes daytime on Earth.)

Thinking about association links to a word is useful because associations often elicit words that are used together with the original word. For example, associations often create collocations.

Look at the two target words and their five associations. See how the associations have meaning links to the target words.

	Association	**Meaning Link**

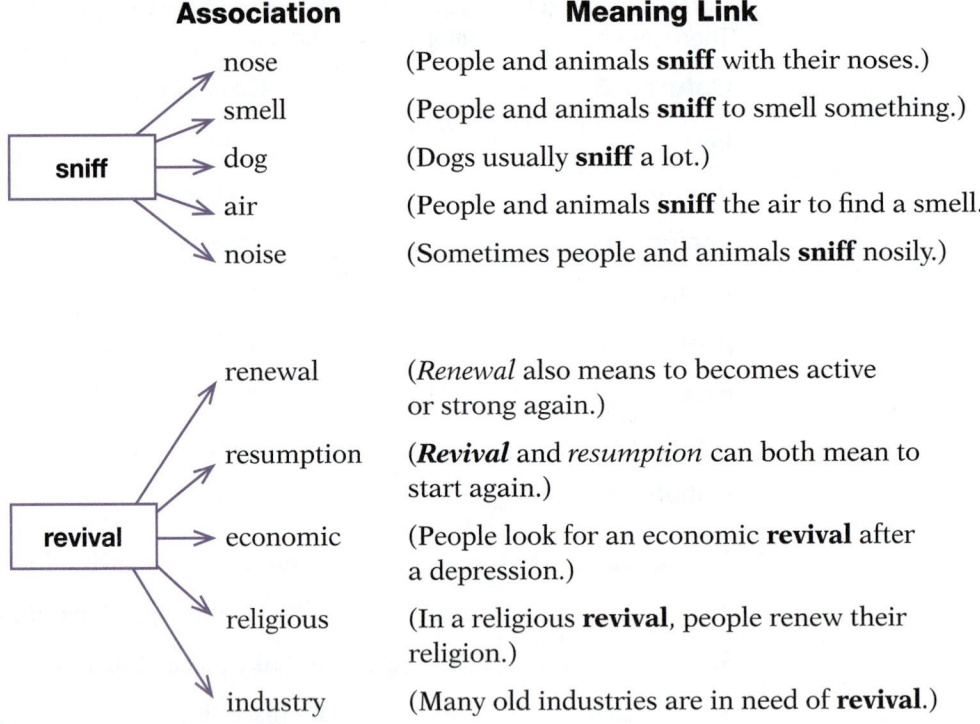

nose	(People and animals **sniff** with their noses.)
smell	(People and animals **sniff** to smell something.)
dog	(Dogs usually **sniff** a lot.)
air	(People and animals **sniff** the air to find a smell.)
noise	(Sometimes people and animals **sniff** nosily.)

renewal	(*Renewal* also means to becomes active or strong again.)
resumption	(***Revival*** and *resumption* can both mean to start again.)
economic	(People look for an economic **revival** after a depression.)
religious	(In a religious **revival**, people renew their religion.)
industry	(Many old industries are in need of **revival**.)

A. Each of the word boxes has associations that belong to one of the target words. Match each box of associations to a target word. Then explain the meaning links.

champagne	gas	personality	sparkling	voice

bright	electricity	lightning	storm	thunder

Association **Meaning Link**

1. **bolt**
(_____)
(_____)
(_____)
(_____)
(_____)

2. **bubbly**
(_____)
(_____)
(_____)
(_____)
(_____)

B. Now add your own associations to the following target words. Then explain the meaning links.

Association **Meaning Link**

1. **auditory**
(_____)
(_____)
(_____)
(_____)
(_____)

2. **buzz**
(_____)
(_____)
(_____)
(_____)
(_____)

A number of famous people have been identified as synesthetes. Choose one of these people. After doing some background research, write a 300-word biography about your chosen famous person.

Revisiting the Target Words

Now that you have completed this chapter, use the scale to describe your knowledge of the target words.

1 I still don't know anything about this word.

2 I am still not sure of the meaning of this word even after studying it.

3 I understand this word when I see it or hear it in a sentence, but I don't know how to use it in my own speaking and writing.

4 I know this word and can use it in my own speaking and writing.

TARGET WORDS			
____abnormality	____disillusioned	____perception	____rose
____auditory	____flavor	____personality	____seep
____bee	____frequent	____portrayal	____simultaneous
____bolt	____ink	____prominent	____sniff
____bubbly	____inspiration	____refined	____spontaneously
____buzz	____orchestra	____revival	____wobbly

KNOWLEDGE CHECK 2

Select examples from the words you now give a score of **3** or **4**, but didn't at the start of the chapter, to complete the sentences.

1. I didn't know that _____ meant _____ before reading this chapter.

2. I wasn't sure that I knew the meaning of _____, but I am now.

3. I now am confident that I know what _____ means, but I would like more practice with how to use it in my speaking and writing.

4. I now know that _____ collocates with _____.

Did You Have Trouble Getting Up This Morning?

Getting Started

Discuss the questions with your classmates.

✦ When you were a teenager, did you have trouble getting along with your parents?

✦ In high school, what was your attitude toward studying and hobbies?

✦ As a teenager, did you like to try out new things? Were you a risk-taker?

Assessing Your Vocabulary Knowledge: TARGET WORDS

Look at the words in the box. These are the target words for this chapter. Use the scale to score yourself on each word.

1 I don't know this word.

2 I have seen or heard this word before, but I am not sure of the meaning.

3 I understand this word when I see it or hear it in a sentence, but I don't know how to use it in my own speaking and writing.

4 I know this word and can use it in my own speaking and writing.

TARGET WORDS

____aggravation	____consequence	____hobby	____prune
____alert	____constructive	____laboratory	____rehearse
____alien	____deprivation	____leisure	____speculate
____caretaker	____enthusiasm	____moody	____temper
____caution	____executive	____prompt	____translate
____circuit	____habit	____provisional	____trim

Check your progress in learning the vocabulary in this chapter.

- First, look at your scores in the table on page 63. Write the number of words for each score (1–4) in the "at the beginning" column. For example, if you scored eight words as **1** ("I don't know this word"), then write **8**.

- At the end of the chapter, score yourself again. Then compare the two sets of scores. Are you showing improvement on most of the words in the chapter?

Your score	Number of words ...		
	at the beginning:	at the end:	
		showing improvement	no improvement yet
1			
2			
3			
4			

Reading

The passage reports on findings from several new areas of research on the teenage brain. As you read, pay special attention to the target vocabulary words in **bold**.

The Teenage Brain

1   Think back to when you were entering high school. Did you have trouble getting up in the morning? Did your teachers think you were **moody**? Did your parents think you had turned into an **alien**? These changes in your behavior were probably because you were a teenager and your brain was playing havoc with your life.

2   Let's start with waking up in the morning. This is often a source of conflict and **aggravation** for teenagers and parents. In this case, science is on teens' side. Researchers have found that the body's sleep-wake cycle is governed by something called our circadian clock. This determines when our body is ready to fall asleep and when it is ready to wake up. During the teenage years, the circadian clock shifts forward about four hours. For example, the child, who used to go to bed at 8:30 P.M. and rise at 6 A.M., now wants to stay up past midnight and sleep in until 10 A.M. This change puts teens' sleep cycles out of sync with the sleep **habits** of the rest of their family. If teens are forced to get up at the same time as everyone else, then they begin to build up a sleep debt. Researchers **speculate** that this sleep **deprivation** may provide one explanation for why teens feel unable to concentrate at home or stay **alert** at school and are generally bad-**tempered**. Lack of sleep also has serious **consequences** with respect to learning. During sleep, we **rehearse** all of the learning from our day and assign it to long-term memory. Without enough sleep, we aren't able to learn effectively.

3   Research is providing **provisional** insights

into other areas of teenage brain development, too. Until recently, many researchers believed that most important brain development took place in the womb and during the first three years of life. However, a large-scale study of 145 children and adolescents, carried out by Dr. Jay Giedd and colleagues at the National Institute for Mental Health, has shown that the teenage years are also an important period for brain development. We know that the brain grows like a tree. Just before puberty, the brain overproduces lots of new brain cells. Then, during the teenage years, it **prunes** away any cells that are unused. This **trimming** of brain cells has **prompted** scientists to propose a "use it or lose it" theory of brain development. Giedd believes that which **leisure** activities teens participate in during these years—from playing video games to undertaking more demanding **hobbies** such as photography and karate—determine which connections survive into adulthood.

4   Meanwhile, in Boston, researchers in the **laboratories** at McLean Hospital are carrying out exploratory research on how the teen brain processes facial expressions. Teens and adults were asked to view a series of pictures showing a variety of facial expressions. The researchers found that the teens used a different part of the brain than the adults when processing the pictures. This resulted in them misreading the emotions being expressed. Teen brains showed more activation in the brain **circuits** that respond emotionally. In other words, the teens' responses were more like gut reactions. Adults, on the other hand, processed the facial expressions using the prefrontal part of the brain. This area is responsible for the **executive** functions of the brain including planning, decision making, reasoning, and judgment. The researchers **speculate** that this area regulates the more emotional part of the brain and helps to control reactions. The fact that the teen brain is not interacting with the emotional region in the same way as the adult brain could provide clues to understanding adolescent behavior. Therefore, rather than expecting teenagers to act like grown-ups, parents and **caretakers** need to be aware that teenage brains process the world differently than adult brains.

5   While brain researchers are full of **enthusiasm** regarding these new findings, they are also quick to **caution** against **translating** them into educational policies or new teaching fads without first considering whether this is truly justified. One point that all researchers agree on is that the most **constructive** thing adults can do to ensure healthy brain development in their children is to spend loving, quality time with them.

(693 words)

READING COMPREHENSION

Respond to the questions in writing. Base your responses on the reading and your own personal experiences.

1. Why do teenagers have such difficulty waking up in the morning?

2. What are some consequences of not getting enough sleep?

3. Describe how the brain grows and develops.

4. Why did the teenagers in the Boston study react to facial expressions differently from adults?

5. What practices could parents or schools put in place, based on these research results?

6. Do you think teenagers should be treated like adults by their parents or in the eyes of the law?

Focusing on Vocabulary

WORD MEANING

A. Read the sentences and choose the phrase that best matches the meaning of the target word. Use context clues to determine the correct meaning. Check your dictionary if you are not sure of the answer.

1. The SETI Institute is dedicated to searching for evidence of **alien** life in the universe.

   a. the air, water, and land on a planet
   b. a creature from another world
   c. the ability to learn and understand about things

2. The noise from the roadwork was causing so much **aggravation** for nearby residents that they made a formal complaint to the city council.

   a. feeling of being annoyed
   b. quality of being useful for a particular purpose
   c. feeling of not being satisfied

3. Eat more carbohydrates than protein if you are nervous and want to be more relaxed or eat more protein than carbohydrates if you are tired and wish to be more **alert**.

   a. ready to go out and do things
   b. giving all your attention to what is happening or being said
   c. healthier, stronger, and calmer

4. One stage in confidence building is to prepare, **rehearse**, and role-play a different, more self-assured response to an everyday situation.

   a. practice something you are going to say or do
   b. decide how and when you will do something
   c. behave as if something is true, even when it is not

5. At this early stage in the semester, you only need to give your teacher a **provisional** topic for your final presentation.

   a. suitable for a particular time, situation, or purpose
   b. something that is well known to you
   c. likely or able to be changed in the future

6. The government's plan to **trim** spending included cuts to the higher education budget.

   a. make something bigger in amount, number, or degree
   b. make something so that it is exactly right for someone's needs
   c. reduce the number, amount, or size of something

7. The cold weather has **prompted** a rush to travel websites to book warm-weather vacations.

   a. prevented something from happening
   b. made a product available to the market
   c. caused something to happen or be done

8. If exercise bores you but you still want to be healthy, take up a **hobby** that engages you in physical activity, such as dancing or hiking.

    a. process of being taught the skills for a particular job or activity
    b. activity you enjoy in your free time
    c. process of moving or way that something moves

9. The international space station is essentially a **laboratory** that orbits Earth to allow researchers to carry out specialized experiments in space.

    a. building where tools and machines are used for making and repairing things
    b. building with rooms where people can work at desks
    c. special building where scientists do tests

10. Children who become **caretakers** of other family members often feel satisfied and proud of the contribution they are making to their family's livelihood.

    a. people who accept what is being offered
    b. people who look after other people
    c. people who try hard to avoid doing anything wrong

11. The crowd showed little **enthusiasm** for the speaker, and only a few people clapped when he finished his speech.

    a. strong feeling of interest and enjoyment about something
    b. help or protection
    c. close relationship between two things

12. You can improve the second draft of your essay if you pay attention to the **constructive** feedback from your teacher on your first draft.

    a. given at once and without delay
    b. intended for anyone to know, see, or hear
    c. useful and helpful, or likely to produce good results

B. Read the target words and definitions. Then read the sentences. Circle the sentence in which the target word is NOT used correctly.

1. **moody**: often changing quickly from having a good temperment to having a bad temperment

    a. The actress played a **moody**, self-absorbed woman who took advantage of her friends and family to advance her own career.
    b. A poor diet can have a negative effect on children's energy levels, causing them to become **moody** and out of sorts.
    c. My sister is always happy, **moody**, and a little bit silly; that's why everyone likes her.

2. **habit**: something that you do regularly or usually, often without thinking about it because you have done it so many times before

    a. Putting good sleep **habits** into practice is particularly difficult for teenagers.
    b. Watching movies is one of my favorite **habits**; I try to go to the movies every weekend.
    c. She has a **habit** of biting her lip when she is concentrating on something.

3. **speculate**: to guess about the possible causes or effects of something, without knowing all the facts or details

    a. I really shouldn't **speculate**, but I do think that the coach is thinking of cutting your son and mine from the baseball team.

    b. That lawyer **speculates** in cases involving workplace problems and employee rights.

    c. The police refused to **speculate** on a motive for the crime at this early stage in the investigation.

4. **deprivation**: a lack of something that you need in order to be healthy, comfortable, or happy

    a. The small town offered much in the way of social **deprivation**—a community center, a public library, a swimming pool, and a tennis court.

    b. Researchers have found that even short-term sensory **deprivation** quickly leads to a reduced ability to carry out even simple tasks.

    c. Healthy eating doesn't have to be about **deprivation**. You can include anything in your diet as long as it isn't eaten to excess.

5. **temper**: the way you feel at a particular time, especially when you feel angry

    a. You need to control your **temper**, or it is going to get you into trouble.

    b. I had a high **temper** all through my classes today, so I finally went home, took some aspirin, and went to bed.

    c. My sister is very sensitive and easily loses her **temper** if she thinks she has been wronged.

6. **consequence**: something that happens as a result of a particular action or set of conditions

    a. Babe Didrikson's success as a female athlete and golfer opened up many **consequences** for the women who followed her in these sports.

    b. The **consequences** of her mistake were far more serious than she could have imagined.

    c. Meeting the doctor who became her husband was a welcome **consequence** of breaking her ankle.

7. **prune**: to get rid of something you do not need or want, especially in order to reduce size or cost

    a. The life coach advised her to **prune** her schedule to make more time to do things that she really enjoyed.

    b. We had to call a tree specialist to come in and **prune** our oak tree because the neighbors complained it blocked their sun.

    c. The company decided to **prune** off its most successful hotels by adding fitness centers and other leisure facilities.

8. **leisure**: the time when you are not working or studying and can relax and do things you enjoy

    a. The city's public **leisure** facilities need upgrading so that all residents can easily and economically travel around the town.

    b. Airlines often offer discounted fares to **leisure** travelers in order to fill extra seats.

    c. Puzzles became very popular at the time of the Industrial Revolution because workers had more time available for **leisure** activities.

9. **circuit**: the complete circle that an electric current travels through

    a. The microprocessor is an integrated **circuit** that processes all information in the computer.

    b. If all of the connections in a **circuit** are not intact, then the electrical current will be stopped on its way through the **circuit**.

    c. There was only one electricity outlet in the bedroom, so she had to use an extension **circuit** to plug in her computer.

10. **executive**: concerned with making decisions and ensuring that decisions are carried out

    a. The **executive** functions of the company were carried out by a group of managers who set plans and policies for all of the employees.

    b. The directions for operating the machines were written out in **executive** detail to avoid any accidents.

    c. The kings and queens of Norway, Sweden, and Denmark are all heads of state, but none of them have any **executive** powers.

11. **caution**: to warn someone that something might be dangerous or difficult

    a. Brain experts **caution** that the training gains made from playing computerized brain games rarely lead to improved performance in everyday life.

    b. Doctors **caution** that everyone should eat five portions of fruit and vegetables a day in order to maintain a healthy diet.

    c. Public health experts **caution** that both the UVA and UVB rays in sunlight can do serious damage to our skin.

12. **translate**: to change something into a different form or to express something in a different way

    a. Ordinary people are hoping that the recent economic recovery will **translate** into more jobs.

    b. A raise in pay doesn't always **translate** into more spending money, as much of it ends up going to taxes.

    c. The cake recipe stated it was okay to **translate** honey for sugar.

WORD FAMILIES

A. The table contains word families for some of the target words in the reading. Complete the table. An **X** indicates that there is no form or that the form is not common. Sometimes more than one form may be possible. If you are unsure about a form, check your dictionary.

Verb	Noun	Adjective	Adverb
	aggravation	1. 2.	
caution	1. 2.	1. 2.	
	deprivation		X
	enthusiasm	1. 2.	
X	habit		
X	1. 2.	moody	
X	X	provisional	
rehearse			X
speculate			
translate			X

B. Read the sentences. In eight of the sentences, an incorrect form of the target word has been used. If the form of the target word is incorrect, cross it out and write the correct form. If the form is correct, put a checkmark (✔). Use the word families table to help you.

_____ **1.** Although the food at that restaurant is excellent, the service is **aggravation** slow.

_____ **2.** After breaking her leg skiing last winter, she was very **caution** about wanting to go again this year.

_____ **3.** A first child sometimes feels **deprivation** of his or her mother's attention when a new baby comes into the home.

_____ **4.** We had a very **enthusiasm** and knowledgeable guide for our tour of Istanbul.

_____ **5.** I **habit** get a stiff back from spending too much time sitting in front of the computer.

_____ **6.** Her **moodiness** almost ruined our whole vacation because we could never be sure whether she was going to want to join in any of our activities.

_____ **7.** The football game has **provision** been rescheduled for November 1, after it was canceled today due to poor weather.

_____ **8.** The cast members of the play were very nervous because their final **rehearse** had not gone well.

_____ **9.** After the exam was finished, the students went off to a coffee shop where they had a **speculate** conversation about their grades.

_____ **10.** A survey of Indian workers shows that employees spend an average of one hour per day on various social networking sites. This **translates** to a 12.5 percent loss in productivity.

COLLOCATION

In each set of sentences, the target word is paired with different words to form different collocations. Choose the collocation that best fits the last sentence and write it in the blank. You may need to change the form of one word in the collocation to fit the sentence.

1. a. Science fiction books and films fuel our imaginations by introducing us to a wide range of superhuman heroes, futuristic technology, and **alien worlds**.
  b. When the radio play *War of the Worlds* was first aired in 1938, many people believed it was a real newscast and that Earth was under **alien attack**.
  c. *Close Encounters of the Third Kind* is one of the most famous Hollywood movies focusing on the topic of **alien abduction**.
  d. Special effects have made it easier for filmmakers to create more realistic and varied _____ instead of simply showing deserts.

2. a. Regional differences between language users is a **natural consequence** of humans' ability to use language creatively.
  b. The massive population loss in North and South America after the arrival of Columbus was a **direct consequence** of the introduction of European diseases.
  c. The Special Olympics clearly show that leading a limited life is not an **inevitable consequence** of disability.
  d. The changes to the library's opening hours were a(n) _____ of suggestions put forward by regular library users.

3. a. The negotiators were hoping for a **constructive dialogue** between the company and union representatives in order to avoid a strike.
  b. Improving the public transport system may offer a more **constructive approach** to dealing with traffic problems than building more roads.
  c. When teachers introduce peer editing into writing classrooms, they need to be sure that peer readers are trained to offer **constructive criticism**.
  d. The ability to give and take _____ is an important part of good employer-employee relationships.

4. a. Although the applicant lacked some basic skills, everyone on the interview panel agreed that her **youthful enthusiasm** more than made up for these gaps.

   b. For many people, the **initial enthusiasm** they had for their New Year's resolution has already worn off by early February.

   c. My math teacher had such an **infectious enthusiasm** for his subject that even the most uninterested learners began to see its usefulness.

   d. The _____ for the new park project quickly dried up when everyone saw how difficult it was going to be to raise the necessary money.

5. a. Susan wasn't willing to wait for the others to make up their minds, so she made an **executive decision** to order pizza and garlic bread for dinner.

   b. In some countries, the office of the president holds **executive power**, while in others the president is mainly a figurehead, and real power belongs to the prime minister.

   c. National emergencies such as floods, tornados, and wildfires require prompt **executive action** to ensure the quick arrival of needed supplies.

   d. The careful _____ the management team made during the economic slowdown ensured the company's survival.

6. a. My little brother had strange **eating habits**. He would only eat one food at a time, and he never allowed two different foods to touch each other on his plate.

   b. My wife has the **annoying habit** of setting her alarm clock to go off early and then hitting the snooze button about ten times before getting up.

   c. Alison has the **nervous habit** of repeatedly clearing her throat whenever she has to give a presentation or speak at a meeting.

   d. I've noticed that my boss tugs at his moustache whenever he is asked a difficult question. It is a(n) _____, and I doubt he even knows he does it.

7. a. The city hopes to regenerate the industrial area along the river by bringing in more restaurants, parks, and other **leisure facilities**.

   b. In England, spending time with friends and family, listening to music, and watching TV are the top **leisure activities** of 80 percent of people between 16 and 24.

   c. My father travels a lot for his job, but always makes sure to have some **leisure time** to go sightseeing in the places he visits.

   d. According to the U.S. Bureau of Labor Statistics, on an average day, adults 75 and over spent 7.6 hours engaged in _____—more than any other age group.

8. a. The physical and mental health problems experienced by retired NFL football players has **prompted a** congressional **investigation** into football brain injuries.

   b. The reformation of the rock band after so many years **prompted the question** "Why did they break up in the first place?"

   c. Concerns about pedestrian safety **prompted the** city council's **decision** to put up new traffic lights at the corner of Lincoln Avenue and Broad Street.

   d. The price of tuition and a fear of missing her family _____ to study at a college in her home state.

Expanding the Topic

Try to answer the trivia questions about the brain and mental health.

1. **True** **False** There is evidence that yawning helps your brain be more **alert**.

2. **True** **False** The **caretakers** of pets are generally both physically and psychologically healthier than people who do not have pets.

3. **True** **False** **Circuits** in the brain are links between brain cells called *neurons*. There are about 1 billion neurons in a human brain.

4. **True** **False** Some things you can do to promote mental health include daydreaming, exercising, enjoying **hobbies**, keeping a journal, and volunteering.

5. **True** **False** The speech production area of the brain was first identified in a **laboratory** experiment in 1905.

6. **True** **False** The number of neurons babies have has been **pruned** back by 20 percent by the time they are adults.

7. **True** **False** High blood pressure can directly cause bad **temper**.

8. **True** **False** **Trimming** one's weight can lead to better mental health.

 Given that the research reported here indicates that the teen brain is clearly different from the adult brain, should teenagers continue to be treated as young adults? Write a 500-word essay expressing your views. Be sure to provide supporting evidence.

Revisiting the Target Words

Now that you have completed this chapter, use the scale to describe your knowledge of the target words.

1 I still don't know anything about this word.

2 I am still not sure of the meaning of this word even after studying it.

3 I understand this word when I see it or hear it in a sentence, but I don't know how to use it in my own speaking and writing.

4 I know this word and can use it in my own speaking and writing.

TARGET WORDS			
_____aggravation	_____consequence	_____hobby	_____prune
_____alert	_____constructive	_____laboratory	_____rehearse
_____alien	_____deprivation	_____leisure	_____speculate
_____caretaker	_____enthusiasm	_____moody	_____temper
_____caution	_____executive	_____prompt	_____translate
_____circuit	_____habit	_____provisional	_____trim

KNOWLEDGE CHECK 2

Go back to the beginning of the chapter and complete the Knowledge Check 1 table.

Strategy Practice

Getting Started

Look at the three images taken from Chapters 5–7. Without looking back at the chapters, how many target words can you remember from each chapter?

Focusing on Skills: ESSAY WRITING

One of the most effective ways to learn and remember new vocabulary words is to practice using them. Writing is a great way to practice vocabulary, and that's why there are writing tasks at the end of each chapter in this book. This chapter presents a variety of useful vocabulary designed to help you with these tasks and future essay assignments.

UNDERSTANDING ESSAY STRUCTURE

Whether you are writing an essay for a college assignment or for a TOEFL or IELTS exam, essay structure is an important element to keep in mind. Most essays have the following structure:

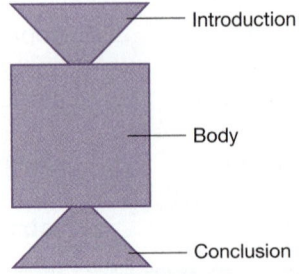

Introduction

Body

Conclusion

In order to demonstrate a clear essay structure, it is a good idea to use a selection of words and phrases that teachers and examiners expect to see. This vocabulary is presented in the following sections.

WRITING THE INTRODUCTION

The purpose of an essay introduction is to lead the reader into your essay topic. An introduction usually includes three key elements:

    (1) a general statement that states the topic of the essay
    (2) a sentence that presents your main argument or opinion
    (3) a section that outlines how you are going to organize your essay

① The example phrases in the table are used to state the topic of an essay. They are divided into groups according to their specific function.

A. Match the functions with the example phrases in the table.

Functions

a. introducing a contrasting viewpoint
b. emphasizing the importance of a topic
c. making a general statement

Example phrases

＿＿ 1.	It is said that … It is a fact that … For many people … Most scientists agree that … Some say that …
＿＿ 2.	However, others believe that … Nevertheless, some claim that … On the other hand, people say that …

＿＿ 3.	The idea of (topic) …	is one of the most important issues in … is probably the biggest …

B. Look back at the three writing tasks from Unit 2. For each task, write a sentence that states the topic.

② The second element of an essay introduction usually indicates the purpose of the essay and frequently includes the main argument. The example phrases in the box can be used to do that.

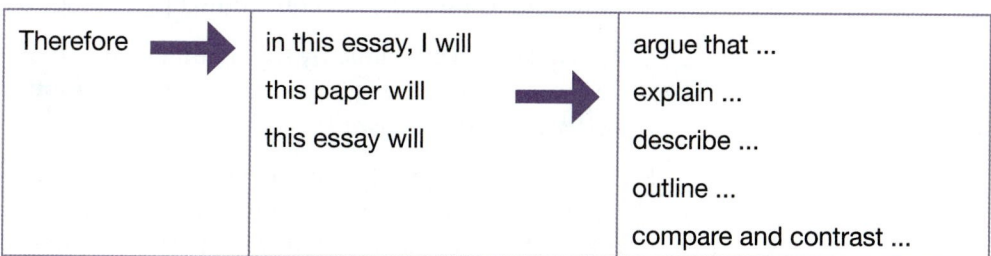

| Therefore | ➡ | in this essay, I will

 this paper will

 this essay will | ➡ | argue that …

 explain …

 describe …

 outline …

 compare and contrast … |

Look back at the three writing tasks from Unit 2. For each task, write a sentence that states the purpose / argument.

③ The final element of an essay introduction usually tells the reader how you are going to organize your essay. Example phrases are listed in the box.

A. Use the phrases in the box to complete the table.

Finally,	will conclude by saying that …
will be followed by …	will summarize the main points and conclude.
will begin by …	will then go on to …

I This essay This paper	1.
I It	2.
This	3.

4.	I this essay this paper	5. 6.

Now that you know the formulaic language of essay introductions, you can combine the standard phrases with the target words from previous chapters. It is important that you pay attention to word order and word form when adding your own words to these useful phrases.

B. Complete each sentence with the correct form of the word in parentheses. Use the chapter number in parentheses to locate and reread the word in context. Also, use the word families tables in Unit 2 to help you. Then identify what part of the essay introduction the sentence is (1, 2, or 3).

_____ **1.** Most _____ (**biological**) would agree that humans and apes have evolved from the same source. (5)

_____ **2.** It is a well-known fact that the ability to think is _____ (**uniquely**) to human beings. (5)

_____ **3.** The idea of _____ (**multiple**) intelligences is one of the most important issues in educational psychology today. (5)

_____ **4.** This essay will conclude by saying that research on synesthesia should be given greater _____ (**prominent**) if we are to develop a better understanding of this condition. (6)

_____ **5.** However, others believe that teenagers are _____ (**deprivation**) of sleep, which may provide one explanation for why teens are unable to concentrate for long periods of time. (7)

WRITING THE BODY

Once you have identified your topic, argument, and organizational plan, you can begin the body. The body is composed of paragraphs that reflect your main point. Each paragraph should include (a) a topic sentence that introduces the reader to the topic of your paragraph, (b) sentences demonstrating your main idea, and (c) supporting evidence depending on the type of essay you're writing.

The following example phrases can be used in the body of your essay. They are divided into groups according to their specific function.

A. Match the functions with the example phrases in the table.

Functions

a. expressing other people's opinions
b. beginning topic sentences
c. introducing additional points
d. expressing your opinion
e. giving examples

Example phrases

____ 1.	First of all, To begin with,	let's look at ...
	Before I ... ,	I think it is useful to ...
	Let's begin by ...	

____ 2.	There are a number of	points issues ideas opinions	to consider.	First of all, ... Secondly, ... In addition, ... In addition to ... , Furthermore, ... Moreover, ... However, ... On the other hand, ... In contrast, ... Finally, ... Last but not least, ... Lastly, ...

____ 3.	For example, ... To take another example, ... For instance, ... such as ...

____ 4.	In my view, … I am convinced that …	
	I (completely) agree with … It is difficult to disagree with …	because … for the following reasons …
	I disagree with the idea that … I do not share the view that … It is wrong to … The problem with …	

____ 5.	According to		(the author),		…
	In his / her	book, article, chapter,	(the author)	claims … states … points out …	
	On his / her website,			mentions …	
	As			argues …	

B. Read the target words in the box. Complete each sentence with the target word that matches the meaning of the words in parentheses.

alien	enthusiasm	possess	primary	rehearse

1. First of all, let's look at the _____ reason for the development of
(most important)
human thought.

2. In addition to the ability to see sounds, people with synesthesia
_____ other unusual abilities.
(have)

3. For example, parents consider the behavior of their teenage children to be
completely _____.
(strange)

4. I do not share the view that teenagers lack _____ because they
(eagerness)
are not getting enough sleep.

5. According to Robert Stickgold of the Massachusetts Institute of Technology,
sleep allows us to _____, restructure, and reclassify all of the
(practice)
learning from our day—and then assign it to long-term memory.

WRITING THE CONCLUSION

The final part of an essay is the conclusion. The purpose of most essay conclusions is to summarize the main points made in the body and, in some cases, to recommend some action. The following example phrases are all commonly used in essay conclusions.

In sum, …	Therefore …	there is a need for further …
To sum up, …	Thus …	it is possible to argue that …
To conclude, …		it can be said that …
In conclusion, …		this essay has found that …
		I believe that …

Read the target words in the box. Choose the target word that best completes the collocation and write it in the blank. You may need to change the form of one word in the collocation to fit the sentence.

consequence	prompt	speculate
explore	provisional	

1. Therefore, there is a need to _____ the **possibility** of making significant changes to school timetables to better suit teenagers.

2. In sum, the **likely** _____ of sleep deprivation include poor concentration levels, mood swings, and ineffective learning.

3. Therefore, it can be said that there is **growing** _____ that art may be the key to understanding when humans first began to think.

4. Therefore, the _____ **findings** of this study are that synesthesia is a far more common condition than originally thought and that it comes in a wide variety of forms.

5. Thus, I believe that _____ **action** is required if we are to develop a better understanding of this condition.

Focusing on Vocabulary Cards: TARGET WORDS IN WRITING GAME

At the beginning of this book, you were introduced to the idea of making vocabulary cards and how useful they are as a strategy for learning new vocabulary. If you have completed Units 1 and 2, you should already have a collection of 144 vocabulary cards. In addition, you should have already completed six writing tasks.

Use your vocabulary cards to check how many words you have used in your writing tasks. Follow these steps.

Instructions

1. Form pairs or teams (Team A and Team B).

2. Each team selects a total of ten vocabulary cards from its stack of 144 vocabulary cards. Team members each select a piece of writing that they have done. (Choose pieces of writing that use as many of the target words as possible.) For example, a team of five people should have ten vocabulary cards and five pieces of writing.

3. Team A then selects one of its own vocabulary cards and asks Team B members if they have used that target word in any of their writing tasks.

4. Team B is given time to skim their pieces of writing to see if they have used the target word.

5. If Team B has used the target word, it receives five points for each team member who has used the word correctly (not for how many times the word has been used in each piece of writing). For example, if the target word is "buzz" and three members of Team B have used "buzz" correctly in their writing tasks, the team is awarded fifteen points (three members x five points).

6. If the target word has not been used by any members of Team B, or has been used incorrectly, Team A scores five points.

7. Once the scores have been tallied, Team B chooses one of its vocabulary cards and the process is repeated. The team with the highest score at the end of the game wins.

UNIT

3

Design

Science Fiction into Reality

Getting Started

Discuss the questions with your classmates.

✦ Do you like science fiction in general? Why or why not?

✦ Was *Star Trek* popular where you grew up? Are you a fan?

✦ Do you think science fiction can inspire the creation of new technology in the real world?

Assessing Your Vocabulary Knowledge: TARGET WORDS

Look at the words in the box. These are the target words for this chapter. Use the scale to score yourself on each word.

1 I don't know this word.

2 I have seen or heard this word before, but I am not sure of the meaning.

3 I understand this word when I see it or hear it in a sentence, but I don't know how to use it in my own speaking and writing.

4 I know this word and can use it in my own speaking and writing.

TARGET WORDS

____accent	____dissolve	____magnetic	____scan
____battery	____dubious	____mission	____software
____convenient	____feasible	____mobile	____spark
____cope	____flip	____oral	____tablet
____crew	____global	____portable	____trek
____dialect	____graphic	____refrigerator	____viable

KNOWLEDGE CHECK 1

Complete the sentences with words that you have scored as **1**.

1. I am not familiar with the word / term _____.

2. I have no idea what _____ means.

Fill in the first blank with a word that you have scored as **2**. Then complete the sentence.

3. I think _____ could mean _____.

Reading

The passage discusses how science fiction can inspire the creation of new technology, using *Star Trek* as an example. As you read, pay special attention to the target vocabulary words in **bold**.

Star Trek Technology

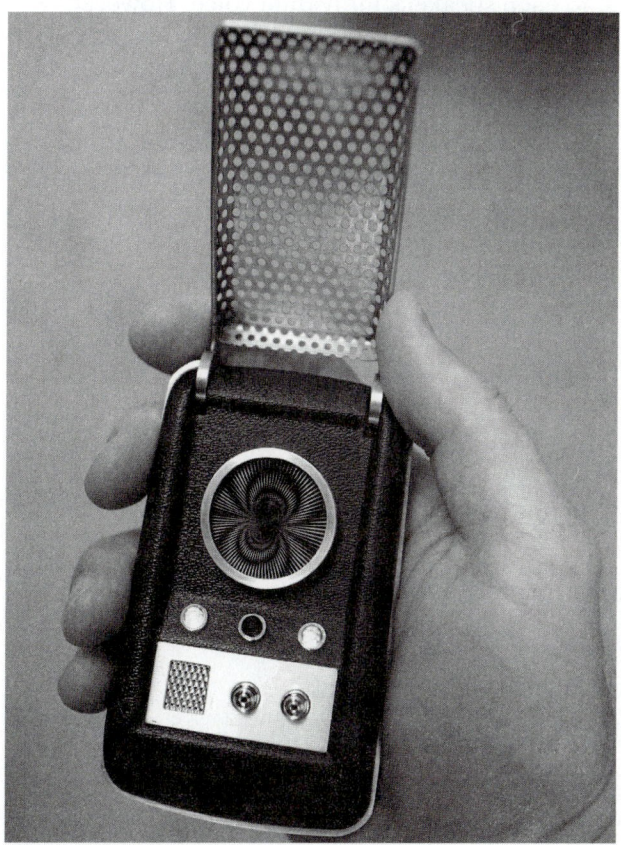

1   One of the most successful science fiction programs of all time is *Star Trek*. The original television series was first broadcast from 1966 to 1969. This **sparked** the "Trekkie" phenomenon, with a total of six television series and eleven movies as of 2009. A large part of *Star Trek's* ongoing popularity with science fiction fans is the futuristic gadgets found in the various episodes. Although transporters, time-travel machines, and the like are not currently **feasible**, other equipment seems **viable** and may be developed during our lifetimes. Consider the advanced hologram technology on the ships' "holodecks," which allowed characters to create simulated realities. Scientists are working to develop similar technology today and Tele-immersion is one such application. Tele-immersion will create a simulated virtual room that allows people to come together and interact

without leaving their own physical location. In fact, many of the *Star Trek* technologies that seemed **dubious** or impossible only a few decades ago now are available for use in the real world.

2   Probably the most notable of these gadgets was the handheld **flip**-open communicator, often used by Captain Kirk to summon help when he and his **crew** were in danger on some alien world. It allowed **portable** and lightweight communication wherever a person was. The appearance of this device started Martin Cooper and his team at Motorola thinking about how to develop a **mobile** phone. The first **mobile** phones were hardly **convenient**: They weighed 2.2 pounds, and the **batteries** allowed only thirty-five minutes of talk time. However, once the technology was introduced, it advanced and miniaturized until it was developed into the small cell phones we have today, which not only allow voice communications, but also allow access to all of the textual and **graphic** riches of the Internet. As a result, cell phones are now commonplace, with at least 85 percent of adults in the U.S. and the U.K. owning one.

3   A number of other electronic devices from *Star Trek* are also now commonplace. Many of the *Star Trek* computerized gadgets featured touch screens, including the *Starship Enterprise's* controls. Nowadays, touch screens appear on everything from cell phones to smart **refrigerators**. Our modern e-book readers and BlackBerries were also foretold by the small computerized **tablets** that the *Star Trek* **crew** used for reading and storing data. And just as the *Star Trek* **crew** could always find its location when on **missions** to foreign planets by using **scanners**, we can now do this on Earth by using a GPS (**Global** Positioning System) device.

4   Some of the medical technologies on *Star Trek* have also become reality. In the show, brain surgery was performed by attaching a gadget to someone's head, which healed internal injuries without cutting into the

brain. There is now a similar procedure called *gamma ray surgery*, where a number of beams of gamma radiation are precisely focused at a single target—for example, a brain tumor. This **dissolves** and eliminates the diseased area. Since the procedure is noninvasive, there is little pain and much less chance for infection. *Star Trek* doctors also diagnosed patients using the versatile handheld tricorder **scanners**. (In fact, the *Star Trek* tricorder seemed to do everything, from checking a planet's atmosphere to diagnosing a broken engine!) Modern patients are **scanned** in essentially the same way, by **magnetic** resonance imaging (MRI) and CAT **scans**, although the equipment is much larger than a handheld device. Even the crusty Dr. McCoy would be impressed.

5   Another *Star Trek* technology that appears to be within reach is the universal communicator. A number of translators already are available on the Internet, and they do a fair (although far from perfect) job of translating written texts. But translating speech is much more difficult. People speak with a wide variety of **dialects** and **accents**, which current voice recognition systems simply cannot **cope** with. For the best results, the **software** must be trained to each speaker's individual voice. However, improvements gradually are being made, and it may be years rather than decades before sufficiently powerful voice recognition **software** makes simultaneous **oral** translations possible.

6   With advances such as these, it is fair, exciting, and perhaps a bit frightening to ask, how far behind can Mr. Spock's telepathic "mind-meld" communication be?

(698 words)

READING COMPREHENSION

Respond to the questions in writing. Base your responses on the reading and your own personal experiences.

1. List four inventions from *Star Trek* programs that are available for use today.

2. What two inventions are not yet available, but may be within our lifetimes?

3. How does modern medical technology compare with that shown in *Star Trek*?

4. If a universal translator is eventually developed, will there still be value in learning a second language?

5. How does a science fiction story or program, such as *Star Trek*, lead to the creation of new technology?

6. Will it ever be possible to visit other stars using spaceships that travel faster than the speed of light?

Focusing on Vocabulary

WORD MEANING

A. Match the target words with their definitions. If you are unsure about a word's meaning, try to figure it out from the context by rereading the passage. Then check your dictionary.

Set 1

_____ 1. crew
_____ 2. battery
_____ 3. refrigerator
_____ 4. tablet
_____ 5. mission
_____ 6. accent
_____ 7. software

a. an important job that involves traveling somewhere
b. a large piece of electrical equipment, used for keeping food and drink cool
c. a pad of paper for writing on
d. a group of people with special skills who work together
e. an object that provides a supply of electricity for something such as a radio, car, or toy
f. the way someone pronounces the words of a language
g. the sets of programs that tell a computer how to do a particular job

Set 2

_____ 1. viable
_____ 2. flip
_____ 3. portable
_____ 4. graphic
_____ 5. scan
_____ 6. magnetic
_____ 7. dialect

a. able to be done or worth doing
b. connected with or including drawing, printing, or designing
c. able to be carried or moved easily
d. to use a piece of equipment that passes an electrical beam over something; to take a picture of what is inside
e. to move something with a quick sudden movement so that it is in a different position
f. capable of attracting iron objects
g. a form of a language that is spoken only in one area, with words or grammar that is slightly different from other forms of the same language

B. Read each target word and the list below it. One word or phrase in each list is NOT a synonym for the target word. Cross it out.

1. **trek**

| journey | trick | long trip | voyage |

2. **spark**

| start | launch | set in motion | flame |

3. **feasible**

| practical | workable | trouble-free | possible |

4. **dubious**

| unhelpful | doubtful | questionable | unpromising |

5. **mobile**

| moveable | renewable | not fixed | transportable |

6. **convenient**

| handy | practical | old-fashioned | useful |

7. **global**

| community | international | large-scale | worldwide |

8. **dissolve**

| melt | liquefy | knock down | soften |

9. **cope**

| unite | handle | deal with | manage |

10. **oral**

| spoken | verbal | by mouth | heard |

Word Tip

Although many people believe that *accent* and *dialect* refer to the same thing, it's useful to be aware of how they are different. *Accent* refers only to pronunciation, while *dialect* refers to grammar and vocabulary as well. For example, speakers from Boston and Dallas have different **accents**, but not different **dialects**. Although there are differences in their pronunciation, the words and grammar they use are the same.

In England, people from Newcastle speak a different **dialect** than people from London. In addition to using different pronunciation, they also use a range of different vocabulary.

WORD FAMILIES

A. The table on the next page contains word families for some of the target words in the reading. Complete the table. An **X** indicates that there is no form or that the form is not common. Sometimes more than one form may be possible. If you are unsure about a form, check your dictionary.

Verb	Noun	Adjective	Adverb
X		convenient	
X		dubious	
X		feasible	
	1. 2.	global	
X		1. graphic 2.	
	1. 2. 3.	magnetic	
X		portable	X
	1. 2. refrigerator		X
scan	1. 2.		X
X		viable	

B. Choose the correct form of the word in **bold** in sentence **a** to complete sentence **b**. Use the word families table you just completed as a guide.

1. **a.** It is often more **convenient** to drive a car than to take public transportation, but public transportation is usually the greener alternative.

   b. _____ stores make it easier for busy people to buy food, but the foods they carry are often lacking in nutritional value.

2. **a.** Although John D. Rockefeller was one of the richest men in American history, much of his wealth was gained by rather **dubious** business practices.

   b. He looked _____ at his friend's rusty old car and wondered whether it was safe to get into.

3. **a.** Although the plan had many critics, the CEO still believed that it was **feasible**.

   b. The U.S. government ran a _____ study to determine whether it was possible to begin sending astronauts to the moon again, but decided that it was simply too expensive.

4. a. There is now overwhelming evidence that **global** warming exists.

   b. The trend toward the _____ of banking has made it much more difficult for individual governments to regulate international banks.

5. a. Newspaper advertising is heavily dependent on **graphic** design for its visual appeal.

   b. *Persepolis* by Marjane Satrapi is a _____ novel that tells the story of the author growing up in Iran.

6. a. The North **Magnetic** Pole, which compasses point to, is situated in Canada and moves about 25 miles per year.

   b. _____ are attracted to certain metals such as iron and steel.

7. a. The exploration of the oceans has been made possible by a **portable** air supply system called SCUBA (Self-Contained Underwater Breathing Apparatus).

   b. Their small size and _____, along with good sound quality, is what makes MP3 players popular.

8. a. American homes have **refrigerators** that are much larger than those in most homes in Europe.

   b. Alexander Twining is credited with developing the first commercially **viable** method of _____ in the United States in the mid-1850s.

9. a. When the checkout boy **scans** your purchases at the supermarket, he's sending valuable information to the store manager about sales and inventory.

   b. Veterinarians are now able to reunite owners with their lost pets by using handheld _____ to read microchips implanted under the pet's skin.

10. a. For a young singer struggling to get noticed, YouTube offers a **viable** option for self-promotion.

    b. Although many questioned the _____ of professional women's soccer, successful leagues now exist in the United States, Australia, and a number of European countries.

COLLOCATION

Read the common collocations in the column on the left. Give two examples of things associated with each collocation.

	Example 1	Example 2
1. regional **accent**	_____	_____
2. spark debate	_____	_____
3. cope with a situation	_____	_____

4. upward
mobility _____   _____

5. rescue
mission _____   _____

6. crew
member _____   _____

7. software
application _____   _____

8. oral
examination _____   _____

Expanding the Topic

This is a list of a number of devices commonly seen on *Star* **Trek**.

Devices

a. a handheld communicator   **f.** replicators
b. the matter-antimatter engine   **g.** the ship's computer
c. the phaser   **h.** a transporter
d. the photon torpedo   **i.** the tricorder
e. reading pads   **j.** a universal communicator

A. Complete the descriptions of the devices using the target words from the box. You many need to change the form of the word to fit the sentence.

battery	dissolve	mission	refrigerator	tablet
dialect	flip	oral	scan	trek

Descriptions

1. _____ This was activated by _____ command.

2. _____ This is a weapon on *Star* _____ ships that creates large explosions.

3. _____ This **portable** device is used for a variety of _____ purposes.

4. _____ As the main power for the ship, it may have been supplemented by _____ for backup power.

5. _____ There was no need for _____ to preserve food because these devices created any type of food on command.

6. _____ This weapon shot large energy bursts that would _____ enemy ships, rocks, and virtually anything else.

7. _____ Originally this was a device that _____ open, but later was incorporated into the Star Fleet badge.

8. ____ This device could instantly translate any alien language or _____.

9. ____ The **crew** read a variety of things from these _____, which look very much like modern digital book readers.

10. ____ This device could instantly move the crew to _____ on planets by turning the crew members into energy.

B. Now try to match the devices to the descriptions.

This chapter discusses the technology from *Star Trek* and how **feasible** it is in today's world. Write a 500-word essay on the technology from some other science-fiction book, movie, or TV show, and discuss how **feasible** these devices are.

Revisiting the Target Words

Now that you have completed this chapter, use the scale to describe your knowledge of the target words.

1 I still don't know anything about this word.

2 I am still not sure of the meaning of this word even after studying it.

3 I understand this word when I see it or hear it in a sentence, but I don't know how to use it in my own speaking and writing.

4 I know this word and can use it in my own speaking and writing.

TARGET WORDS

____accent	____dissolve	____magnetic	____scan
____battery	____dubious	____mission	____software
____convenient	____feasible	____mobile	____spark
____cope	____flip	____oral	____tablet
____crew	____global	____portable	____trek
____dialect	____graphic	____refrigerator	____viable

KNOWLEDGE CHECK 2

Select examples from the words you now give a score of **3** or **4**, but didn't at the start of the chapter, to complete the sentences.

1. I didn't know that _____ meant _____ before reading this chapter.

2. I wasn't sure that I knew the meaning of _____, but I am now.

3. I now am confident that I know what _____ means, but I would like more practice with how to use it in my speaking and writing.

4. I could next use _____ when I am _____.

CHAPTER 10

How Choice Architects Can Help You!

Getting Started

Discuss the questions with your classmates.

✦ Have you ever found a choice difficult to make because there were too many options to choose from?

✦ What kind of products cause this "choice overload" for you?

✦ What or who do you turn to for advice in these situations?

Assessing Your Vocabulary Knowledge: TARGET WORDS

Look at the words in the box. These are the target words for this chapter. Use the scale to score yourself on each word.

1 I don't know this word.

2 I have seen or heard this word before, but I am not sure of the meaning.

3 I understand this word when I see it or hear it in a sentence, but I don't know how to use it in my own speaking and writing.

4 I know this word and can use it in my own speaking and writing.

TARGET WORDS			
____adopt	____diet	____handy	____layout
____architect	____donate	____hint	____lifestyle
____beware	____encounter	____impose	____menu
____clash	____gently	____indulge	____professor
____classify	____glance	____infrequently	____relieve
____consumer	____grab	____label	____shelf

KNOWLEDGE CHECK 1

Fill in the first blank with a word that you have scored as **2**. Then complete the second sentence.

1. I have seen / heard _____. I saw / heard it while I was

_____.

Fill in the first blanks with words that you have scored as **4**. Then complete the sentences.

2. One meaning of _____ is _____.

3. I last used the word _____ while I was _____.

Reading

A Nudge in the Right Direction

1   Freedom, independence, choice—these are all good things, right? Some might even argue that these are basic human rights, and that having laws that dictate behavior **clashes** with our right to choose for ourselves.

2   But is there such a thing as too much choice? Yes, some say. Being free and independent requires us to make choices, and sometimes those choices can be difficult.

3   Let's say you've decided you want to eat more healthfully. You've read books, blogs, and magazine articles about healthy **diets** and listened to news reports about what is and isn't good for you. However, you don't have time to carefully plan **menus** for meals or read food **labels** at the supermarket. Since you really are committed to a healthier **lifestyle**, a little help would come in **handy**, wouldn't it? This is where a "choice **architect**" can help **relieve** some of the burden of doing it all yourself.

4   Choice **architects** are people who organize the contexts in which **consumers** make decisions. For example, the person who decides the **layout** of your local supermarket—including which **shelf** the peanut butter goes on, and how the oranges are stacked—is a choice **architect**. So is the person who organizes where the salad and dessert bars are in your school or work cafeteria. And, believe it or not, the arrangements they **adopt** will influence

the selections you make, according to Richard Thaler and Cass Sunstein, **professors** at the University of Chicago.

5   Thaler and Sunstein say that governments don't have to **impose** healthier **lifestyles** through laws—for example, smoking bans and transfat boycotts. Rather, they say, that if given an environment created by a choice **architect**—one that encourages us to choose what is best—we will do the right thing. In other words, Thaler and Sunstein would like to see designs that **gently** push, or nudge, customers toward making healthier choices, without removing freedom of choice. They call this idea "nudge" because it combines the idea of freedom to choose with **gentle hints** from choice **architects**, who aim to help people live longer, healthier, and happier lives.

6   For example, the British and Swedish governments have introduced a so-called "traffic light system" to **classify** foods as healthy or unhealthy. This means that shoppers can see at a **glance** how much fat, saturated fat, sugar, and salt each product contains simply by looking at the lights on the package. A green light indicates that the amounts of the four nutrients are healthy; yellow signals that the shopper should **beware**; and red means that the food is high in at least one of the four nutrients and should be eaten in moderation. The shopper is given important health information, but is still free to decide whether to **grab** an apple or **indulge** in that chocolate brownie.

7   Moreover, Thaler and Sunstein believe that ordinary people would *especially* benefit from nudges when **encountering** any of the following five situations. When
- we have to choose now, but deal with the consequences later
- the degree of difficulty is great
- it is a decision that is made **infrequently**
- there is no immediate feedback
- the choice is about something unfamiliar.

8   Actual situations include things as ordinary

as deciding which car to buy, how much insurance to get, and which charities to **donate** to.

9   But, as we all know, despite our best intentions, we don't always make good decisions. So, couldn't we all benefit from a little nudge in the right direction every now and then?

(602 words)

Summarized from Thaler, R. and Sunstein, C. (2008). *Nudge.* London: Penguin Books.

READING COMPREHENSION

Respond to the questions in writing. Base your responses on the reading and your own personal experiences.

1. What is a *choice* **architect**?

2. Describe Thaler and Sunstein's idea of "nudge."

3. The passage suggests that people can benefit from help in making choices in five particular cases. List them.

4. The passage illustrates the idea of "nudging" people to better choices with the example of food **labeling** (green, yellow, and red signals). Can you think of two other examples of nudging?

5. A recent trend is the growing number of Internet comparison and advice sites. Have you ever used such a site? Did you find it helpful?

6. Do you think the government should require us to make healthier choices, for example, not drink alcohol or smoke? Or should this be totally left to individual choice?

Focusing on Vocabulary

WORD MEANING

A. Read the target words. Use the paragraph number in parentheses to locate and reread the word in context. Then read the dictionary definitions below each word and choose the one that reflects how the word is used in the reading.

_____ **1. clash** (1)
   a. to be in conflict because of very different ideas, beliefs, or opinions
   b. to look bad together, as with colors or designs

_____ **2. diet** (3)
   a. the kind of food that a person or animal eats each day
   b. a way of eating in which you only eat certain foods in order to lose weight

_____ **3. menu** (3)
   a. a list of things on a computer screen that you can ask the computer to do
   b. a list of all the kinds of food that are available for a meal

_____ **4. label** (3)
   a. a word or phrase used to describe a person, group, or thing, but is unfair or not correct
   b. a piece of paper or other material attached to something that gives information about it

_____ **5. handy** (3)
   a. good at using something, especially a tool
   b. useful

_____ **6. relieve** (3)
   a. to reduce pain or problems
   b. to replace someone when he or she has completed a duty or needs a rest

_____ **7. layout** (4)
   a. the way in which writing and pictures are arranged on a page
   b. the way objects in an area are arranged

_____ **8. shelf** (4)
   a. a long, flat, narrow board attached to a wall or in a frame or cupboard, used for putting things on
   b. a flat, narrow surface of rock, especially under water

_____ **9. adopt** (4)
   a. to take someone else's child into your home and legally become his or her parent
   b. to decide to start using a particular method, plan, or idea

_____ **10. hint** (5)
   a. a very small amount or sign of something
   b. something that you say or do to suggest an idea to someone, without telling them directly

_____ **11. grab** (6)
   a. to get some food or sleep quickly because you are busy
   b. to take hold of someone or something with a sudden or violent movement

_____ **12. encounter** (7)
   a. to experience or deal with something
   b. to meet someone without planning to

B. Read the target words in the box. Complete each sentence with the target word that matches the meaning of the words in parentheses. You may need to change the form of the word to fit the sentence.

architect	consumer	glance	infrequently
beware	donate	impose	lifestyle
classify	gently	indulge	professor

1. The mother took a quick _____ behind her to see that her
(quick look, glimpse)
children were following.

2. The old _____ was well known for writing the most popular
(university teacher, lecturer)
university textbook on chemistry.

3. Tim Berners-Lee is credited with being the _____ of the World
(designer, builder)
Wide Web.

4. After a hard week of work, it is good to _____ yourself on the
   (have something nice, treat)
   weekend.

5. Andrew Carnegie _____ millions of dollars to build over 2,500
   (give, contribute)
   public and university libraries in at least nine different English-speaking
   countries.

6. The International Monetary Fund _____ stricter lending
   (force, oblige)
   conditions on the country because of its corruption.

7. The nurse _____ gave the newborn baby to its mother to hold
   (softly, carefully)
   for the first time.

8. Visitors to Australia should _____ of the Sydney funnel-web
   (be careful, be cautious)
   spider, which is highly poisonous to humans.

9. _____ have benefited from better food labeling, as they can
   (customer, user)
   make more informed decisions about the food they eat.

10. Environmental groups urge people to adopt a "greener" _____.
   (way of life, existence)

11. A "blue moon" (a second full moon in a month) occurs _____,
   (rarely, seldom)
   only about once every two to three years.

12. Ancient Greek philosophy _____ the world into four main
   (categorize, group)
   elements: earth, water, fire, and wind.

WORD FAMILIES

A. The table contains word families for some of the target words in the reading. An
   X indicates that there is no form or that the form is not common. Study the table.
   Look for spelling patterns for the noun, adjective, and adverb forms of the words.
   List the patterns in the space on the next page.

Verb	Noun	Adjective	Adverb
adopt	adoption	adopted	X
clash	clash	X	X
classify	1. class 2. classification	classified	X
donate	donation	X	X
encounter	encounter	X	X
X	gentleness	gentle	**gently**
glance	**glance**	X	X
impose	imposition	X	X
indulge	indulgence	indulgent	indulgently
X	infrequency	infrequent	**infrequently**

nouns _____

adjectives _____

adverbs _____

B. Complete each sentence with the correct form of the word in parentheses. Use the word families table to help you.

1. The _____ (**adopt**) plan had the support of all the members of the committee.

2. Much of the last century was defined by the _____ (**clash**) between communism and capitalism.

3. The _____ (**classify**) of smallpox as an "eradicated disease" occurred in 1979; it is the only human disease to be completely eliminated.

4. The _____ (**donate**) of blood is one of the most valuable things anybody can do.

5. The _____ (**encounter**) with the bear in the forest left him shaken and scared.

6. She spoke to the dog with a _____ (**gently**) voice in order to calm him down.

7. The spy _____ (**glance**) around the corner to see if anyone was following him.

8. The _____ (**impose**) of taxes by England was the main cause of the American War for Independence.

9. The athlete ate very carefully, with an occasional chocolate bar being his only _____ (**indulge**).

10. After moving to Australia from America, she was only able to make _____ (**infrequently**) visits home to see her parents.

COLLOCATION

Combine a word from Column A with a word from Column B to form a collocation. Then match the collocation to its definition.

Column A	Column B
chief	goods
comfortable	**menu**
relieve	pain
subtle	**architect**
grab	a bite
designer	**lifestyle**
dinner	**hint**
consumer	**label**

1. _____ the main person responsible for a plan or idea

2. _____ fashionable products

3. _____ a list of food available for the evening meal

4. _____ a life in which you have enough money to buy the things you want

5. _____ to quickly get something to eat

6. _____ things that people buy for their own use

7. _____ to make something hurt less

8. _____ an indirect suggestion that is not very easy to understand

Expanding the Topic

A. If you were completely free, what kind of life would you choose? Complete the sentences and phrases with the target words from the box. You may need to change the form of one word in the collocation to fit the sentence. There are three extra words.

adopt	encounter	indulge
architect	gently	layout
beware	glance	lifestyle
classify	handy	professor
consumer	hint	relieve
donate	impose	shelf

1. Which _____ would you like?

   a. eating at nice restaurants with fancy **menus** every evening
   b. eating at home in the dining room with your family
   c. eating on the sofa watching TV

2. Which kind of career would you prefer?

   a. working outdoors in forests and gardens
   b. being a(n) _____ at a university
   c. being an entertainer such as an actor or musician

3. If you wanted to _____ yourself, which kind of treat would you prefer?

   a. going shopping to buy yourself something nice
   b. going out to an expensive restaurant
   c. taking some time off to _____ stress and just relax

4. If you did not have to worry about health issues, which type of **diet** would you
_____?

    a. a vegetarian **diet**
    b. a "Mediterranean" **diet** with lots of fruit, vegetables, olive oil, fish, and dairy
       products
    c. a rich **diet** with lots of meat, creamy sauces, and desserts

5. What would be the _____ of your ideal house?

    a. very open, with a few large rooms and modern furniture
    b. lots of smaller rooms with traditional furniture
    c. medium-size rooms with lots of _____ to put books and
       plants on

6. On an ideal vacation, what would you most like to _____?

    a. distant drum music _____ reaching your ears on a moon-lit
       Tahitian beach
    b. a(n) _____ of spice in the air as you walk through an Indian
       garden
    c. catching a(n) _____ of a beautiful "bird-of-paradise" in a New
       Guinean forest

7. If you could be known as the _____ of a new development that
would benefit the whole world, which would you choose?

    a. new, fast-growing foods that could **relieve** hunger
    b. a cure for cancer
    c. a machine that could control the weather and eliminate disastrous winds and
       floods

8. If you could _____ one law that would help reduce global
warming, which would you choose?

    a. _____ cars according to size, and severely tax the largest ones
    b. limit the amount of _____ goods packaging, including plastic
       grocery bags
    c. require all homes to install improved insulation so that they keep their heat
       better

B. Now think about the pros and cons of each choice and decide which you would
prefer. Discuss the reasons for your answers with a classmate. Did he or she make
the same choices as you? Why or why not?

Choose one of the topics in Exercise A and write a 500-word essay describing the
advantages and disadvantages of each option and which one you support.

Revisiting the Target Words

Now that you have completed this chapter, use the scale to describe your knowledge of the target words.

1 I still don't know anything about this word.

2 I am still not sure of the meaning of this word even after studying it.

3 I understand this word when I see it or hear it in a sentence, but I don't know how to use it in my own speaking and writing.

4 I know this word and can use it in my own speaking and writing.

TARGET WORDS

____adopt	____diet	____handy	____layout
____architect	____donate	____hint	____lifestyle
____beware	____encounter	____impose	____menu
____clash	____gently	____indulge	____professor
____classify	____glance	____infrequently	____relieve
____consumer	____grab	____label	____shelf

KNOWLEDGE CHECK 2

Select examples from the words you now give a score of **3** or **4**, but didn't at the start of the chapter, to complete the sentences.

1. I didn't know that _____ meant _____ before reading this chapter.

2. I wasn't sure that I knew the meaning of _____, but I am now.

3. I now am confident that I know what _____ means, but I would like more practice with how to use it in my speaking and writing.

4. I now know that _____ collocates with _____.

Positive Design

Getting Started

Discuss the questions with your classmates.

✦ Think of your favorite gadget. What do you like about it?

✦ Have you ever had an experience where the design of a machine or product has made it difficult for you to use?

✦ Do you find it difficult to be creative if you are frustrated or angry?

Assessing Your Vocabulary Knowledge: TARGET WORDS

Look at the words in the box. These are the target words for this chapter. Use the scale to score yourself on each word.

1 I don't know this word.

2 I have seen or heard this word before, but I am not sure of the meaning.

3 I understand this word when I see it or hear it in a sentence, but I don't know how to use it in my own speaking and writing.

4 I know this word and can use it in my own speaking and writing.

TARGET WORDS			
_____appliance	_____frustration	_____kettle	_____passionate
_____bulb	_____hassle	_____loyalty	_____persist
_____classic	_____humor	_____offset	_____resolve
_____craft	_____idiot	_____opt	_____squeeze
_____curiosity	_____illustrate	_____ornamental	_____sting
_____device	_____irritated	_____panic	_____tolerate

KNOWLEDGE CHECK 1

Check your progress in learning the vocabulary in this chapter.

- First, look at your scores in the table on page 100. Write the number of words for each score (1–4), in the "at the beginning" column. For example, if you scored eight words as **1** ("I don't know this word"), then write **8**.

- At the end of the chapter, score yourself again. Then compare the two sets of scores. Are you showing improvement on most of the words in the chapter?

Your score	Number of words ...		
	at the beginning:	at the end:	
		showing improvement	no improvement yet
1			
2			
3			
4			

Reading

The passage looks at the impact of design on the usability of products. As you read, pay special attention to the target vocabulary words in **bold**.

Easier on the Eye—Easier to Use?

1 *"More and more people buy objects for intellectual and spiritual nourishment. People do not buy my coffee makers, **kettles**, and lemon squeezers because they need to make coffee, to boil water, or to **squeeze** lemons, but for other reasons."* — Alberto Alessi, designer

2 Have you ever stood in front of a cash machine and been unsure of how to make it work? Your **frustration** mounts as you try different buttons, and you begin to **panic** because if you make another mistake, the machine will eat your card. How can a machine make you feel like such an **idiot**? Alternatively, have you ever seen a Mini? These **classic** little British cars may not seem terribly practical because they cannot carry many people or much stuff. Nonetheless, there is something about their style that attracts people. In fact, their owners are so **passionate** about them that they actually have their own international association of Mini enthusiasts. What these cases have in common is that they both **illustrate** the effects of design—bad and good—on human emotions.

3 William Morris, a key figure in the English arts and **crafts** movement in the late 1800s, famously stated, "Have nothing in your houses that you do not know to be useful, or believe to be beautiful." Even today aesthetics (beauty) and functionality (usability) remain the two key features of design, whether we are talking about the design of a building or a light **bulb**.

However, the question of which is more important may never be **resolved**.

4 This is **illustrated** by another well-known saying in design: "form follows function." This normally means that the usability and practicality of a design should always take priority over the beauty of a design. For those of us who have encountered bad design, this seems to make perfect sense. Remember the **hassle** of the cash machine or times when you have stood in front of a door pulling on an **ornamental** doorknob when the door actually opened with a simple push. Naturally, we might prefer a more functional product regardless of what it looks like.

5 However, researchers have found that aesthetics really do matter. For example, in a study of how people use computers, researchers found that early impressions influenced people's long-term attitudes about the computers' quality and use. People perceive that more beautiful and attractive designs are easier to use than their less attractive counterparts. Because these designs look easier to use, people are more likely to use them even though a less attractive **device** may have superior usability features.

6 According to Donald Norman, a cognitive scientist, this is because positive emotions aid learning, promote creativity, and encourage **curiosity**. This means that how well we are able to deal with a difficulty—such as an unfamiliar machine—is partially dependent on how we perceive the machine itself. Thus, how a **device** looks or feels can play an important role in fostering positive attitudes toward it and toward users' willingness to **persist** with difficult instructions or less than perfect performance. Take cell phones, for instance. They are plagued with problems such as difficulty getting a network connection and batteries that run out midway through important calls. Nokia was one of the first cell phone companies to realize that aesthetics could take some of the **sting** out of these

inconveniences and **offset** negative feelings when they do occur. It began to design phones in a variety of colors and with customizable ringtones. The result was a more positive appraisal by users who were more willing to **tolerate** the phones' limitations.

7   Google is another company that has **opted** to take this effect into account in its design. Consider how Google plays with its logo to celebrate holidays or recognize famous people or events. The use of **humor** puts users in a good mood, which can have a positive effect on their search for information. This, in turn, fosters **loyalty** to the Google search engine. Likewise, drivers **irritated** by the standard faceless voice of a GPS **device** may well be charmed by that same **device** speaking in their granddaughter's voice.

8   Product designers recognize that consumers have a variety of reasons for preferring one design over another and look for ways to **offset** potential negative aspects of their products. It should therefore come as no surprise that the iPhone, home espresso machines, and other popular **appliances** are now designed as much for their style as for their functionality. It might even be said that the new design motto is "Beauty is in the eye of the consumer."

(745 words)

READING COMPREHENSION

Respond to the questions in writing. Base your responses on the reading and your own personal experiences.

1. What are the two most important factors that designers of new products must consider?

2. What relationship between these factors have researchers found?

3. What are the specific effects of positive and negative feelings on learning?

4. What lesson have modern designers learned from these findings? Give an example.

5. Think of a difficult or problematic machine or gadget you have had to learn to use. Were you successful in learning to use it? What do think contributed to your success?

6. Make a list of other products that combine style and functionality.

Focusing on Vocabulary

WORD MEANING

A. Read the sentences and choose the word or phrase that best matches the meaning of the target word. Use context clues to determine the correct meaning. Check your dictionary if you are not sure of the answer.

1. You can either use your maple syrup immediately, or you can store it in a plastic bottle so that you can easily **squeeze** it onto pancakes later.

   a. put food into your mouth, and chew and swallow it
   b. get liquid from something by pressing it
   c. put a soft substance over the surface of something

2. Even an **idiot** should know that if you rob a bank, you should not take photos of yourself with the money.

   a. clever person
   b. stupid person
   c. criminal

3. Record Store Day is a campaign by people who are **passionate** about records to get other people reacquainted with their local record shops.

   a. knowledgeable about something because you have seen it, read it, or used it
   b. liking something a lot
   c. not considered modern or fashionable anymore

4. Council members will try to **resolve** parking problems on High Street, which have led to complaints about traffic congestion.

   a. take something away from the place that it is
   b. say that you are annoyed or unsatisfied with something
   c. find a satisfactory way of dealing with a problem or difficulty

5. When my computer broke down, I had to go to the library to do all of my homework. It was such a **hassle**.

   a. something that is annoying, because it causes problems or is difficult to do
   b. busy and noisy activity
   c. failure of a relationship or system

6. The mind is like a muscle that becomes stronger through continual exercise, so the mental exercise caused by **curiosity** makes your mind stronger and stronger.

   a. staying completely still
   b. extreme tiredness
   c. desire to know about something

7. Dance Island surprised spectators at today's race. Few would have assumed that when the 7-year-old horse began to chase the leader, he would **persist** and race to a brilliant second-place finish.

   a. continue to do something, although it is difficult or other people oppose it
   b. be the best or most successful in a race, game, election, or competition
   c. quickly follow someone or something, in order to catch them

8. The **sting** of not being invited to the party upset her until she realized she was now free to go to the play she wanted to see.

   a. something that happens, especially a strange event
   b. great happiness or pleasure
   c. sharp but usually temporary physical or emotional pain

9. I like wearing wool, but my mother and sister cannot **tolerate** the scratchiness of it on their skin.

   a. be able to accept something unpleasant or difficult, even though you don't like it
   b. move slowly and with great effort
   c. have enough money to buy or pay for something

10. Students who study modern languages may **opt** to study one language or two.

   a. become a member of an organization, society, or group
   b. choose one thing or do one thing instead of another
   c. refuse to accept, believe in, or agree with something

11. My favorite high school teacher used to use **humor** to help us relax before an important test.

   a. something frightening or scary
   b. something funny that makes people laugh
   c. lack of food

12. I understood that the delay was not the airline's fault, but I was **irritated** that it did not make any announcements to explain what was going on.

   a. trying or intending to achieve something
   b. feeling annoyed or impatient
   c. no longer worried

B. Read the target words and definitions. Then read the sentences. Circle the sentence in which the target word is NOT used correctly.

1. **kettle:** a container with a lid, handle, and spout, used for boiling and pouring water

   a. Using the Eco **Kettle** will save electricity, water, and time (it comes to a boil really fast), and it will save you money.
   b. Transfer the meat mixture to a preheated dish. Top with the mashed potatoes and bake in a preheated **kettle** at 190 degrees Celsius or 375 degrees Fahrenheit for thirty minutes.
   c. In the mornings, the maid fried bacon and eggs, filled the **kettle** for tea, and sliced bread for toast. When it was ready, she carried it to her master's bedchamber.

2. **frustration:** the feeling of being annoyed, upset, or impatient because you cannot control or change a situation, or achieve something

   a. We need to raise the levels of academic **frustration** in public schools.
   b. The players' **frustration** mounted as their repeated attempts to score were all expertly stopped by the goalie.
   c. His sense of **frustration** increased when he again failed to receive the promotion he felt he deserved.

3. **panic:** to suddenly feel so frightened that you cannot think clearly or behave sensibly

   a. Some people feel like they are going to **panic** when speaking to a large audience for the first time.
   b. Filmmakers have always known that one way to capture an audience is to **panic** the life out of them.
   c. I was maybe four minutes into my first triathlon when I swallowed too much water. I began to **panic**. I wasn't sure how I'd manage to finish the swim.

4. **classic:** admired by many people, and having a value that has continued for a long time.

   a. If you want to sip coffee in a **classic** café, go to Vienna, where the coffeehouses offer fabulous cakes along with amazing coffee.
   b. Maurice Sendak's **classic** picture book *Where the Wild Things Are* is one of the best-loved children's books of all time.
   c. Lee Iacocca rose from **classic** beginnings to become boss of Ford Motor Company.

5. **illustrate:** to make the meaning of something clearer by giving examples

   a. The costumes in the "Marriage in the Movies" exhibition are being used to **illustrate** the development of the wedding dress since the eighteenth century.
   b. A small path was **illustrated** by low yellow lamps hidden in the flower beds.
   c. In reflexology, maps have been drawn to **illustrate** which body organ is linked to which part of the sole of the foot.

6. **craft:** a job or activity in which you make things with your hands, and that you usually need skill to do

   a. Many jobs today require computer **crafts**.
   b. Hobby **crafts** such as knitting have become fashionable leisure pursuits.
   c. Dudley Library will be holding a children's **craft** activity from 10:30 to 11:30 A.M. on Thursday.

7. **bulb:** the glass part of an electric light

   a. They keep knocking down old paper **bulbs** and putting up new ones.
   b. A dim light came from a tiny electric **bulb** hanging from the ceiling.
   c. Thomas Edison patented everything from the first phonograph player in 1877 to the first practical light **bulb** in 1879.

8. **ornamental:** designed to make something look attractive rather than to be used for a particular purpose

   a. The **ornamental** lions that sit outside City Hall are a popular meeting spot for friends going out for the evening.
   b. My job is to think up creative and **ornamental** advertising ideas.
   c. The buttons on the dress were purely **ornamental**—there was a zipper on the side for putting the dress on and taking it off.

9. **device:** a machine or tool that does a special job

   a. Apple has revealed plans for a new **device** that will allow consumers to watch 3-D films on the inside of a pair of glasses.

   b. The ceiling is bordered with a beautiful, hand-painted, floral **device**.

   c. Many restaurants are replacing paper pads and pens with handheld **devices** that allow waitstaff to record and process orders electronically.

10. **offset:** to use one cost, payment, or amount of something to cancel or reduce the effect of another

   a. Many people believe that we can **offset** the effects of our polluting lifestyles by planting trees that take carbon dioxide from the atmosphere.

   b. The company used profits from the sale of the land to **offset** losses from low sales.

   c. We were worried that we would **offset** the children if we told them in advance that we were not going to Disneyland.

11. **loyalty:** the quality of always supporting something or somebody

   a. Many companies hope that by building brand **loyalty** in children today, those children will stay committed to their products as adults.

   b. I've always had great **loyalty** for people who can speak more than one language.

   c. Although the choir director felt that the younger woman had a stronger singing voice, she gave the solo to her old friend out of **loyalty**.

12. **appliance:** a piece of equipment, especially electrical equipment, such as a stove or washing machine, used in the home

   a. The new shop, Papercraft, sells a number of multicolored **appliances** that are great for sending invitations and thank-you cards.

   b. Missouri is encouraging the use of energy-efficient **appliances** by offering $5.6 million in rebates to residents who buy energy-efficient clothes washers, dishwashers, furnaces, and air conditioners.

   c. The wedding registry industry is worth a whopping $12 billion annually, and **appliances** continue to be the most-asked-for category of gift.

WORD FAMILIES

A. The table contains word families for some of the target words in the reading. Complete the table. An **X** indicates that there is no form or that the form is not common. Sometimes more than one form may be possible. If you are unsure about a form, check your dictionary.

Verb	Noun	Adjective	Adverb
	frustration	1. 2.	
X	**idiot**		
illustrate	1. 2.		**X**
opt			
	1. 2.	**ornamental**	**X**
panic			**X**
X		**passionate**	
persist			
resolve	1. 2.	**X**	**X**
tolerate			

B. Read the sentences. In eight of the sentences, an incorrect form of the target word has been used. If the form of the target word is incorrect, cross it out and write the correct form. If the form is correct, put a checkmark (✔). Use the word families table to help you.

_____ **1.** Although the coach found the referee's decisions **frustration**, he had to admit that the loss was due to his team's poor quality of play.

_____ **2.** The movie we saw last night was **idiot**. It was supposed to be a serious historical drama, but there were too many factual errors.

_____ **3.** The hard work by the band members in preparing for the parade is **illustrate** of their commitment to music and each other.

_____ **4.** The cruise price was all inclusive for everything on the ship. But since the land tours were **opt**, you had to pay extra if you wanted to go.

_____ **5.** Many of the finest traditional Christmas tree **ornamental** from Germany and Eastern Europe are made of glass.

_____ **6.** The young man tried to hide his **panic** as he waited his turn to bungee jump.

_____ **7.** The lawyer argued **passionate** in defense of his client.

_____ **8.** Although my mother never nagged, she still managed to be **persist** and normally got what she wanted.

_____ **9.** His poor performance in today's race simply strengthened his **resolve** to train harder for the next race and win a medal.

_____ **10.** The fan produced just enough air movement to make the room feel **tolerate** despite the heat and humidity.

COLLOCATION

In each set of sentences, the target word is paired with different words to form different collocations. Choose the collocation that best fits the last sentence and write it in the blank. You may need to change the form of one word in the collocation to fit the sentence.

1. a. In the early part of the twentieth century, when electricity was still new, lightbulbs represented luxury, which is why you see fixtures with **bare bulbs** in historic houses.
   b. A **fluorescent bulb** is four to six times more efficient than an ordinary incandescent bulb.
   c. General Electric, the granddaddy of lightbulb producers, has developed an LED replacement for 40-**watt bulbs** that can last for seventeen years.
   d. An ENERGY STAR-qualified compact _____ will save about $30 over its lifetime and pay for itself in about six months.

2. a. John Ford's magnificent film of John Steinbeck's **classic novel** *The Grapes of Wrath* is on Channel 4 at 2 P.M.
   b. The Rolling Sculpture Car Show will bring **classic cars** to Main Street, Ann Arbor, on the first weekend in July.
   c. In a **classic study** of product development, Booz-Allen and Hamilton reported that only two out of ten new products were a commercial success.
   d. Morrison's _____ tells the story of a woman who escapes from slavery to freedom in Cincinnati, but remains haunted by her daughter's murder.

3. a. The school decided to hold a **craft fair** to raise money for new choir robes.
   b. There is an excellent choice of **craft** courses and **workshops** in the U.K., covering a huge range of subjects in all areas of arts and crafts.
   c. Parkway **Craft Center** is one of the five shops of the Southern Highland Craft Guild and features work from 300 Southern Appalachian craftspeople.
   d. The _____ aims to educate the community through events and activities arranged to accompany its lively exhibition program.

4. a. The actions of the old man in the library **aroused my curiosity**, so I decided to follow him when he left.

  b. Since no one was allowed into the building while it was being remodeled, we had to **satisfy our curiosity** by looking at drawings made by the architect and interior designer.

  c. Babies **show their curiosity** by putting objects into their mouths in order to feel their texture and to learn something about them.

  d. Working in academia offers an incredible amount of freedom to _____ intellectual _____. I don't know of any other job that allows you the freedom to get up in the morning with a new idea and go into work to research it.

5. a. Leaders in the automotive industry want people to realize that the main **safety device** in the front seat of a car is the seat belt, not the airbag.

  b. There is a wide range of home **security devices** on the market. You can get alarms, panic buttons, and window and door sensors, to name just a few.

  c. Some **medical devices**, such as X-ray machines and thermometers, diagnose diseases or conditions. Others, such as pacemakers and inhalers, are used for prevention or treatment.

  d. Parents must decide whether cell phones for children are actually a _____ or just another must-have consumer product.

6. a. I wanted to **avoid a hassle** when the babysitter came, so I made sure the children were already in bed.

  b. Are the small rewards given by loyalty cards really **worth the hassle** of shopping only at select stores?

  c. Machines that recognize an individual's eyes are intended to **reduce the hassle** of immigration procedures for frequent travelers.

  d. Buying your movie tickets online means that you can _____ of standing in line, and you can be sure that your movie isn't sold out.

7. a. In the novel *Jeff in Venice, Death in Varanasi*, Geoff Dyer uses his typical **wry humor** to tackle love and death in a headlong, entertaining rush.

  b. Garrison Keillor on *A Prairie Home Companion* relies on **self-deprecating humor** all the time, most famously by telling stories of rural Minnesotans.

  c. **Dark humor** is a form of bravery in the face of bad news. The worse things get, the funnier I think they are.

  d. The film *Little Miss Sunshine*, about a little girl's dream to win a beauty pageant, uses lots of _____ to introduce us to her very troubled family.

8. a. One of the characteristics of a great leader is the ability to **inspire loyalty** in his or her followers.

  b. Naturalized citizens are required to **pledge** an oath of **loyalty** to their new country.

  c. The hockey team's championship win **rewarded the loyalty** of fans who had stuck with the team even during its losing seasons.

  d. After undergoing a series of tasks and challenges, new recruits _____ to their chosen fraternity or sorority.

Complete the passage. Use the target words from the box. You may need to change the form of the word to fit the sentence. There is one extra word.

appliance	irritated	offset	squeeze
classic	kettle	ornamental	sting

The Essence of Good Design

1   Over the years, designers and artists have tried to capture the essence of good design in mottos. The aim of these sayings is to help others understand the ideas of good design. We have seen two such mottos already. This passage will explore four more of these mottos.

2   **Less is more.** This saying is associated with the German-born architect Mies van der Rohe. In his Modernist view, beauty lies in simplicity and elegance, and the aim of the designer is to create solutions to problems through the most efficient means. Design should avoid unnecessary (**1**) _____. Japanese interior design is a good example of these beliefs.

3   **More is not a bore.** The American-born architect Robert Venturi concluded that if simplicity is done badly, the result is soulless design. Post-Modernist designers began to experiment with decoration and color again. Product design was heavily influenced by this view and can be seen in kitchen (**2**) _____ such as mixers, juicers, and (**3**) _____.

4   **Fitness for purpose.** Successful product design takes into consideration a product's function, purpose, shape, form, color, and texture. The most important result for the user is that the product does what is intended. For example, think of an adjustable desk lamp. It needs to direct light where it is needed, it needs to be stable, and it needs to be constructed from materials that will withstand the heat of the lamp and regular adjustments by the user. Stylish design alone cannot (**4**) _____ a user's (**5**) _____ at a collapsing lamp.

5   **Form follows emotion.** This phrase is associated with the German designer Hartmut Esslinger. He believes design must take into account the sensory side of our nature—sight, smell, touch, and taste. These are as important as rational thinking. When choosing everyday products such as toothpaste, we appreciate a cool-looking dispenser that still allows us to easily (**6**) _____ the toothpaste onto our brush. Or a handy onion chopper that can take the (**7**) _____ out of slicing onions.

Choose a modern product and research its design. Write a 500-word essay that considers the key design principles reflected in the product.

Revisiting the Target Words

Now that you have completed this chapter, use the scale to describe your knowledge of the target words.

1 I still don't know anything about this word.

2 I am still not sure of the meaning of this word even after studying it.

3 I understand this word when I see it or hear it in a sentence, but I don't know how to use it in my own speaking and writing.

4 I know this word and can use it in my own speaking and writing.

TARGET WORDS

____appliance	____frustration	____kettle	____passionate
____bulb	____hassle	____loyalty	____persist
____classic	____humor	____offset	____resolve
____craft	____idiot	____opt	____squeeze
____curiosity	____illustrate	____ornamental	____sting
____device	____irritated	____panic	____tolerate

KNOWLEDGE CHECK 2

Go back to the beginning of the chapter and complete the Knowledge Check 1 table.

Strategy Practice

Getting Started

Look at the three images taken from Chapters 9–11. Without looking back at the chapters, how many target words can you remember from each chapter?

Learning More about Words: SYNONYMS

When you are introduced to a new word, your teacher or textbook may often link the new word to a synonym that you already know. For example, you may be told that **gently**, a target word from Chapter 10, means the same as *carefully*. However, although synonyms are words that are similar, there are normally key differences in their meanings and uses.

We can say that synonyms share a common meaning. In the table, you can see that all of these synonyms share the meaning "to affect with wonder." However, each word also has an additional meaning sense that is not shared with the others.

	To affect with wonder	Because unexpected	Because difficult to believe	So as to cause confusion	So as to leave one helpless to act or think
surprise	✔	✔			
astonish	✔		✔		
amaze	✔			✔	
astound	✔				✔

There are several other ways that synonyms might differ from one another.

- One word has a wider meaning, whereas the other word has a more specific meaning.

- One word is more formal or informal than the other.

- One word sounds more polite than the other.

- One word is much less frequent than the other.

- One word is only used in British or American English.

- One word is used in technical or medical contexts, whereas the other word is used by ordinary people.

This means that it is important to treat synonyms with care. Try to find out how they are different from each other. Very few pairs of words can be used interchangeably in the same situations.

The descriptions explain why the paired synonyms are not interchangeable. Circle the synonym that matches the description. The first one has been done for you.

Descriptions	Paired Synonyms	
1. One is British.	**a.** mobile phone	**b.** cell phone
2. One is more informal.	**a.** annoyance	**b.** hassle
3. One is more formal.	**a.** doable	**b.** viable
4. One is more polite.	**a.** idiotic	**b.** unwise
5. One is less frequent.	**a.** ornamental	**b.** decorative
6. One is more specific.	**a.** sort	**b.** classify
7. One is more technical.	**a.** diet	**b.** food

IDENTIFYING LINKS

Recognizing synonyms can help you identify related, or linked, ideas within a reading. By identifying the linked ideas, you can better understand the message.

To create links, writers use chains of related words, such as synonyms, superordinates (words used to describe a category), subordinates (words that belong to a category), and co-ordinates (a group of subordinates). These chains connect ideas within and across sentences. In the following passage, the links are shown with arrows.

A. Identify the type of relationship (synonym, superordinate, subordinate, or co-ordinate) between the words in each link.

In 2008, the European Union **(1) imposed** a policy whereby **(2) tire** manufacturers are required to **(3) label** their tires with criteria **(4)** for braking performance, rolling resistance, and rolling noise. The aim is to force manufacturers to provide **consumers** with **convenient** access to information about their products' **performance**.

1. _____   3. _____

2. _____   4. _____

B. Now identify the vocabulary chains in a paragraph taken from the reading in Chapter 10. Notice the words in bold and underline the related words. Then draw lines to connect each chain.

4   Choice **architects** are people who organize the contexts in which **consumers** make decisions. For example, the person who decides the **layout** of your local supermarket—including which **shelf** the peanut butter goes on, and how the oranges are stacked—is a choice **architect**. So is the person who organizes where the salad and dessert bars are in your school or work cafeteria. And, believe it or not, the arrangements they **adopt** will influence the selections you make, according to Richard Thaler and Cass Sunstein, **professors** at the University of Chicago.

Focusing on Vocabulary Cards: LINKS GAME

An important stage in the process of learning new vocabulary is to regularly review and use the target words you have encountered. The more frequently you do this, the more likely it will be that you remember new vocabulary and are able to use them accurately and confidently. This game will help you to do this.

The name of this activity is "Links," and the aim is to create links between target words. This will test your target word knowledge and your ability to use target words. You will need your growing collection of vocabulary cards.

Instructions

1. Form pairs or teams (Team A and Team B).

2. Team A selects four vocabulary cards at random and presents the first three to Team B.

3. Team B is then given time to discuss a way to link all three target words.

4. When Team B is confident that it has found a way to link the target words, it presents its idea to Team A.

5. If all agree that the links are reasonable, Team B is awarded three points.

6. At this stage, Team B is given the opportunity to win an additional two points by linking the fourth vocabulary card to the first three.

7. Once the scores have been noted, Team B chooses four vocabulary cards for Team A, and the process is repeated.

Example:
Here is a model answer to illustrate how you might link three words.

For many years, scientists and archaeologists have studied how **architects** in ancient Egypt designed and built the pyramids. The pyramids contain **chambers** that have air vents that point to particular stars. However, it is still a **mystery** as to why these air vents exist.

A story is just one way to show links. Other ways include word grammar, pronunciation, and collocations.

Face It

What's behind an Attractive Face?

Getting Started

Discuss the questions with your classmates.

✦ What facial feature(s) do you consider to be the most important when deciding if a face is attractive or not?

✦ To what extent does culture play a role when deciding which faces are attractive?

✦ In your opinion, who has a very attractive face? Name a male and a female.

Assessing Your Vocabulary Knowledge: TARGET WORDS

Look at the words in the box. These are the target words for this chapter. Use the scale to score yourself on each word.

1 I don't know this word.

2 I have seen or heard this word before, but I am not sure of the meaning.

3 I understand this word when I see it or hear it in a sentence, but I don't know how to use it in my own speaking and writing.

4 I know this word and can use it in my own speaking and writing.

TARGET WORDS			
____ally	____fertility	____nervous	____reproduce
____ample	____fine	____numerous	____reward
____cheek	____gallery	____obsession	____superior
____chin	____jaw	____perceive	____surgeon
____circulation	____lip	____portrait	____sweat
____convey	____necessity	____rapidly	____tuck

KNOWLEDGE CHECK 1

Complete the sentences with words that you have scored as **1**.

1. I am not familiar with the word / term _____.

2. I have no idea what _____ means.

Fill in the first blank with a word that you have scored as **2**. Then complete the sentence.

3. I think _____ could mean _____.

Reading

The passage introduces the concept of facial beauty. It looks at why we think some faces are more attractive than others. As you read, pay special attention to the target vocabulary words in **bold**.

Facial Attraction

1   We see a certain face, and without knowing why, our hearts begin to beat faster. We may even start to feel **nervous** and begin to **sweat**. Our eyes blink more **rapidly** because we want a better look. What's going on here? Our body is responding to a face that our brain automatically has judged to be attractive.

2   You might think that the idea of facial attractiveness is a relatively new phenomenon, reflected by our growing **obsession** with cosmetics and celebrity. In fact, the origins of facial beauty appear to lie in the biological **necessity** to survive and successfully **reproduce**. What we now call beauty was originally our way of determining who was a potential mate. With limited food resources and ever-present dangers, it was important for our earliest ancestors to choose a mate who would not only pass on successful genes to future generations, but also survive childbirth and live long enough to be able to provide for the family. The face **conveys** information about age, health, and **fertility**, and the better the signals, the more "attractive" a person was to potential mates.

3   Research shows that our primitive ancestors focused on the skin because it is a reliable indicator of a strong immune system. In addition, the **jaw**, **lips**, and eyes signal information about hormone levels. In women, for example, **lips** that have a full shape indicate positive estrogen levels and good blood **circulation**. Symmetrical faces—faces that are similar in shape on each side—also were **perceived** to be a sign of good health and, thus, more attractive.

4   It's reasonable to think that our feelings about facial beauty also would be influenced by our culture, gender, and age. After all, these factors affect everything from the music we prefer, to the clothes we wear, to the food we eat. However, research by Gillian Rhodes at the University of Western Australia has found that we are born with preferences for certain face types. In fact, **numerous** studies have reported that babies prefer to look at attractive faces. This suggests that culture has a very limited effect on what we judge to be a beautiful face. According to Judith Langlois at the University of Texas, not only do different cultures share similar views on facial attractiveness, but men and women from different cultures also have similar facial preferences, and people from different cultures of all ages are attracted to similar "beautiful" faces.

5   The evidence suggests that we are genetically wired to consider certain characteristics more attractive than others. A woman's face should be symmetrical with clear skin, a small **chin** and nose, a narrow **jaw** and slim eyebrows, but full, well-defined **lips** and **cheeks**, and large eyes. An attractive male face also should exhibit many of these features.

6   However, before we all rush to find the nearest plastic **surgeon** to have our chins **tucked**, noses reduced, and eyes widened, we should consider that a growing **number** of studies are beginning to show that physical features can be of secondary importance. Researchers at the University of Aberdeen in Scotland have discovered that women found men who were being smiled at by other women to be more attractive despite the fact that the men lacked the typical characteristics of an attractive face. The opposite was true for

men. At UCLA, a study of art in **galleries** has found that **portraits** that emphasize the right side of the face are judged by viewers to be more attractive. Again, this was despite a lack of typical facial beauty characteristics. Also, there is **ample** evidence indicating that some of the most celebrated female faces do not fit a standard pattern of beauty, such as those of many professional models. Instead, their unique facial features are what cause them to stand out from the crowd.

7   Regardless of how beauty is defined, its **rewards** extend beyond just finding a mate.

Attractive people tend to earn **superior** salaries, are **perceived** as being friendlier, and even get smaller **fines** and lighter prison sentences. In short, we don't appear to have moved on very far from our earliest ancestors. So if we cannot do anything to change our genetics, maybe it is time to evolve our behavior instead. Since most of us don't need to worry about limited resources and ever-present dangers anymore, perhaps we should **ally** ourselves with people based on what they do rather than on how they look.

(730 words)

READING COMPREHENSION

Respond to the questions in writing. Base your responses on the reading and your own personal experiences.

1. The passage describes several facial features that indicate good health and attractiveness. List them.

2. How early in life does the preference for particular facial types begin to appear?

3. There are several advantages to being physically attractive besides finding a mate. What are they, according to the passage?

4. Does the passage suggest that physical beauty is the most important thing?

5. How important do you think physical beauty is compared to personality and intelligence in the way we evaluate other people?

6. Do you think that males evaluate females using the same criteria that females use to evaluate males?

Focusing on Vocabulary

WORD MEANING

A. Match the target words with their definitions. If you are unsure about a word's meaning, try to figure it out from the context by rereading the passage. Then check your dictionary.

Set 1

_____ 1. perceive
_____ 2. chin
_____ 3. cheek
_____ 4. gallery
_____ 5. ample
_____ 6. reward
_____ 7. fine

a. to understand or think of something or someone in a particular way

b. a fee charged because a person has done something wrong or broken the law

c. the soft round part of your face below each of your eyes

d. the front part of your face below your mouth

e. the benefit that you receive as a result of doing something

f. more than enough

g. a building where people can see pieces of art

Set 2

_____ 1. sweat
_____ 2. obsession
_____ 3. jaw
_____ 4. lip
_____ 5. surgeon
_____ 6. tuck
_____ 7. portrait

a. to put something into a small space, especially in order to protect, hide, carry, or hold it

b. a doctor who does operations in a hospital

c. an extreme and unhealthy interest in or worry about something that stops you from thinking about anything else

d. the bone that supports the bottom of your mouth

e. one of the two soft parts around your mouth with redder or darker skin

f. a painting, drawing, or photograph of a person

g. to have drops of salty liquid come out through your skin because you are hot, ill, frightened, or exercising

B. Read each target word and the list below it. One word or phrase in each list is NOT a synonym for the target word. Cross it out.

1. nervous

| anxious | worried | angry | frightened |

2. rapidly

| speedily | quickly | hurriedly | steadily |

3. necessity

| obligation | need | requirement | choice |

4. reproduce

| copy | duplicate | imitate | sample |

5. convey

| pass on | transmit | stop | give |

6. fertility

| emptiness | fruitfulness | richness | productiveness |

7. circulation

| flow | movement | leak | distribution |

8. numerous

| many | few | lots of | countless |

9. superior

| similar | better | greater | advanced |

10. ally

| combine | group | unite | separate |

WORD FAMILIES

A. The table contains word families for some of the target words in the reading. Complete the table. An **X** indicates that there is no form or that the form is not common. Sometimes more than one form may be possible. If you are unsure about a form, check your dictionary.

Verb	Noun	Adjective	Adverb
ally			X
	circulation		X
convey	1. 2.	X	X
	1. fertility 2.		X
	necessity		
X		nervous	
	1. 2. 3.	1. 2. numerous	
X	1. 2.		rapidly
	reward		X
X	1. surgeon 2.		

B. Choose the correct form of the word in **bold** in sentence **a** to complete sentence **b**. Use the word families table you just completed as a guide.

1. **a.** With the threat of war in the region, the small country felt it necessary to **ally** itself to its larger neighbor.

   b. The _____ of women voters and young voters was enough to elect the progressive candidate.

2. **a.** Exercising helps improve blood **circulation** in your body.

   b. He was too shy to _____ around the room and meet new people.

3. **a.** Modern cell phones are not mere telephones; they also **convey** Internet information and function as cameras, video cameras, and game platforms.

   b. It is never nice to be the _____ of bad news.

4. **a.** The **fertility** clinic helped many childless couples have a baby.

   b. The _____ Crescent is an area with rich soil where human civilization began. It is located in the modern-day countries of Iraq, Syria, and Lebanon.

5. **a.** Having a university degree is becoming a **necessity** in today's job market.

   b. The fact that she was beautiful wasn't _____ the main reason why he fell in love with her.

6. **a.** She was extremely **nervous** before her job interview.

   b. They stood up _____ and admitted that it was their mistake.

7. **a.** There are **numerous** reasons why we might be attracted to a particular person.

   b. The sheer _____ of wildebeests attracted lions from miles around.

8. **a.** The supermarket **rapidly** removed the items from its shelves as a result of a health scare.

   b. Having a modern _____ transit system is key to the success of any major city today.

9. **a.** She received a $2,000 **reward** for giving the police the information they needed to catch the criminal.

   b. More often than not, universities _____ hard-working students with higher grades.

10. **a.** The **surgeon** removed the tumor from the sick man.

    b. The pacemaker had to be _____ inserted into the woman's heart.

COLLOCATION

Read the common collocations in the column on the left. Give two examples of things associated with each collocation.

	Example 1	Example 2
1. **ample** space		
2. art **gallery**		
3. pay a **fine**		
4. red **cheeks**		
5. rub your **chin**		
6. **superior** performance		
7. cold **sweat**		
8. family **portrait**		

Expanding the Topic

An important part of developing your vocabulary involves forming and supporting opinions about the topic you are studying. Read the statements and indicate whether you agree (**A**) or disagree (**D**). Then discuss your opinions and reasoning with a partner.

_____ 1. The media is the reason why we are all **obsessed** with our physical appearance.

_____ 2. Cosmetic **surgeons** should be banned from operating on people under the age of 21.

_____ 3. **Fertility** treatment for couples who have no children should be free.

_____ 4. Our **perception** of what is beautiful is a form of discrimination.

_____ 5. Only people with attractive faces should **reproduce**.

_____ 6. A person's **lips** are the most attractive facial feature.

_____ 7. Women's hair looks better loose and down than **tucked** up into a bun, as in many hairstyles from the 1950s and 1960s.

_____ 8. Men with rugged faces (for example, strong **chins** and solid **jaws**) are **perceived** to be more manly than those without these features.

 Choose one of the statements above and write a 500-word essay on why you agree or disagree with it.

Revisiting the Target Words

Now that you have completed this chapter, use the scale to describe your knowledge of the target words.

1 I still don't know anything about this word.

2 I am still not sure of the meaning of this word even after studying it.

3 I understand this word when I see it or hear it in a sentence, but I don't know how to use it in my own speaking and writing.

4 I know this word and can use it in my own speaking and writing.

TARGET WORDS

____ally	____fertility	____nervous	____reproduce
____ample	____fine	____numerous	____reward
____cheek	____gallery	____obsession	____superior
____chin	____jaw	____perceive	____surgeon
____circulation	____lip	____portrait	____sweat
____convey	____necessity	____rapidly	____tuck

KNOWLEDGE CHECK 2

Select examples from the words you now give a score of **3** or **4**, but didn't at the start of the chapter, to complete the sentences.

1. I didn't know that _____ meant _____ before reading this chapter.

2. I wasn't sure that I knew the meaning of _____, but I am now.

3. I now am confident that I know what _____ means, but I would like more practice with how to use it in my speaking and writing.

4. I could next use _____ when I am _____.

Makeup: Painted Faces

Getting Started

Discuss the questions with your classmates.

✦ Do you use any facial cosmetics? If so, make a list of what you use.

✦ Why do people wear makeup?

✦ Should men wear makeup?

Assessing Your Vocabulary Knowledge: TARGET WORDS

Look at the words in the box. These are the target words for this chapter. Use the scale to score yourself on each word.

1 I don't know this word.

2 I have seen or heard this word before, but I am not sure of the meaning.

3 I understand this word when I see it or hear it in a sentence, but I don't know how to use it in my own speaking and writing.

4 I know this word and can use it in my own speaking and writing.

TARGET WORDS

____abandon	____empire	____mineral	____powder
____alongside	____grease	____mud	____recipe
____billion	____honey	____nut	____routine
____civilization	____ingredient	____pale	____shadow
____crushed	____marital	____perfume	____strict
____desert	____mercury	____poisonous	____wax

KNOWLEDGE CHECK 1

Fill in the first blank with a word that you have scored as **2**. Then complete the second sentence.

1. I have seen / heard _____. I saw / heard it while I was

    _____.

Fill in the first blanks with words that you have scored as **4**. Then complete the sentences.

2. One meaning of _____ is _____.

3. I last used the word _____ while I was _____.

Reading

The passage describes the use of makeup throughout history. As you read, pay special attention to the target vocabulary words in **bold**.

Face Paint

1   Animal courtship customs include amazing uses of smells, tastes, sounds, sights, and physical touch to signal health and attractiveness to possible partners. But what signals do humans use to signal youth, health, and attractiveness? We depend mainly on visual signs, with an important one being facial cosmetics, or makeup. In fact, the global makeup industry is now worth many **billions** of dollars per year.

2   Makeup was first used as far back as 100,000 years ago by early humans called Neanderthals. Archaeologists have discovered that Neanderthals used colored **minerals** found in **mud** to decorate their faces. Face paint was used **alongside** tattoos, bone hair accessories, and cave paintings to signal social information. It was the Egyptians, however, who were the first **civilization** to use makeup as a beauty product.

3   When we think of ancient Egyptian faces, the first thing we notice is their dark eye makeup. This early makeup was originally used by both men and women to **shadow** their eyes from the reflection of the bright **desert**. (Today football and baseball players use black **grease** on their cheeks for a similar purpose.) In time, the makeup became a way of showing off the beauty of the wearers' eyes, and Egyptian women began to create their own **recipes**, using combinations of **minerals**, metals, and burned **nuts**. The Egyptians also wore blue eye makeup (also called "eye **shadow**") made from the stone lapis lazuli and red lipstick made from **crushed** beetles.

4   The Egyptians weren't the only ancient **civilization** to use makeup. The ancient Greeks not only gave us the word *cosmos*, from which we get the English word "cosmetics," but they also created the first face creams. Some of these creams even contained **perfumes**. Roman women favored early forms of mascara, eye **shadow**, and rouge. A famous Roman saying translates as "A woman without paint is like food without salt."

5   Although only Roman women used brightly colored makeup, both sexes frequently applied **powder** to their faces to whiten their skin. **Pale** facial skin was considered to be beautiful. **Pale** skin distinguished the higher classes from laborers who had tanned skin from working outside. Although **pale** skin was thought to look healthier and more beautiful, some methods used to get the look were actually deadly. Early forms of white face **powder** contained lead, **mercury**, and arsenic, which are highly **poisonous**. They weren't only **poisonous** for the wearer. Some face **powders** could kill with just one kiss on the cheek!

6   For hundreds of years after the fall of the Roman **Empire**, the use of cosmetics was frowned upon by many Europeans due to **strict** religious views. This changed in the seventeenth century, when the term "makeup" was first used. It was considered highly attractive for men and women to wear white **powder** and paint beauty spots on their faces. The shape and position on the face of a beauty spot could signal the wearer's place in society, **marital** status, or even their desire to flirt.

7   Society's view of makeup changed again in the nineteenth century. Women avoided **powders** and bright colors, and men **abandoned** makeup altogether. Instead, women mixed natural **ingredients**, such as oatmeal, **honey**, and eggs, to improve their natural looks. At one point, women were considered more beautiful if they looked unwell. So they used

cosmetics to make dark circles under their eyes, to redden their lips, and to make their skin look **pale** as **wax**.

8   Modern makeup owes much to the growth of the film industry in Hollywood, which popularized suntans and "the movie star look." Most importantly, the birth of the commercial cosmetics industry has made mass-produced cosmetics much more affordable, and now they are part of the beauty **routine** of all social classes. Today, it is fashionable once again for both sexes to indulge in facial cosmetics, particularly cosmetics made from the same natural **ingredients** used centuries ago.

(645 words)

READING COMPREHENSION

Respond to the questions in writing. Base your responses on the reading and your own personal experiences.

1. How long has makeup been used by humans?

2. Why did the Egyptians originally use dark eye makeup?

3. What effect did the development of the cosmetics industry have on the use of cosmetics?

4. How is the information in the passage organized?

5. Makeup has swung between being popular and unpopular through the ages. In today's world, do you think makeup is becoming more or less popular in general?

6. Do you personally like makeup, or do you prefer the "natural look"?

Focusing on Vocabulary

WORD MEANING

A. Read the target words. Use the paragraph number in parentheses to locate and reread the word in context. Then read the dictionary definitions and choose the one that reflects how the word is used in the reading.

_____ **1. shadow** (3)
   a. darkness caused by something preventing light from reaching a place
   b. the bad effect or influence that something has, which makes other things seem less enjoyable, attractive, or impressive

_____ **2. grease** (3)
   a. a thick oily substance, often put on the moving parts of a machine to make it move smoothly
   b. a fatty or oily substance that comes off meat when it is cooked

_____ **3. recipe** (3)
   a. a set of instructions for making and cooking something, particularly food
   b. (be a **recipe** for something) likely to cause a particular result, often a bad one

_____ **4. nut** (3)
   a. a small piece of metal with a hole through the middle, which is screwed onto a bolt to fasten things together
   b. a dry brown fruit inside a hard shell, which grows on a tree

_____ **5. crushed** (3)
   a. treated so as to have a permanently wrinkled appearance
   b. broken or pounded into small fragments

_____ **6. powder** (5)
   a. a dry substance in the form of very small grains
   b. dry, light snow

_____ **7. pale** (5)
   a. to be made to seem much less important
   b. a skin color that is very white, or whiter than it usually is

_____ **8. mercury** (5)
   a. the planet that is nearest the sun
   b. a heavy, silver-white, poisonous metal that is liquid at ordinary temperatures

_____ **9. abandon** (7)
   a. to stop having a particular idea or belief, or to stop doing a particular thing
   b. to leave someone, especially someone you are responsible for

_____ **10. honey** (7)
   a. a sweet, sticky substance produced by bees, used as food
   b. a term used to address someone you love

_____ **11. wax** (7)
   a. a solid substance made of fat or oil and used to make candles
   b. a natural sticky substance in your ears

_____ **12. routine** (8)

    a. a set of movements that form part of a performance

    b. the usual order in which you do things, or the things you regularly do

B. Read the target words in the box. Complete each sentence with the target word that matches the meaning of the words in parentheses. You may need to change the form of the word to fit the sentence.

alongside	desert	marital	perfume
billion	empire	mineral	poisonous
civilization	ingredient	mud	strict

1. The popularity of ringtone downloads has developed _____ advances in cell phone technology.
    (with, next to)

2. The Roman _____ lasted more than 400 years and finally fell to invading tribes from the north.
    (kingdom, domain)

3. Many villages in Mali consist of _____ huts.
    (dirt, soil)

4. It is predicted that India's population of 1.1 _____ people will continue to grow and will overtake China within twenty years.
    (one thousand million)

5. Chili and coconut are common _____ in Thai cooking.
    (part, component)

6. The _____ of freshly cut flowers completely filled the room.
    (scent, aroma)

7. The Aztecs had a(n) _____ that covered much of what is now Mexico.
    (population, citizenry)

8. When applying for a travel visa, you are frequently asked about your _____ status.
    (marriage, union)

9. Some of the earliest materials used for makeup, such as lead and **mercury**, have been found to be highly _____.
    (lethal, toxic)

10. Due to global warming, there is the very real fear that significant areas of land will turn into _____.
    (wasteland, arid region)

11. One way for some of the poorest countries in the world to improve their economic development is to exploit their rich _____ reserves.
    (rock, raw material)

12. It is typical for exclusive golf clubs to have a(n) _____ dress code for anyone who wants to play there.
    (firm, stern)

Word Tip

The word *billion* is an example of how globalization has affected the English language. For most of the twentieth century, one *billion* in the U.K. was equal to one million x one million (1,000,000,000,000), whereas in the U.S., one billion is one thousand x one million (1,000,000,000). This was because the U.K. used the long-scale, large-number naming system, in which every new term greater than one million is one million times the previous term. However, the U.S. uses the short-scale naming system, in which every new term greater than one million is one thousand times the previous term. In 1974, the U.K. officially adopted the short-scale naming system. However, many people in the U.K. and continental Europe still consider a *billion* to be one million million.

WORD FAMILIES

A. The table contains word families for some of the target words in the reading. An **X** indicates that there is no form or that the form is not common. Study the table. Look for spelling patterns for the adjective forms of the words. List the patterns in the space below the table.

Verb	Noun	Adjective	Adverb
abandon	abandonment	abandoned	**X**
civilize	**civilization**	civilized	**X**
crush	crush	1. **crushed** 2. crushing	**X**
grease	**grease**	greasy	**X**
marry	marriage	1. **marital** 2. married	**X**
muddy	**mud**	muddy	**X**
pale	paleness	**pale**	**X**
perfume	**perfume** perfumery	perfumed	**X**
poison	poison	1. poisoned 2. **poisonous**	**X**
powder	**powder**	1. powdered 2. powdery	**X**

adjectives _____

B. Complete each sentence with the correct form of the word in parentheses. Use the word families table to help you.

1. The climbers _____ (**abandon**) their attempt to climb Mount Everest when the weather became too dangerous to continue.

2. The early Egyptians had a highly _____ (**civilization**) society.

3. We were nearly _____ (**crush**) when the band came on stage.

4. The meat was far too _____ (**grease**) for my liking.

5. Michelle and Barack got _____ (**marital**) on October 18, 1992.

6. Hippopotamuses get their skin _____ (**mud**) to protect it against the sun.

7. Our skin stays _____ (**pale**) if we stay indoors.

8. The oldest _____ (**perfume**) appears to have been created in Cyprus nearly 4,000 years ago.

9. The _____ (**poison**) dart frog skin contains a toxic chemical that sickens or kills any animal that touches or eats it.

10. In the seventeenth century, it was common for men to _____ (**powder**) their faces and hair.

COLLOCATION

Combine a word from Column A with a word from Column B to form a collocation. Then match the collocation to its definition.

Column A	Column B
strict	**wax**
barren	**routine**
colonial	rules
organic	**honey**
daily	**empire**
sweet	**shadows**
long	**ingredients**
hot	**desert**

1. _____ a substance used to make skis go faster

2. _____ the set of things you do every day

3. _____ a group of countries ruled by another country that is far away

4. _____ the effect of the sun when it is low in the sky

5. _____ foods grown without using artificial chemicals that are used in cooking

6. _____ a food that children love to eat

7. _____ a very dry place where little life can exist

8. _____ laws that you must follow exactly

Expanding the Topic

Try to answer the trivia questions about makeup and cosmetics.

1. How many people have **abandoned** their glasses to use contact lenses worldwide?

   a. 125 million
   b. 250 million
   c. 375 million

2. How much money is spent on makeup every year?

   a. $20 **billion**
   b. $30 **billion**
   c. $40 **billion**

3. Which modern makeup uses **mercury alongside** other **ingredients**?

   a. face cream
   b. lipstick
   c. no makeup has **mercury**

4. Which substances were used by Native Americans to make their facial paint?

   a. plant materials such as roots, berries, and tree bark
   b. soil colored by the **minerals** it contained
   c. a and b

5. Why is it important to read the **ingredients** of makeup?

   a. because some makeup goes bad relatively quickly
   b. because some kinds of makeup should not be used together
   c. because some products use **nut** oils, which can cause an allergy in some people

6. What is often used in body lotions and cleaners as well as in food **recipes**?

   a. sugar
   b. honey
   c. chocolate

7. The first American tour of Tutankhamen was a hit, and his famous eye **shadow** inspired the popular "Egyptian eyeliner" look. In which years did the tour take place?

   a. 1955–1957
   b. 1961–1963
   c. 1967–1969

8. What is the world's most expensive **perfume**?

   a. Clive Christian's Imperial Majesty
   b. Chanel No. 5
   c. Jean Patou's Joy

 Decide on some aspect of beauty, makeup, or cosmetics and write a 500-word essay on this topic. Some possible topics include the tattoos that the Maori wear in New Zealand, the heavy dark makeup some groups like "Goths" prefer to wear, or historical uses of makeup not discussed in the reading.

Revisiting the Target Words

Now that you have completed this chapter, use the scale to describe your knowledge of the target words.

1 I still don't know anything about this word.

2 I am still not sure of the meaning of this word even after studying it.

3 I understand this word when I see it or hear it in a sentence, but I don't know how to use it in my own speaking and writing.

4 I know this word and can use it in my own speaking and writing.

TARGET WORDS

_____abandon	_____empire	_____mineral	_____powder
_____alongside	_____grease	_____mud	_____recipe
_____billion	_____honey	_____nut	_____routine
_____civilization	_____ingredient	_____pale	_____shadow
_____crushed	_____marital	_____perfume	_____strict
_____desert	_____mercury	_____poisonous	_____wax

KNOWLEDGE CHECK 2

Select examples from the words you now give a score of **3** or **4**, but didn't at the start of the chapter, to complete the sentences.

1. I didn't know that _____ meant _____ before reading this chapter.

2. I wasn't sure that I knew the meaning of _____, but I am now.

3. I now am confident that I know what _____ means, but I would like more practice with how to use it in my speaking and writing.

4. I now know that _____ collocates with _____.

Facial Recognition: Do You Know Who I Am?

Getting Started

Discuss the questions with your classmates.

✦ What facial features do you think are the most important for facial recognition?

✦ How many different faces do you think a single person can recognize?

✦ What would life be like if you couldn't recognize people's faces?

Assessing Your Vocabulary Knowledge: TARGET WORDS

Look at the words in the box. These are the target words for this chapter. Use the scale to score yourself on each word.

1 I don't know this word.

2 I have seen or heard this word before, but I am not sure of the meaning.

3 I understand this word when I see it or hear it in a sentence, but I don't know how to use it in my own speaking and writing.

4 I know this word and can use it in my own speaking and writing.

TARGET WORDS			
____artificial	____distinguish	____groceries	____remedy
____behave	____elaborate	____hormone	____sequential
____composition	____envisage	____infant	____sneak
____cuddle	____fascinating	____objective	____summon
____database	____former	____offender	____tragic
____disguise	____furnish	____recollect	____wander

KNOWLEDGE CHECK 1

Check your progress in learning the vocabulary in this chapter.

• First, look at your scores in the table above. On the next page, write the number of words for each score (1–4) in the "at the beginning" column. For example, if you scored eight words as **1** ("I don't know this word"), then write **8**.

• At the end of the chapter, score yourself again. Then compare the two sets of scores. Are you showing improvement on most of the words in the chapter?

Your score	Number of words …		
	at the beginning:	at the end:	
		showing improvement	no improvement yet
1			
2			
3			
4			

Reading

The passage describes research on how we recognize faces and the technological applications that have been developed as a result. As you read, pay special attention to the target vocabulary words in **bold**.

I Know That Face

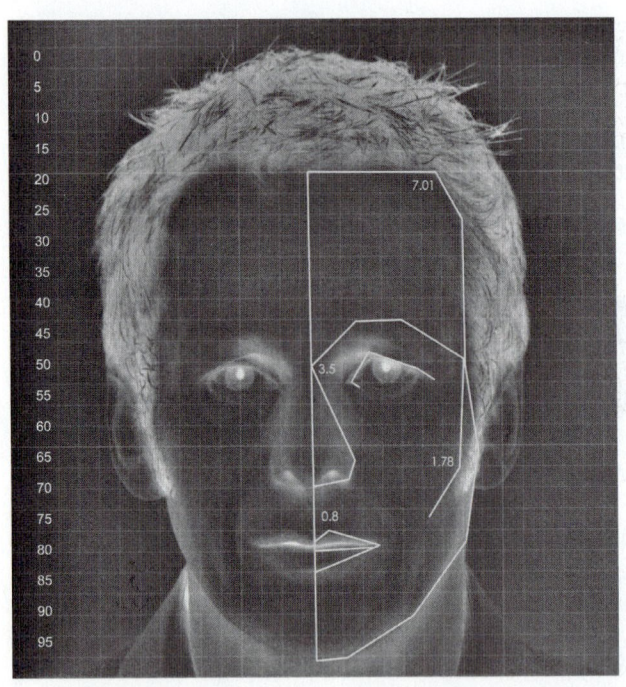

1   **Envisage** walking into a room of people, or **wandering** down a busy sidewalk, watching a TV program—and not knowing who anyone is because you can't recognize faces. Unfortunately, for a small minority of people recovering from a **tragic** illness or accident, this is the world they live in. Thankfully, scientists are now much closer to understanding how facial recognition works, with significance for possible future **remedies**. In the meanwhile,

their work is enjoying immediate application in law enforcement.

2   As **infants**, we can recognize our mothers within hours of birth. In fact, we can recognize the **composition** of our mother's face well before we can recognize her body shape. It's **fascinating** how the brain can carry out such an **elaborate** function at such a young age, especially since we don't learn to walk and talk until we are over a year old. By the time we are adults, we have the ability to **distinguish** around 100,000 faces. How can we remember so many faces when many of us find it difficult to **recollect** something as simple as a phone number? The exact process is not yet fully understood, but research around the world has begun to pinpoint the particular areas of the brain and processes necessary for facial recognition.

3   Researchers at the Massachusetts Institute of Technology believe that they have identified a specific area of the brain called the *fusiform face area* (FFA), which is used only for facial recognition. This means that recognition of familiar objects, such as our clothes or cars, is **summoned** from elsewhere in the brain. Researchers also have found that the brain needs to see the whole face for recognition to take place. Previously, it had been thought that we only needed to see certain facial features.

Meanwhile, research at University College London has found that facial recognition is not a single process, but instead involves three **sequential** steps. The first step appears to be an analysis of the physical features of a person's face, which is similar to how we scan the bar codes on our **groceries**. In the next step, the brain decides whether the face we are looking at is already known or unknown to us. And finally, the brain **furnishes** the information we have collected about the person whose face we are looking at. This complex processing is done in a split second so that we can **behave** quickly when reacting to situations, for instance, **sneaking** into a store when we see a **former** partner coming down the sidewalk.

4   But it isn't just structures and processes within the brain that make recognition possible, according to scientists in Switzerland. They have identified a "**cuddle** chemical" that our body releases to help us **distinguish** between **objective recollection** of a face and the emotional feelings associated with familiar faces. They believe this **hormone**, which is responsible for feelings of love in relationships, particularly between mothers and their babies, in the past helped us to recognize our mothers at birth in order to survive.

5   Despite considerable progress, scientists are still far from developing treatments for patients with recognition difficulties. However, their findings are already being used in the legal field. We have all seen TV crime dramas where an image of a criminal is uploaded onto a police computer, and minutes later the crime team gets the identity of the **offender**. Is this really possible? Although the FBI doesn't solve many crimes in sixty minutes, it does use sophisticated software known as *artificial facial recognition* to compare the likeness of criminal faces caught on closed-circuit TV (CCTV) with driver's license photographs held on government **databases**. There have been doubts regarding its reliability, though, because faces change with age, and criminals can use **disguises** to confuse the computers. Acknowledging this, researchers in Israel have used recent facial recognition studies to develop a more human-like, 3-D facial recognition system that is far more reliable.

6   So, the next time you see a friendly face across the street, take a moment to recognize the enormous importance facial recognition has in our lives. Most of us are lucky enough to be able to do it hundreds of times per day. Then, as you continue to walk down the street past a security camera, consider that it may not be just watching you—it might be *recognizing* you.

(730 words)

READING COMPREHENSION

Respond to the questions in writing. Base your responses on the reading and your own personal experiences.

1. What has prompted the growing amount of research on facial recognition?

2. What discoveries on brain function and structure are referred to in the text?

3. In your own words, how does the **cuddle** chemical help mothers and babies form a loving bond?

4. Is the use of facial recognition software in TV crime shows realistic?

5. Can you think of any arguments against law enforcement agencies using facial recognition technology?

6. Can you think of any other applications it might be useful for?

Focusing on Vocabulary

WORD MEANING

A. Read the sentences and choose the word or phrase that best matches the meaning of the target word. Use context clues to determine the correct meaning. Check your dictionary if you are not sure of the answer.

1. For an hour and a half we **wandered** around the streets of Venice, totally lost.

   a. tried to find someone or something by looking very carefully
   b. spent time in a place or with someone, especially for pleasure or interest
   c. walked slowly across or around an area, usually without a clear direction or purpose

2. The color of a star depends on its chemical **composition** and its mass.

   a. chemical change that happens when two or more substances are mixed
   b. something that is made of only one thing
   c. way that something is made up of different parts

3. Singapore's mix of cultures and history makes it a **fascinating** vacation destination.

   a. extremely interesting
   b. much quicker
   c. very expensive

4. The pages of a book are **sequential**.

   a. occurring in the correct order; one after the other
   b. ordered according to the letters of the alphabet
   c. happening or chosen without any definite pattern

5. Price promotions are mainly used with fast-moving consumer goods such as **groceries**.

   a. luxury items
   b. food and other household items
   c. consumer electronics

6. The thieves **snuck** into the store while the owner had his back turned.

   a. entered a building illegally and by force
   b. visited a place to search for something illegal
   c. went somewhere secretly and quietly to avoid being seen or heard

7. Her **former** boss now works for a computer firm in Los Angeles.

   a. previous
   b. new
   c. first

8. She had fallen asleep **cuddling** her favorite doll.

   a. dreaming about a particular object
   b. letting something slip out of your hands
   c. holding someone or something very close to you with your arms

9. It's always difficult to be **objective** about an issue as sensitive as the death penalty.

   a. unfairly against or in favor of a particular group
   b. according to what everyone in a group agrees with or accepts
   c. based on facts rather than on your feelings or beliefs

10. Parents usually blame teenagers' moody behavior on teens' **hormones**, their choice of friends, or the lyrics of the music they listen to.

    a. people who are never satisfied and always complaining
    b. chemical substances produced by your body that influences growth, development, and condition
    c. illnesses that results in an inability to sleep

11. Putting a young **offender** in prison is not an effective deterrent against that person repeating the crime.

    a. someone who is waiting to go on trial or to court
    b. someone who is guilty of a crime
    c. someone who is very rude or insulting

12. The U.K. government has a **database** for a wide range of topics, including agriculture, business, crime, population, and transportation.

    a. large amount of data stored in a computer system so that you can find and use it easily
    b. person hired by the government to provide a service
    c. company that sells information for a profit

B. Read the target words and definitions. Then read the sentences. Circle the sentence in which the target word is NOT used correctly.

1. **envisage**: to form a picture or idea in your mind about what something might be like

   a. Scientists **envisaged** a sharp drop in ozone levels over the Antarctic region throughout the past five years.
   b. The new football stadium cost a lot more than had been originally **envisaged**.
   c. I cannot **envisage** what life will be like in fifty years.

2. **tragic**: a tragic event or situation makes you feel very sad, especially because it involves death or suffering

   a. Are you insured against **tragic** damage to your property?
   b. The court was told that the ski instructor was not to blame for the **tragic** death of one of her students.
   c. The earthquake rescue team was deeply moved by the **tragic** stories it heard.

3. **remedy**: a way of dealing with a problem or making a bad situation better

   a. There are a number of possible **remedies** to this problem.
   b. The collapse of major banks and growing unemployment are yet more **remedies** of the global financial crisis.
   c. She tried some herbal tea and other anti-stress **remedies**, but none of them worked.

4. **infant**: a baby or very young child

   a. Health experts advise mothers not to smoke during pregnancy to protect **infants**.
   b. Our cat has just had a litter of six **infants**.
   c. There are clear differences in speed of learning between **infants** and teenagers.

5. **elaborate:** having a lot of small parts or details put together in a complicated way

   a. Sociologists have developed increasingly **elaborate** theories to explain teenage behavior.
   b. **Elaborate** paintings by the aboriginal people of Australia are extremely valuable.
   c. The builder was only able to give us an **elaborate** estimate of how much it was going to cost to extend the kitchen.

6. **distinguish**: to recognize and understand the difference between two or more things or people

   a. It was a complex process trying to **distinguish** all the similarities in the three sets of data.
   b. A tiny baby soon learns to **distinguish** its mother's face from other adults' faces.
   c. They had to **distinguish** between problems due to lack of ability and problems due to lack of motivation.

7. **recollect**: to be able to remember something

   a. I do not **recollect** ever having been to Fargo, although my mother says we went there when I was a child.
   b. The events of 9/11 were so dreadful that even now it is painful to **recollect** them.
   c. After twenty-five years of **recollecting** recipes, Barbara has compiled them into a cookbook.

8. **summon**: to gather or call forth (your courage, memories) especially with effort

   a. The music of the ice cream truck **summoned** memories of childhood vacations at the seashore.
   b. I had to **summon** all of my courage to walk past the barking dogs.
   c. The new computers were **summoned** after consumers failed to show any interest.

9. **furnish**: to supply or provide something

   a. Applicants for a driver's license must **furnish** proof of their identity.
   b. International aid organizations **furnish** supplies to whatever part of the world is in need of them.
   c. The family **furnished** money from the bank to buy a new car.

10. **behave**: to act in a particular way

    a. A police spokesperson said the demonstrators were well **behaved**.
    b. Eventually, the children themselves may begin to understand their own feelings, and why they **behave** as they do.
    c. The portrait of the old man **behaves** as though it were a photograph.

11. **artificial**: not real or not made of natural things, but made to seem like something that is real or natural

   a. The advantage of **artificial** Christmas trees is that they last forever.
   b. Nowadays, I only buy meat that is **artificial**.
   c. My dad is trying to lose weight, so he uses **artificial** sweetener in his coffee.

12. **disguise**: something that you wear to change your appearance and hide who you are

   a. The thief used a wig and false moustache as a **disguise**.
   b. My daughter wanted a new cheerleader **disguise** for her birthday.
   c. The mystery guest turned out to be my friend in **disguise**.

WORD FAMILIES

A. The table contains word families for some of the target words in the reading. Complete the table. An **X** indicates that there is no form or that the form is not common. Sometimes more than one form may be possible. If you are unsure about a form, check your dictionary.

Verb	Noun	Adjective	Adverb
X		artificial	
cuddle			X
	disguise		X
		1. 2. fascinating	
furnish			X
X		objective	
	1. offender 2. 3.	1. 2. 3.	
		sequential	
X		tragic	
wander	1. 2.		X

B. Read the sentences. In eight of the sentences, an incorrect form of the target word has been used. If the form of the target word is incorrect, cross it out and write the correct form. If the form is correct, put a checkmark (✔). Use the word families table to help you.

_____ **1.** The economic crisis has kept prices **artificial** low.

_____ **2.** She loved to **cuddle** with her fluffy teddy bear.

_____ **3.** Dan wore an amazing **disguise**. He had me completely fooled.

_____ **4.** I was **fascinating** when we visited the Egyptian exhibit at the museum.

_____ **5.** Their house was **furnish** with expensive rugs, sofas, and vases bought on their recent trip to Morocco.

_____ **6.** The jury's task is to weigh the evidence **objective** and impartially.

_____ **7.** There are many new methods to prevent criminals from committing other **offender**.

_____ **8.** The dance is basically a **sequentially** of steps that you repeat over and over again.

_____ **9.** William Shakespeare wrote many **tragically**.

_____ **10.** With their parents at work, the kids were left to **wanderer** the streets.

COLLOCATION

In each set of sentences, the target word is paired with different words to form different collocations. Choose the collocation that best fits the last sentence and write it in the blank. You may need to change the form of one word in the collocation to fit the sentence.

1. a. Learning to behave is a key part of growing up.
   b. Only after their teacher shouted at them did the students **start to behave** themselves.
   c. Mom asked if we could **try to behave**, even though she knew we hated visiting the dentist.
   d. I'm really worried about Jimmie. He's _____ really strangely.

2. a. The travel company has **created** an online **database** of 23,000 hotels that allow pets.
   b. In-store computers allow customers to **search** the **database** to see if their books are in stock.
   c. Good companies in today's market **update** their customer **databases** on a regular basis to ensure high levels of customer service.
   d. The new computerized library system makes it possible for students to _____ several _____ at once in order to find assigned reading material.

3. a. Living on a farm in Colorado, we were a million miles away from our **former life** in Boston.

  b. Susan was still on good terms with her **former boss**.

  c. Michael Schumacher is one of the most famous **former** Formula One **world champions**.

  d. It can be helpful to keep in contact with your _____ just in case you need a job reference.

4. a. Hormone replacement therapy is a method used to replace hormones that your body is no longer producing by itself due to either age or illness.

  b. Some patients may benefit from **hormone treatment** in their fight against certain diseases.

  c. Maintaining a healthy body weight can help to keep **hormone levels** under control.

  d. Growth _____ start off low in early life and peak just before puberty, after which they gradually decline with age.

5. a. If you find it hard to live on your current salary, the **best remedy** would be to change jobs.

  b. There are many doctors who argue that there is little evidence to support the idea that **herbal remedies** are effective alternatives to prescribed drugs.

  c. In Brazil, mint tea is a **traditional remedy** to treat various problems, from headaches and stomach pain to fever and flu.

  d. Chinese _____ have been tested as supplements to conventional treatments and have been shown to give promising results

6. a. The story of the boy in a balloon hundreds of feet above ground ended up being an **elaborate hoax**.

  b. Ancient Egyptians created an **elaborate system** of ditches and canals to irrigate their crops.

  c. Archaeological evidence shows that the First Peoples of Canada practiced **elaborate rituals** and celebrations.

  d. Stories of UFOs and alien abduction are frequently dismissed as examples of _____.

7. a. Futurologists are employed by leading technology companies to **envisage the** exciting **future** of high-tech gadgets.

  b. I tried to **envisage** how my life would **change** once I moved to the United States.

  c. He couldn't **envisage** a **plan** that would work in reality.

  d. Climate experts are trying to _____ to stop glaciers and polar ice caps from melting.

8. a. The disappointment she felt at not winning the talent competition was so great that she found it difficult to **summon a smile** for the photographers at the end of the show.

  b. The rower **summoned the strength** to reach the finish line just ahead of the next boat.

  c. I needed to **summon** all of **my courage** to get on the roller-coaster ride.

  d. After hiking all day and then setting up my tent, I couldn't _____ to make a fire to cook, so I simply opened some beans and ate them directly from the can.

Expanding the Topic

Complete the passage. Use the target words from the box. You may need to change the form of the word to fit the sentence. There is one extra word.

composition	distinguish	groceries	recollect
cuddle	furnish	infants	sneak

1   For social animals, such as humans, the ability to (1) _____ different faces from one another is important since this skill (2) _____ us with important social information, such as whether the person is our partner and therefore someone we can (3) _____ with, or whether the person is a stranger and an introduction would be more appropriate.

2   But how do we (4) _____ the faces we know? The first step to facial recognition is the processing of visual information in the brain, which is thought to rely on the orientation of features such as lines.

3   By manipulating images of celebrities, such as Coldplay's Chris Martin and actor George Clooney, researchers have found that nearly all the information we need to recognize a face is contained in horizontal lines, such as the lines of the eyebrows, the eyes, and the lips. Further analysis of facial (5) _____ has revealed that these features could be simplified into black and white lines of information, similar to bar codes.

4   Bar codes, such as those found on (6) _____ in supermarkets, were developed as an efficient way of obtaining information from food packages: Straight, one-dimensional lines are far easier to process than two-dimensional characters such as numbers. Our faces may have evolved in a similar way—for example, to allow parents and (7) _____ to recognize each other.

5   The researchers analyzed various natural images, such as flowers and landscapes, and found that faces are unique in conveying all their useful information in horizontal stripes. The bar-code pattern has many advantages: It allows a face to be recognized efficiently by the visual parts of the brain; it is easy to locate in complex scenes; and it appears to be resistant to changes in the overall appearance of the face.

Adapted from http://www.sciencedaily.com/releases/2009/04/090413202728.htm.

 Imagine that for one day you have lost the ability to recognize people's faces. Write a 500-word story that describes your day, your feelings, and the consequences.

Revisiting the Target Words

Now that you have completed this chapter, use the scale to describe your knowledge of the target words.

1 I still don't know anything about this word.

2 I am still not sure of the meaning of this word even after studying it.

3 I understand this word when I see it or hear it in a sentence, but I don't know how to use it in my own speaking and writing.

4 I know this word and can use it in my own speaking and writing.

TARGET WORDS

____artificial	____distinguish	____groceries	____remedy
____behave	____elaborate	____hormone	____sequential
____composition	____envisage	____infant	____sneak
____cuddle	____fascinating	____objective	____summon
____database	____former	____offender	____tragic
____disguise	____furnish	____recollect	____wander

KNOWLEDGE CHECK 2

Go back to the beginning of the chapter and complete the Knowledge Check 1 table.

Strategy Practice

Getting Started

Look at the three images taken from Chapters 13–15. Without looking back at the chapters, how many target words can you remember from each chapter?

Learning More about Words: SYNONYMS

One of the main benefits of building a larger vocabulary is that it makes it possible for you to be more precise. In other words, you are able to say exactly what you want to say instead of being limited to simple ideas because you don't have the vocabulary you need.

A helpful tool for finding more precise words is a thesaurus. A thesaurus is a book or an online resource that provides lists of words and their synonyms. However, a list of synonyms is not very useful if you do not know the meanings of each of the words and what makes them different from one other.

In Chapter 12, we saw that there can be important differences between the meanings and uses of synonyms. This is also true for the grammatical behavior of synonyms. Take a look at the set of words. These words all share the same core meaning.

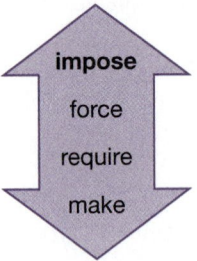

impose
force
require
make

core meaning: *to make someone do something*

However, if we look at sentences in which these words are used, we see that *impose* is not followed by the same grammatical pattern as the others.

Example:

Teachers should not **impose** <u>their personal beliefs on their students.</u>
(impose something on somebody)

Teachers should not <u>force their students to adopt new beliefs</u>.
(force somebody to do something)

School policy <u>requires all students to wear uniforms</u>.
(require somebody to do something)

Our teacher <u>made us study fifty new words</u> every week.
(make somebody do something)

What this means is that when you choose a synonym from a list, you have to think about the grammar that goes with it and whether the synonym and the structure work well in the piece you are writing.

A. Look back at how **_impose_** is used in the reading in Chapter 10. Try replacing **_impose_** with one of the synonyms on page 146. What kind of changes do you need to make to the sentence? Discuss these changes with a partner.

B. Look at the synonyms for **_donate_**. What is the core meaning for this set of words?

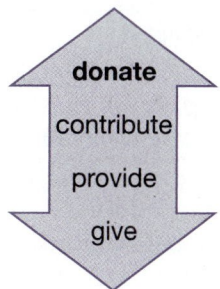

core meaning: _____

C. Identify the grammatical pattern that follows each verb in the sentences. Discuss the differences.

1. My father donated one of his kidneys to his sister.

donate _____

2. His grandfather contributed $2,000 toward his tuition fees.

contribute _____

3. Local companies provided summer jobs for area students.

provide _____

4. Wells Fargo Bank gave my brother a small business loan.

give _____

Some words may be followed by more than one grammatical pattern. Look at the model sentences for **ample** and its synonyms: *enough*, *sufficient*, and *plenty*.

am·ple *adjective* ◄))
[thesaurus] [listen and repeat]

1 more than enough
◄)) *There will be ample opportunity to ask questions.*

THESAURUS

enough, plenty, sufficient

2 **ample belly/bosom etc.** a big stomach, etc., in a way that is attractive or pleasant
—**amply** *adverb*

---

e·nough *adverb, determiner, pronoun* ◄))

1 as big, as many, as far, as much, etc. as necessary
◄)) *This bag isn't big **enough to** hold all my stuff.*
◄)) *He doesn't even earn **enough to** pay the rent.*
◄)) *Is he old **enough for** school?*
◄)) *Do we have **enough** food **for** everybody?*

suf·fi·cient [Ac] *adjective (formal)* ◄))

as much as you need for a particular purpose

[SYN] **ENOUGH** [ANT] **INSUFFICIENT**
◄)) *Will $100 be sufficient?*
◄)) *They had **sufficient** evidence **to** send him to prison.*

—**sufficiency** *noun* [singular, noncountable]
Is there a sufficiency of time to analyze the data?

---

plen·ty[1] *pronoun* ◄))

a large amount that is enough or more than enough
◄)) *Eat **plenty of** fruits and vegetables.*
◄)) *We have **plenty to** worry about.*

Other words may differ in other ways still. You can find information about the grammatical behavior of words in a good learners' dictionary.

Focusing on Skills: READING

USING CONTEXT TO WORK OUT WORD MEANING

When you encounter an unknown word while you are reading, you can use context clues to work out the unknown word's meaning. Texts offer a variety of different clues to help you. Below are five such clues.

Match the clues with the samples taken from Chapters 13, 14, and 15 on the next page. The "unknown" words are underlined.

Clues

_____ **1.** There is a word in the sentence with a similar meaning to the unknown word.

_____ **2.** The text provides examples of the unknown word.

_____ **3.** The text develops an idea that is closely linked to the meaning of the unknown word.

_____ **4.** The text uses punctuation to signal that a definition of the unknown word is provided nearby.

_____ **5.** The unknown word(s) are part of a word or idea you already know well.

Samples

a. A woman's face should be symmetrical with clear skin, a small <u>chin</u> and nose, a narrow jaw and slim <u>eyebrows</u>, but full, well-defined lips and cheeks, and large eyes. An attractive male face also should exhibit many of these features.

b. In fact, the origins of facial beauty appear to lie in the biological necessity to survive and successfully <u>reproduce</u>. What we now call beauty was originally our way of determining who was a potential mate. With limited food resources and ever-present dangers, it was important for our earliest ancestors to choose a mate who would not only pass on successful genes to future generations, but also survive childbirth and live long enough to be able to provide for the family.

c. <u>Symmetrical</u> faces—faces that are similar in shape on each side—also were perceived to be a sign of good health, and, thus, more attractive.

d. Women avoided powders and bright colors, and men abandoned makeup altogether. Instead, women mixed natural <u>ingredients</u>, such as oatmeal, honey, and eggs, to improve their natural looks.

e. How can we remember so many faces when many of us find it difficult to <u>recollect</u> something as simple as a phone number?

Focusing on Vocabulary Cards: QUESTION TIME

The name of this activity is "Question Time," and the aim is to practice using target words. This will help you review your target word knowledge and your ability to use target words. You will need your growing collection of vocabulary cards.

Instructions

1. Choose five vocabulary cards at random.
2. On a separate piece of paper, write five questions. Each question should include one target word.
3. Get a teacher to check your questions.
4. Ask a partner your five questions and write down his or her answers.
5. Report back to the rest of the class your questions and the answers you wrote down.

Technology

Techno-Doping

Getting Started

Discuss the questions with your classmates.

✦ What sports do you play and / or watch?

✦ What equipment is needed for the sports you take part in?

✦ Is the equipment you need necessary for safety or performance reasons?

Assessing Your Vocabulary Knowledge: TARGET WORDS

Look at the words in the box. These are the target words for this chapter. Use the scale to score yourself on each word.

1 I don't know this word.

2 I have seen or heard this word before, but I am not sure of the meaning.

3 I understand this word when I see it or hear it in a sentence, but I don't know how to use it in my own speaking and writing.

4 I know this word and can use it in my own speaking and writing.

TARGET WORDS			
____alike	____controversial	____gambling	____launch
____ban	____crash	____giant	____participation
____barrier	____cushioned	____glory	____scandal
____boxing	____dedicated	____glove	____silk
____broadcast	____dwelling	____gravel	____unprecedented
____champion	____exposure	____helmet	____wool

KNOWLEDGE CHECK 1

Complete the sentences with words that you have scored as **1**.

1. I am not familiar with the word / term _____.

2. I have no idea what _____ means.

Fill in the first blank with a word that you have scored as **2**. Then complete the sentence.

3. I think _____ could mean _____.

Reading

The passage examines the use of technology in sports and the implications for fairness and participation. As you read, pay special attention to the target vocabulary words in **bold**.

Sports Technology: Is It Unfair?

1   Throughout history, competitive sports have been a source of **glory** for both athletes and fans. But the sports world is not without **controversy**, with **gambling**, drug use (also known as doping), and **scandals** now almost commonplace. However, some believe another threat to sports requires equal attention: *techno-doping*. This is the use of technology to obtain an unfair advantage, to unfairly lessen the challenges faced by modern-day athletes, and to limit the field of competitors.

2   Some claim that the design of sports equipment damages sports because it noticeably improves athletic performance above natural athletic development. For example, in 1928 a well-known swimsuit manufacturer introduced a **controversial** swimsuit made of **silk** instead of the usual **wool**, which many believe led to the world freestyle record being broken. Eighty years later that same manufacturer created another **controversial** swimsuit, and an **unprecedented** 108 swimming world records were broken in the same year. Sports writers and researchers **alike** argue that the occurrence of the performance improvement at the same time as the **launch** of the swimsuit could not be just chance. The swimsuit has since been **banned**. In addition to over enhancing performance, sports equipment technology may even make sports more dangerous, some experts claim. For example, **boxing gloves** and head

guards have resulted in more brain injuries. Boxers are more willing to hit and to take a hit to the head because of the new equipment.

3   Such improvements in equipment design and performance in sports also have had an effect on **participation**. Competitive sports in the twenty-first century require vast amounts of money. Athletes without enough money are unable to compete at the highest levels because they lack access to the technology that would make them competitive. A sportsperson starting out who has limited commercial support cannot compete against a **champion** supported by **giant** sponsorship deals worth millions of dollars. Money influences **participation** at all levels of all sports. Research carried out in 2001 found that in U.S. households with a yearly income of less than $40,000, only 49 percent of the children played sports, whereas if a family earned more than $80,000, **participation** in sports rose to 73 percent. A key reason is the high cost of technology in modern sports.

4   However, there are those who argue that it is unfair to say that technology has had only a negative role in modern sports. Overall, technology has dramatically improved safety, not just for the competitors but also for spectators. For example, in motor sports, carbon-fiber technology has greatly improved **crash** survival rates for drivers. High-tech track designs with larger **gravel** run-off areas and **cushioned** safety **barriers** have reduced spectator risk. And without developments in **helmet** design, Brazilian F1 star Felipe Massa, who suffered a serious head injury while racing in Hungary in 2009, would not be still driving today.

5   It is also argued that rather than limiting **participation**, technology is, in fact, widening it. It is true that technology can add to the cost of equipment; however, technology is the very reason that sports equipment can be mass-produced making it cheaper and therefore easier for a wider public to buy. Technology has also brought a broader variety of sporting events

from around the world into our **dwellings**, be it hut, cottage, or mansion. Technological advances include **broadcasts** of live and recorded sporting events on TV, radio, and the Internet, which means greater **exposure** to sports. There are at least fifty TV channels **dedicated** to sports in the United States alone. Taking a single sporting event as an example, in 2009 more than 150 million people watched the Super Bowl on TV.

6   Finally, technology has brought about an increase in fairness in sports as well. Not only has **broadcast** technology made refereeing sports more accurate thanks to video playback facilities, but developments in timing devices have reduced the number of inconclusive results—for instance, the number of draws in track and field events. Technology gains have also made drug testing in sports far more comprehensive and reliable, so it could be said that rather than techno-doping, technology is actually responsible for anti-doping.

7   In sum, there are always two sides to every issue, and the techno-doping argument certainly shows no sign of going away anytime soon. As for which side of the argument you support, consider how the fan or athlete in you would feel if golf balls were still filled with feathers, tennis rackets crafted from wood, and swimsuits made of **wool**.

(734 words)

READING COMPREHENSION

Respond to the questions in writing. Base your responses on the reading and your own personal experiences.

1. In your own words, how would you define "techno-doping"?

2. Explain in your own words the relationship between falling **participation** rates and techno-doping in U.S. households.

3. Research has shown that a new **boxing glove** design and new head guards have resulted in more brain injuries. What is the reason for this?

4. Can you think of any sports not mentioned in the text that might be negatively affected by techno-doping?

5. Can you think of any additional arguments in support of technology's role in sports?

6. List as many sports stars as you can whose performances you believe have not been the result of unfair technological advances.

Focusing on Vocabulary

WORD MEANING

A. Match the target words with their definitions. If you are unsure about a word's meaning, try to figure it out from the context by rereading the passage. Then check your dictionary.

Set 1

_____ 1. glory
_____ 2. controversial
_____ 3. gambling
_____ 4. scandal
_____ 5. silk
_____ 6. wool
_____ 7. unprecedented

a. never having happened before, or never having happened so much
b. something shocking, usually involving someone important behaving badly
c. a thin, smooth, soft cloth made from a very thin, thread-like material produced by a worm
d. the importance, honor, and praise that people give someone they admire a lot
e. when people risk money or possessions on the result of something that is not certain, such as a card game or a horse race
f. a serious argument about something that often involves many people and continues for a long time
g. the soft, thick hair that sheep and some goats have on their body

Set 2

_____ 1. launch
_____ 2. boxing
_____ 3. glove
_____ 4. gravel
_____ 5. cushioned
_____ 6. barrier
_____ 7. helmet

a. the sport of fighting while wearing big, leather hand protectors
b. small stones used to make a surface for things such as paths and roads
c. designed to soften the impact of one thing hitting another
d. a physical object that keeps apart two areas, people, etc.
e. when a new product, such as a book, is made available or made known
f. a strong hard hat that people such as soldiers, motorcyclists, and police wear to protect their heads
g. a piece of clothing that you wear on your hand in order to protect it or keep it warm

B. Read each target word and the list below it. One word or phrase in each list is NOT a synonym for the target word. Cross it out.

1. alike

| comparable | different | equal | similar |

2. ban

| disallow | forbid | outlaw | permit |

3. participation

| doing | involvement | taking part | watching |

4. champion

| fan | title holder | victor | winner |

5. giant

| enormous | huge | massive | miniature |

6. crash

| collision | dive | pile-up | smash |

7. dwelling

| abode | home | store | residence |

8. broadcast

| play | program | show | transmission |

9. exposure

| awareness | contact | enjoyment | familiarity |

10. dedicated

| devoted | ambivalent | enthusiastic | fanatical |

WORD FAMILIES

A. The table contains word families for some of the target words in the reading. Complete the table. An **X** indicates that there is no form or that the form is not common. Sometimes more than one form may be possible. If you are unsure about a form, check your dictionary.

Verb	Noun	Adjective	Adverb
X		controversial	
		cushioned	X
		dedicated	X
	exposure		X
	glory		
	gravel	1. 2.	X
	1. 2. **participation**	1. 2.	X
	scandal		
X	1. **silk** 2.	1. 2.	
X	wool	1. 2.	X

B. Choose the correct form of the word in **bold** in sentence **a** to complete sentence **b**. Use the word families table you just completed as a guide.

1. **a.** Banning smoking in public places in New York was a **controversial** measure.

   b. There has been a huge _____ over where to put the war memorial.

2. **a.** Mattresses on the ground **cushioned** the stuntman's fall.

   b. It's a very comfortable shoe with good, firm _____, specially designed for jogging on the road.

3. **a.** Being a **dedicated** sportsman, Steve trained every day of the week.

   b. To reach a high level of skill requires talent, _____, and a lot of hard work.

4. **a.** The failure of Brad and Jen's marriage received a lot of media **exposure**.

   b. The shark opened its mouth and _____ rows of sharp white teeth.

5. **a.** The old city hall needed a lot of repairs to get it back to its former **glory**.

   b. Movies that _____ violence may be responsible for some of the rise in crime.

6. **a.** Every major construction site needs a constant supply of cement, stones, **gravel**, and water.

   b. Their new garden contains _____ courtyards, green lawns, and pretty flower beds.

7. **a.** The new management structure offers more opportunities for **participation** in decision making.

   b. Everyone in the class is expected to _____ actively in these discussions.

8. **a.** Newspapers only seem interested in gossip and **scandal**.

   b. In the 1800s, writer George Sand—really a woman—_____ society by dressing like a man.

9. **a.** Jockeys wear colored shirts made of **silk**.

   b. Many shampoos and hair conditioners claim that they will leave your hair feeling soft and _____.

10. **a.** Sheep's **wool** contains lanolin, a fatty substance that waterproofs the **wool**.

    b. One hundred years ago, it was more common for people to wear _____ underwear than underwear made of cotton.

COLLOCATION

Read the common collocations in the column on the left. Give two examples of things associated with each collocation.

	Example 1	Example 2
1. global **ban**		
2. boxing ring		
3. news **broadcast**		
4. Olympic **champion**		
5. plane **crash**		
6. safety **helmet**		
7. residential **dwelling**		
8. unprecedented demand		

Expanding the Topic

An important part of developing your vocabulary involves forming and supporting opinions about the topic you are studying. Read the statements and indicate whether you agree (**A**) or disagree (**D**). Then discuss your opinions and reasoning with a partner.

_____ **1.** The cost of equipment acts as a **barrier** to **participation** in sports at all levels.

_____ **2.** Professional boxers should not be allowed to wear **gloves**.

_____ **3.** Swimming **giants**, such as Michael Phelps, should return their medals and financial rewards if they wore swimsuits that have subsequently been found to give unfair performance advantage.

_____ **4.** Olympic athletes, from rich and poor countries **alike**, should be required to use standard equipment when competing.

_____ **5. Gambling** on sporting events should be made illegal.

_____ **6.** Humans have physically evolved as far as we possibly can, so the future of competitive sports relies upon the continued **launch** of improved technology alone.

 Choose any piece of sporting equipment—for example: the tennis racket, the golf club, soccer footwear—and write a 500-word essay on how this equipment has developed over time as a result of advances in technology.

Revisiting the Target Words

Now that you have completed this chapter, use the scale to describe your knowledge of the target words.

1 I still don't know anything about this word.

2 I am still not sure of the meaning of this word even after studying it.

3 I understand this word when I see it or hear it in a sentence, but I don't know how to use it in my own speaking and writing.

4 I know this word and can use it in my own speaking and writing.

TARGET WORDS

____alike	____controversial	____gambling	____launch
____ban	____crash	____giant	____participation
____barrier	____cushioned	____glory	____scandal
____boxing	____dedicated	____glove	____silk
____broadcast	____dwelling	____gravel	____unprecedented
____champion	____exposure	____helmet	____wool

KNOWLEDGE CHECK 2

Select examples from the words you now give a score of **3** or **4**, but didn't at the start of the chapter, to complete the sentences.

1. I didn't know that _____ meant _____ before reading this chapter.

2. I wasn't sure that I knew the meaning of _____, but I am now.

3. I now am confident that I know what _____ means, but I would like more practice with how to use it in my speaking and writing.

4. I could next use _____ when I am _____.

Connected or Disconnected?

Getting Started

Discuss the questions with your classmates.

✦ How much time do you spend online / using the Internet per week?

✦ How does this compare with the time you spend socializing with friends?

✦ Do you think that keeping in touch with friends online is as good as seeing them face-to-face?

Assessing Your Vocabulary Knowledge: TARGET WORDS

Look at the words in the box. These are the target words for this chapter. Use the scale to score yourself on each word.

1 I don't know this word.

2 I have seen or heard this word before, but I am not sure of the meaning.

3 I understand this word when I see it or hear it in a sentence, but I don't know how to use it in my own speaking and writing.

4 I know this word and can use it in my own speaking and writing.

TARGET WORDS			
____anxious	____exaggeration	____network	____sensitive
____approximately	____grumble	____privacy	____shrink
____charming	____inclined	____questionnaire	____silence
____chunk	____isolation	____retail	____verify
____console	____modest	____rip	____vigorous
____devastating	____mounting	____sacrifice	____vital

KNOWLEDGE CHECK 1

Fill in the first blank with a word that you have scored as **2**. Then complete the second sentence.

1. I have seen / heard _____. I saw / heard it while I was

_____.

Fill in the first blanks with words that you have scored as **4**. Then complete the sentences.

2. One meaning of _____ is _____.

3. I last used the word _____ while I was _____.

Reading

The passage is about the impact electronic media has had on social interaction. As you read, pay special attention to the target vocabulary words in **bold**.

Will They Call Us "Generation Isolation"?

1   **Retail** sales of cell phones and MP3 players are rising year after year. More people are spending sizable **chunks** of their lives in virtual worlds. And the use of social **networking** websites is continually increasing. Now, amid fears of the dangers of decreased social interaction, a backlash has begun. With parents and teachers alike **grumbling** about youngsters being stuck indoors by themselves, kids are being told to put away their game **consoles** and have more face-to-face fun with their friends. Likewise, kids are complaining about their parents taking work calls and e-mails during family time and so are forcing adults to **rip** themselves away from their cell phones and laptops. However, is there any scientific evidence to **verify** that we are, in fact, interacting less? Is it an **exaggeration** to say we are becoming "Generation **Isolation**"?

2   According to psychologists, social **isolation** occurs when people have only **modest** amounts of interaction or no interaction with their peers. Frequent use of the Internet, video games, and MP3 players might contribute to this. For example, results from a **questionnaire** sent out to more than 4,000 American adults found that the more time the respondents spent online, the more socially **isolated** they became. Of those who spent five-plus hours per week online, **approximately** 10 percent attended fewer social events than they had in the past. Nearly 15 percent found that the time they spent with family and friends had **shrunk**. And nearly 25

percent spent less time talking to family and friends on the phone.

3   Another study found that there are **mounting** numbers of people living by themselves, couples spending time apart, and parents spending time away from their children. In fact, face-to-face interaction has halved over the past twenty years, whereas use of electronic media has doubled. Likewise, the number of people with "core partners" (people with whom you discuss your most **sensitive** issues) is 30 percent lower than a generation ago.

4   This evidence seems to suggest that if we limit the use of electronic media, we can avoid social **isolation**. Yet research shows that the occurrence of "*severe* social **isolation**" has not changed over the past twenty-five years. In fact, research indicates that technology users have larger discussion **networks** than non-users. For instance, if you own a cell phone, your number of core partners is likely to be 25 percent higher than if you don't, and your core partners are likely to be more diverse. For Internet users, the figure is closer to 15 percent and significantly more for those who use the Internet more frequently. Researchers also have discovered that using the Internet doesn't stop people from visiting public places, as originally thought. Because the Internet is such a convenient way to find information about places such as libraries, museums, and bars, Internet users are more **inclined** to visit these places—places where they are more likely to meet new and **charming** people from a variety of backgrounds.

5   There is also evidence to suggest that social **networking** websites, blogs, and chat rooms are having a positive impact on democratic politics. This is because they are solutions to the so-called "spiral of **silence**" problem. Some people find it difficult to express their views face-to-face because they are **anxious** about what their peers may think. This is bad enough when it happens with children, but when it happens with adults, it can have a **devastating** effect on political engagement. It is **vital** that there be

opportunities for adults to share diverse ideas and opinions. Active participation in political debate is a key feature of a **vigorous** democracy. The advantage of communications technology is that it facilitates equal access to discussions and an equal right to be heard without **sacrificing privacy**. This, in turn, means greater social participation and decreased **isolation**.

6   So, is the use of social **networking** websites putting us at risk of greater social **isolation**? It seems that there isn't a simple yes or no answer to this. As technology develops, it becomes ever more sophisticated, which allows greater social interaction. However, we need to remember that in order to send a friend an e-mail, text message, or chat invitation, we need to have met them in the first place. So perhaps this is as good a time as any to log off and go out.

(714 words)

READING COMPREHENSION

Respond to the questions in writing. Base your responses on the reading and your own personal experiences.

1. How would you define "backlash"? According to the text, why has there been a backlash against online social interaction? Have you experienced this backlash yourself?

2. What evidence is given to support the idea that we are becoming "Generation **Isolation**"?

3. Why do you think people with cell phones and access to the Internet have more core partners?

4. In your own words, explain what is meant by the "spiral of **silence**."

5. Do you value electronic media, such as music downloads and online films, as much as you value CDs and DVDs? Why or why not?

6. How do you think social interaction will develop over the next fifty years? Will we stop meeting face-to-face altogether?

Focusing on Vocabulary

WORD MEANING

A. Read the target words. Use the paragraph number in parentheses to locate and reread the word in context. Then read the dictionary definitions and choose the one that reflects how the word is used in the reading.

_____ 1. **chunk** (1)
   a. a large, thick piece of something that does not have an even shape
   b. a large part or amount of something

_____ 2. **grumble** (1)
   a. to keep complaining in an unhappy way
   b. to make a low, continuous sound

_____ 3. **console** (1)
   a. to make someone feel better when they are feeling sad or disappointed
   b. the control unit of a mechanical, electrical, or electronic system

_____ 4. **rip** (1)
   a. to copy music from a CD to an MP3 player or computer
   b. to remove something quickly and violently

_____ **5. isolation** (1)
    a. the state of being far away from any others
    b. something that happens only once, and is not likely to happen again

_____ **6. modest** (2)
    a. unwilling to talk about abilities or achievements
    b. not very great, big, or expensive

_____ **7. inclined** (4)
    a. sloping or leaning in a particular direction
    b. likely to do something or behave in a particular way

_____ **8. silence** (5)
    a. complete absence of sound or noise
    b. failure or refusal to discuss something or answer questions about something

_____ **9. devastating** (5)
    a. very damaging or destructive
    b. very impressive or effective

_____ **10. vital** (5)
    a. full of energy in a way that is exciting and attractive
    b. extremely important and necessary for something to succeed or exist

_____ **11. sacrifice** (5)
    a. to offer something to a god, especially in the past, by killing an animal or person in a religious ceremony
    b. to decide not to have something valuable in order to get something that is more important

_____ **12. privacy** (5)
    a. the state of being able to be alone and not seen or heard by other people
    b. the state of being free from public attention

B. Read the target words in the box. Complete each sentence with the target word that matches the meaning of the words in parentheses. You may need to change the form of the word to fit the sentence.

anxious	exaggeration	questionnaire	shrink
approximately	mounting	retail	verify
charming	network	sensitive	vigorous

1. It is a(n) _____ to say that he earns more money than
(overstatement, embellishment)
anyone I know, but he is certainly very well paid.

2. The disease affects _____ 10 percent of the adult population.
(about, around)

3. The _____ asks students how they feel about access to computer
(survey, opinion poll)
facilities on campus.

4. The senator admitted that documents containing highly _____
(delicate, private)
information had been passed on to a newspaper journalist.

5. There was _____ pressure for the president to tackle the issue of
(growing, escalating)
health care reform.

6. Scientists are able to show that the Canadian ice cap has begun to

_____ at an alarming rate.
(reduce in size, get smaller)

7. The core of this international _____ consists of computers
(system, set of connections)

permanently joined through high-speed links.

8. She thought her friend's new boyfriend was very _____.
(appealing, charismatic)

9. Environmentalists have launched a(n) _____ campaign to fight
(strong, energetic)

against the timber company's plan to cut down the whole forest.

10. Alex was a bit _____ because he'd never flown before.
(worried, apprehensive)

11. Sam Walton opened his first Wal-Mart _____ outlet in 1962.
(store, market)

12. Journalists have to _____ that their story is factually correct
(confirm, check)

before it goes to print.

WORD FAMILIES

A. The table contains word families for some of the target words in the reading. An
X indicates that there is no form or that the form is not common. Study the table.
Look for spelling patterns for the verb, noun, adjective, and adverb forms of the
words. List the patterns in the space on the next page.

Verb	Noun	Adjective	Adverb
X	anxiety	**anxious**	anxiously
approximate	approximation	approximate	**approximately**
devastate	devastation	1. devastated 2. **devastating**	devastatingly
exaggerate	**exaggeration**	exaggerated	**X**
incline	1. inclination 2. incline	**inclined**	**X**
isolate	1. **isolation** 2. isolationism 3. isolationist	1. isolated 2. isolationist	**X**
X	**privacy**	private	privately
1. sense 2. sensitize	1. sensibility 2. sensitivity 3. sensitization 4. sensor	1. **sensitive** 2. senseless 3. sensory	1. senselessly 2. sensitively
verify	verification	1. verifiable 2. verified	**X**
X	vigor	**vigorous**	vigorously

verbs _____

nouns _____

adjectives _____

adverbs _____

B. Complete each sentence with the correct form of the word in parentheses. Use the word families table to help you.

1. They waited _____ (**anxious**) by the phone for news of their daughter.

2. Statisticians can use _____ (**approximately**) when calculating probabilities.

3. The international response to the _____ (**devastating**) caused by the tsunami was immediate.

4. The costs of the Olympic stadium have been wildly _____ (**exaggeration**) in the media.

5. I have no _____ (**inclined**) to believe anything I read in the newspapers.

6. _____ (**isolation**) has been a recurrent theme in U.S. political and economic history.

7. It is increasingly common for movie stars, singers, and politicians to complain about the invasion of their _____ (**privacy**) lives.

8. Street lamps use light _____ (**sensitive**) to know when to switch on and off.

9. Online payment systems rely on _____ (**verify**) technology to make sure that transactions are secure.

10. He _____ (**vigorous**) denied rumors that he was planning to leave the city's football team.

COLLOCATION

Combine a word from Column A with a word from Column B to form a collocation. Then match the collocation to its definition.

Column A	Column B
let	**charming**
modest	**network**
old boy	**rip**
prince	**sacrifice**
retail	statistics
shrinking	sum
ultimate	**therapy**
vital	violet

1. _____ a perfect man who a young woman might dream about meeting

2. _____ the giving up of something valued, usually one's life, for a cause one believes in

3. _____ the system by which men who went to the same school, belong to the same club, etc., use their influence to help each other

4. _____ the act of buying things that you do not need when you are unhappy because you think it will make you feel better

5. _____ facts about birth, death, marriage, and health, collected by the state

6. _____ to get very angry

7. _____ a relatively small amount of money

8. _____ someone who is very shy

Expanding the Topic

Complete the passage. Use the target words from the box. You may need to change the form of the word to fit the sentence.

chunk	exaggeration	mounting	sensitive
console	grumble	questionnaire	silence

Harmful Effects of Video Games

1   It is no (**1**) _____ to say that the rate of violence and aggression among children and teenagers is on the rise. But instead of just (**2**) _____ about this problem, it is important to try to find the causes and address them.

2   Entertainment media—TV, video games, movies—seem to be one cause. In particular, video games, first introduced in 1970, have taken over the world of child entertainment and have become a subject of considerable research, including a number of detailed (**3**) _____, for their presumed role in influencing child behavior and psychology.

3   There is (**4**) _____ evidence that video games can have greater negative effects on children than TV and movies. As video games are more engaging in nature, children usually actively participate in these games and also identify themselves with the aggressor. Besides, video games often contain scenes of incredible violence, which further puts children at risk of developing aggressive thoughts and behavior. In addition, children play these games over and over, and, according to psychologists, repetition and reward along with active involvement enhance learning. Therefore, video games can be more effective in instilling aggressive behavior in young children, as compared to passive media such as TV and movies.

4   Violence and aggression depicted in video games, if practiced in the real world, can cause serious injury and even death. It is believed that excessive video game playing may reduce a child's (**5**) _____ to others. Besides, excessive gaming can have an adverse impact on the academic performance of a child. It can also result in social **isolation**, as children tend to spend more time playing games in (**6**) _____ and less time conversing with family members and friends. Another important harmful effect of video games is that they can affect a child's perceptions about gender roles, as women are often portrayed as the victim or the weaker person in many of these games.

5   Finally, spending large (**7**) _____ of time playing on computers and game (**8**) _____ can significantly reduce physical activity in children and teenagers, thereby increasing the risk of obesity. Besides obesity, other health related issues associated with playing video games include video-induced seizures, muscular and skeletal disorders, and nerve damage.

Adapted from http://www.buzzle.com/articles/harmful-effects-of-video-games.html.

 You have just read a text about video games and their harmful effects on children. Write a 500-word response that takes an opposing viewpoint to the text.

Revisiting the Target Words

Now that you have completed this chapter, use the scale to describe your knowledge of the target words.

1 I still don't know anything about this word.

2 I am still not sure of the meaning of this word even after studying it.

3 I understand this word when I see it or hear it in a sentence, but I don't know how to use it in my own speaking and writing.

4 I know this word and can use it in my own speaking and writing.

TARGET WORDS

____anxious	____exaggeration	____network	____sensitive
____approximately	____grumble	____privacy	____shrink
____charming	____inclined	____questionnaire	____silence
____chunk	____isolation	____retail	____verify
____console	____modest	____rip	____vigorous
____devastating	____mounting	____sacrifice	____vital

KNOWLEDGE CHECK 2

Select examples from the words you now give a score of **3** or **4**, but didn't at the start of the chapter, to complete the sentences.

1. I didn't know that _____ meant _____ before reading this chapter.

2. I wasn't sure that I knew the meaning of _____, but I am now.

3. I now am confident that I know what _____ means, but I would like more practice with how to use it in my speaking and writing.

4. I now know that _____ collocates with _____.

CHAPTER 19

Evolution v 2.0: Shared Humanity

Getting Started

Discuss the questions with your classmates.

✦ List different examples of machine technology that you use in a typical day.

✦ In your opinion, what has been the most significant advance in technology in your lifetime? Why?

✦ Do you consider advances in machine technology to be more of an opportunity or a threat to our future?

Assessing Your Vocabulary Knowledge: TARGET WORDS

Look at the words in the box. These are the target words for this chapter. Use the scale to score yourself on each word.

1 I don't know this word.

2 I have seen or heard this word before, but I am not sure of the meaning.

3 I understand this word when I see it or hear it in a sentence, but I don't know how to use it in my own speaking and writing.

4 I know this word and can use it in my own speaking and writing.

TARGET WORDS			
____colonize	____forever	____protest	____sophisticated
____crumble	____halt	____publicize	____steal
____drown	____lens	____receiver	____stumble
____electronic	____merge	____ruin	____thorny
____error	____novel	____salvation	____trial
____filter	____outline	____sergeant	____virus

Check your progress in learning the vocabulary in this chapter.

- First, look at your scores in the table on page 168. Write the number of words for each score (1–4) in the "at the beginning" column. For example, if you scored eight words as **1** ("I don't know this word"), then write **8**.

- At the end of the chapter, score yourself again. Then compare the two sets of scores. Are you showing improvement on most of the words in the chapter?

Your score	Number of words ...		
	at the beginning:	at the end:	
		showing improvement	no improvement yet
1			
2			
3			
4			

Reading

The passage considers how future advances in technology might impact human existence. As you read, pay special attention to the target vocabulary words in **bold**.

Rise of the Machines

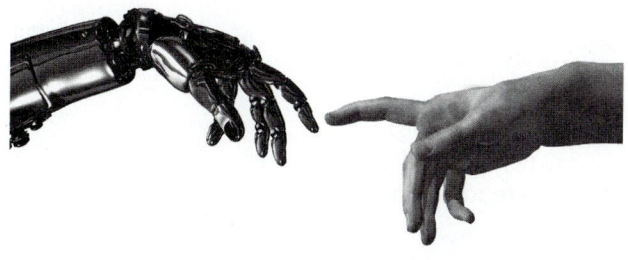

1   The complex relationship between humans and technology has been a constant feature of modern life: from real-life **protests** during the Industrial Revolution in the seventeenth century, to the imaginary worlds of early science fiction **novels** of the late nineteenth century and movies in the twentieth and twenty-first centuries. During this time, technology has divided us into two basic groups: those who think technology will revolutionize humanity in a positive way and those who believe it will bring about our downfall.

2   One area where technology could have a positive impact is human evolution. Life forms have evolved over millions of years, surviving by constantly adapting to environmental changes. However, the conditions for continuing human evolutionary change are beginning to **crumble** away. Humans have **colonized** most parts of the world and have become extremely mobile, thus limiting opportunities for human genes to develop, **filter**, and mutate—all of which is necessary for us to keep up with environmental changes. Some scientists believe that technology has the power to overcome this. They say that at some point, human biology and machine technology will **merge**, thus allowing human evolution to continue **forever**.

3   In 2009, the case of an American army **sergeant** who lost his leg in the Afghan war was **publicized**. He was fitted with a leg that contains a computerized (or bionic) knee that is able to monitor and adjust its own movement. In the same year, doctors implanted **electronic** devices into the eyes of a U.K. man who had been blind for thirty years. These high-tech

receivers have enabled him to see the **outlines** of objects and to read text. Other exciting new possibilities include contact **lenses** that enable wearers to see computer displays and computer chips that could replace the part of the brain that stores short-term memories.

4   A **thornier** vision of future human-technology relationships is based less on partnerships and more on technology taking over. For example, some writers refer to an idea called "the technological singularity." This is the point when computers with sufficient intelligence are able to create even better, faster, more intelligent machines than humans would ever be capable of creating. This development of artificial intelligence (AI) would be beyond the control and understanding of human creators and could mark the beginning of our end.

5   However, the development of more advanced computer intelligence is proving to be more challenging than anticipated. One **trial** to determine whether a computer appears to "think" involves a human judge having two conversations, one with a human and one with a machine. If the human judge is unable to distinguish between them, then the machine has passed the test. To date, no computer has succeeded. The key area where AI **stumbles** is the ability to make connections between seemingly unconnected things in order to generate creative thought. However, AI is getting more **sophisticated**: Machines have created music and played games that have fooled

human judges; devices tell lifeguards if someone is **drowning**; and computers control traffic flow in our cities.

6   But, as for computers actually taking over, there is currently very little evidence to support this. Despite fears of computer **viruses stealing** personal information, computers communicating between themselves, and computer systems replacing human workforces, there is no evidence of computers actually taking over our lives any time soon. Keeping on top of the situation is a new organization called the Association for the Advancement of Artificial Intelligence (AAAI). This group looks at the potential impact of current advances in AI. A similar group was set up in the 1970s to look at emerging advances in DNA technology and accurately predicted the emergence of genetic engineering in humans and genetically modified crops, which were hitherto unknown. So, maybe the AAAI knows something we don't.

7   To sum up, we are still some ways off from making an informed prediction about whether technology will be our **salvation** or will **ruin** our lives. But it would be an **error** to assume that advances in technology will ever **halt**, as computer scientist John von Neumann did fifty years ago when he stated, "It would appear we have reached the limits of what is possible to achieve with computer technology."

(692 words)

READING COMPREHENSION

Respond to the questions in writing. Base your responses on the reading and your own personal experiences.

1. According to the text, why is human evolution at risk?

2. How might humans benefit from **merging** with machines?

3. Why is "the technological singularity" considered a threat to humans?

4. Why does the text reference the organization called the Association for the Advancement of Artificial Intelligence?

5. Apart from the field of bionics, in what other areas could technology be of benefit to us?

6. After reading the text, do you consider technological advances to be more of an opportunity or a threat? Has your opinion changed since the beginning of the chapter?

Focusing on Vocabulary

WORD MEANING

A. Read the sentences and choose the word or phrase that best matches the meaning of the target word. Use context clues to determine the correct meaning. Check your dictionary if you are not sure of the answer.

1. Because of the economic recession, the two companies decided to **merge** into one.

   a. close a factory, business, or piece of machinery, either permanently or for a short time
   b. come together in a group
   c. combine or join things together to form one thing

2. The troops trusted that their **sergeant** knew how to get them home safely.

   a. anyone who is not a member of the military forces or the police
   b. lower-ranking officer in the army, air force, police, etc.
   c. individual who develops and manufactures goods and services used for military purposes

3. It is so annoying when you pick up the telephone **receiver**, dial the number, and then get a recorded voice message.

   a. piece of equipment that blocks signals
   b. equipment that converts signals into sounds or pictures
   c. sound made by electronic equipment

4. The newspaper photographer relied on her long **lens** to get pictures of celebrities.

   a. piece of equipment that emits a special bright light when you press the button on a camera to take a photograph
   b. piece of equipment used for climbing up to or down from high places
   c. piece of curved glass or plastic that makes things look bigger, smaller, or clearer when you look through it

5. New drugs must go through extensive **trials** before they can be used to treat people.

   a. process of testing to find out if something works effectively
   b. long line or a series of marks that have been left by someone or something
   c. series of things that are difficult to deal with

6. Every few years computer software manufacturers release more **sophisticated** versions of their best-selling titles.

   a. very well designed and very advanced, and often working in a complicated way
   b. unusual
   c. primitive or more basic

7. The lifeguards pulled the man who was **drowning** from the water and tried to revive him.

   a. moving or dropping down from a higher position to a lower position
   b. dying from being underwater for too long, or killing someone in this way
   c. staying or moving on the surface of a liquid without sinking

8. Kim was convinced he'd picked up the **virus** from his friend's laptop.

    a. set of instructions secretly put onto a computer or computer program, which can destroy information
    b. very small organisms
    c. piece of computer software that does a particular job

9. Juan saw the youths trying to **steal** the car and called the police immediately.

    a. strong metal that can be shaped easily
    b. prepare yourself to do something that you know will be unpleasant or upsetting
    c. take something that belongs to someone else

10. Getting the more interesting and better paying job was my **salvation**.

    a. something that prevents or saves someone or something from danger, loss, or failure
    b. substance that you put on sore skin to make it less painful
    c. something that causes a complete failure or loss of someone's money, moral standards, or social position

11. Air accident investigators were able to rule out human **error** as a cause of the crash.

    a. mistake
    b. why something happens
    c. way of solving a problem or dealing with a difficult situation

12. Danica Patrick's progress in the stock car race was **halted** by a technical failure.

    a. allowed to carry on
    b. slowed down
    c. prevented from continuing

B. Read the target words and definitions. Then read the sentences. Circle the sentence in which the target word is NOT used correctly.

1. protest: words or actions that show that you do not want someone to do something or that you dislike something very much

    a. The police gathered in numbers at the antiglobalization **protest**.
    b. The teachers were concerned about the students' poor **protest** over the semester.
    c. Political **protests** were an all too common feature of the 1960s.

2. novel: a long written story in which the characters and events are fictional

    a. The professor published his research in the academic **novel**.
    b. The *Matrix* films were loosely based on a sci-fi **novel** by William Gibson.
    c. In North America, romance **novels** are the most popular genre of modern literature.

3. crumble: to lose power, become weak, or fail

    a. My determination to finish the marathon **crumbled** when I saw the "15 miles to go" sign.
    b. The quarterback was hit and **crumbled** the ball.
    c. The Roman Empire began to **crumble** in 180 C.E.

4. **colonize**: to start living somewhere in large numbers

   a. Plans for humans to **colonize** Mars have been put on hold for the time being.
   b. Dead trees are frequently **colonized** by ants.
   c. My family started to **colonize** this house way back in the nineteenth century.

5. **filter**: to remove unwanted substances, objects, or people from something

   a. Some villages in sub-Saharan Africa use sand to **filter** their water.
   b. There is a huge choice of software available that can be used to **filter** e-mails to avoid spam.
   c. We use our front teeth to **filter** food when eating.

6. **forever**: for all future time

   a. Sherry was doing the job **forever** until she decided what she really wanted to do.
   b. Some of the documents from the ancient library in Alexandria have been lost **forever**.
   c. Environmentalists are worried that continued destruction of forests may result in the loss of some species **forever**.

7. **publicize**: to give information about something to the public so that they know about it

   a. The Dalai Lama's visit to the U.K. was highly **publicized**.
   b. Sam had to make a few changes to his assignment before he **publicized** it and handed it in.
   c. These days, too many guests on talk shows are only there to **publicize** their latest book or film.

8. **electronic**: involves the use of equipment, such as computers and TVs, that use electricity

   a. My dad still uses an **electronic** alarm clock that he has to wind up every night.
   b. Music in the 1980s was dominated by the use of **electronic** keyboards.
   c. Most of the **electronic** components in our household appliances are made in China.

9. **outline**: a line around the edge of something that shows its shape

   a. An **outline** of the murder victim's body was still visible on the sidewalk.
   b. Prehistoric hunters carved the **outlines** of animals into rock.
   c. I once saw a newspaper **outline** that said Elvis was living on the moon.

10. **thorny**: complicated and difficult

   a. Delegates at the climate change conference failed to come to an agreement on the **thorny** issue of limiting carbon emissions.
   b. He had the **thorny** honor of accepting the Academy Award for best actor.
   c. What to buy them for their wedding gift was a **thorny** issue since there were so many choices.

11. stumble: to stop or make a mistake

    a. I was so nervous during the first performance that I kept **stumbling** over my words.

    b. She recited the whole poem without **stumbling** once.

    c. The new printer was able to **stumble** over twenty pages per minute.

12. ruin: to destroy

    a. Stella's chances of going to Harvard were **ruined** by her straight-A grade average.

    b. The rapid fall in sales **ruined** any chance of keeping the company going.

    c. The accusations of an affair with his personal assistant **ruined** his reputation in Washington.

Word Tip

Military officers throughout the world are given titles according to their level of command and the number of personnel they are responsible for. This title is known as a *rank,* and the insignias (symbols) for each rank are displayed on officer uniforms. The U.S. Army has the following ranks within its command structure, from lowest to highest: corporal, **sergeant**, second lieutenant, first lieutenant, captain, major, lieutenant colonel, colonel, brigadier general, major general, lieutenant general, and general.

WORD FAMILIES

A. The table contains word families for some of the target words in the reading. Complete the table. An **X** indicates that there is no form or that the form is not common. Sometimes more than one form may be possible. If you are unsure about a form, check your dictionary.

Verb	Noun	Adjective	Adverb
colonize	1. 2. 3.		**X**
crumble	**X**	1. 2.	**X**
drown		1. 2.	**X**
X		**electronic**	
filter	1. 2.		**X**
halt		1. 2.	
merge		1. 2.	**X**
	1. **protest** 2.		**X**
publicize			**X**
	receiver	1. 2.	**X**

B. Read the sentences. In eight of the sentences, an incorrect form of the target word has been used. If the form of the target word is incorrect, cross it out and write the correct form. If the form is correct, put a checkmark (✔). Use the word families table to help you.

_____ **1.** Within fifty years of Columbus's arrival, nearly all of Central America was under Spanish **colony** control.

_____ **2.** He decided to **crumbling** the mixture using his hands.

_____ **3.** The passerby dived in and saved the **drown** man.

_____ **4.** It's much more convenient to bank **electronic**.

_____ **5.** When recording a music track, it's important to **filter** out any background noise.

_____ **6.** The engine cut out, and they were brought to a rapid **halted**.

_____ **7.** This is the point at which both freeways **merger**, causing huge slowdowns.

_____ **8.** As he was taken from the courtroom, he continued to **protest** his innocence.

_____ **9.** The rock group went on college radio to generate **publicize** for their forthcoming tour.

_____ **10.** The device **receiver** signals from the transmitter and relays them to the user.

COLLOCATION

In each set of sentences, the target word is paired with different words to form different collocations. Choose the collocation that best fits the last sentence and write it in the blank. You may need to change the form of one word in the collocation to fit the sentence.

1. a. The investigation found that there had been a **catalog of errors**.
   b. We couldn't withdraw money from the bank because there had been a **computer error**.
   c. The _Challenger_ space shuttle disaster was due to **human error**.
   d. _____ was partially to blame for the nuclear accident at Three Mile Island.

2. a. **Classic novels**, such as _Pride and Prejudice_, are featured on many school reading syllabuses.
   b. The author Jackie Collins has written twenty-five **romance novels** and has sold over ten million copies.
   c. The first **paperback novel** in America sold in 1938.
   d. _____ are much cheaper than books with hard covers and so sell much better.

3. a. He could see the **blurred outline** of an intruder through the shower curtain.
   b. They only need a **rough outline** of your business plan at this stage.
   c. As the archaeologists dug down, it was possible to **trace the outline** of the building.
   d. The blind man _____ of her face using his hands.

4. a. It was such a silly mistake to eat all of that chocolate before dinner because it **ruined my appetite**.
   b. Seeing her ex-boyfriend with his new girlfriend totally **ruined her day**.
   c. Excessive federal debt has **ruined the economy**.
   d. Wall Street speculation has _____, according to some.

5. a. The early portable phones housed in large briefcases would have been considered **sophisticated technology** in the 1980s.
   b. Free applications for the iPhone are less **sophisticated versions** of the ones you have to pay for.
   c. She impressed the board of directors with her more **sophisticated approach** to tackling the problem.
   d. Our ever-growing dependence on _____ is a major cause of concern for some scientists.

6. a. Every so often I would try and **steal a glance** of her as she sat on the other side of the classroom.
   b. Each year *The X Factor* contestants hope to **steal the** nation's **heart**.
   c. She **stole the limelight** at the Oscars ceremony thanks to her stunning dress.
   d. He tried to _____ at the answers during the test, but was caught by the teacher.

7. a. The new cancer drug underwent five years of **clinical trials** before it was launched onto the market.
   b. Every year colleges **run trials** to select the best athletes for their teams.
   c. The racing yacht **underwent** months of **trials** at sea before it was entered in the America's Cup race.
   d. The pharmaceutical company had to consider the financial consequence of the vaccine failing its _____.

8. a. Immigration controls were stepped up to stop the spread of the **deadly virus**.
   b. **Computer viruses** cost the U.S. economy $18 billion in 2001.
   c. The school was shut due to the outbreak of a **mystery virus**.
   d. The football star missed the training session because of a _____ no doctor could diagnose.

Expanding the Topic

A. Each of the boxes has associations that belong to one of the target words. Match each box of associations to a target word. Then explain the meaning links.

| camouflage | military | rank | stripes | uniform |

| contact | glass | paparazzi | telescope | view |

Association　　　　　　　　　　**Meaning Link**

1. **lens**
   - _____ (_____)
   - _____ (_____)
   - _____ (_____)
   - _____ (_____)
   - _____ (_____)

2. **sergeant**
   - _____ (_____)
   - _____ (_____)
   - _____ (_____)
   - _____ (_____)
   - _____ (_____)

B. Now add your own associations to the target words. Then explain the meaning links.

Association　　　　　　　　　　**Meaning Link**

1. **forever**
   - _____ (_____)
   - _____ (_____)
   - _____ (_____)
   - _____ (_____)
   - _____ (_____)

2. **salvation**
   - _____ (_____)
   - _____ (_____)
   - _____ (_____)
   - _____ (_____)
   - _____ (_____)

	Association	**Meaning Link**

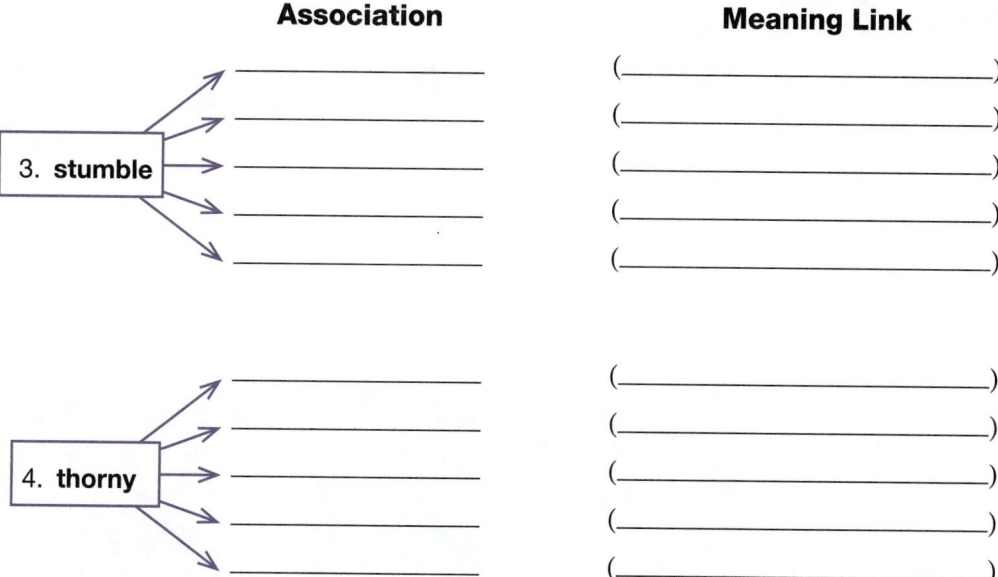

3. **stumble**

4. **thorny**

Read this statement: "Technology will be our **salvation**." Do you agree or disagree with the statement? Write a 500-word essay explaining why.

Revisiting the Target Words

Now that you have completed this chapter, use the scale to describe your knowledge of the target words.

1 I still don't know anything about this word.

2 I am still not sure of the meaning of this word even after studying it.

3 I understand this word when I see it or hear it in a sentence, but I don't know how to use it in my own speaking and writing.

4 I know this word and can use it in my own speaking and writing.

TARGET WORDS

____colonize	____forever	____protest	____sophisticated
____crumble	____halt	____publicize	____steal
____drown	____lens	____receiver	____stumble
____electronic	____merge	____ruin	____thorny
____error	____novel	____salvation	____trial
____filter	____outline	____sergeant	____virus

KNOWLEDGE CHECK 2

Go back to the beginning of the chapter and complete the Knowledge Check 1 table.

Strategy Practice

Getting Started

Look at the three images taken from Chapters 17–19. Without looking back at the chapters, how many target words can you remember from each chapter?

Learning More about Words: METAPHORICAL MEANING

Many words have metaphorical meanings in addition to their literal meanings. In this unit, some of the words have metaphorical meanings. This exercise explains these different types of meaning and gives you a chance to practice using them.

The *literal meaning* is the basic or original meaning of a word.

> **Example:**
> Green is a color. It is a mixture of blue and yellow.

The *metaphorical meaning* is when a word is used to describe something other than itself. In this case, the thing being described will share similar qualities or characteristics with the word used to describe it. For example, many things to do with the environment are green: grass, trees, and plants. Thus, people or activities that protect the environment are also called *green*.

> **Example:**
> Green shopping bags = reusable shopping bags
> Green party = a political party that places a lot of importance on environmental issues

A. Read the literal and metaphorical meanings and examples. Match the words with their metaphorical meanings. Then complete the sentences. You may need to change the form of the word to fit the sentence. The first one has been done for you. (To reread the word in context, use the chapter number in parentheses.)

Words and literal meanings

_e_ **1. crash** (17) to have an accident and hit something else violently: *The plane* **crashed** *into the mountain.*

___ **2. drown** (19) to die because one is trapped under water: *The man* **drowned** *in the river.*

___ **3. filter** (19) to remove unwanted substances from water, air, etc., by passing it through a special substance or piece of equipment: *The air was* **filtered** *before reaching the engine to remove any dust.*

___ **4. giant** (17) a very big man, animal, or plant: *Many children's stories have a* **giant** *in them, such as "Jack and the Beanstalk."*

___ **5. lens** (19) a piece of glass or plastic that makes things look bigger, smaller, or clearer when you look through it: *A* **lens** *in his glasses was cracked.*

___ **6. network** (18) a system of lines, tubes, roads, etc., that cross each other and are connected to each other: *The U.K. railway* **network** *was in desperate need of renewal.*

___ **7. thorny** (19) when a bush, plant, etc., has pointed parts that make it painful to touch: *He scratched his legs badly when walking through the* **thorny** *bushes.*

___ **8. trial** (19) the process of law where a judge or jury decides if someone is guilty of a crime: *He was found guilty of robbery at the* **trial**.

Metaphorical meanings

a. anything that is extremely big: *Toyota is a* _____ *car company, selling over 8 million cars globally per year.*

b. to be in a very difficult situation that feels almost impossible to escape from: *The country is* _____ *in debt.*

c. anything that makes something appear clearer: *Through the* _____ *of hindsight, he knew it was a mistake to invest in the risky company.*

d. a group of people, organizations, etc., that are connected or that work together: *He had a* _____ *of influential friends from his days at Harvard.*

e. to suddenly begin performing very poorly or stop working completely: *The computer* ___*crashed*___ *when I pushed the button.*

f. to remove words, information, etc., that you do not need or want: *The new software* _____ *out all spam before it reached my e-mail account.*

g. a process in which someone (or something) is tested to see if the person (or thing) is satisfactory for a particular purpose: *The new employee was hired on a six-month* _____ *basis.*

h. a question, problem, issue, etc., that is complicated or difficult: *Raising taxes has always been a* _____ *issue for political parties.*

B. Look back at Chapters 17–19. Which of these words were used in a literal sense and which were used in a metaphorical sense?

Focusing on Skills: READING

MAIN AND SUPPORTING IDEAS

Like word meanings, some texts are more direct than others. Writers often start their texts with a main idea that they want to express, however, not all writers provide this so clearly. Nevertheless, we can identify the main idea by studying how they build their text, paragraph by paragraph. We can clearly see how this works if we make a map of the structure of the text.

A. Turn back to the Chapter 17 reading "Sports Technology: Is It Unfair?" on page 152. Complete the text map by identifying the claims and support.

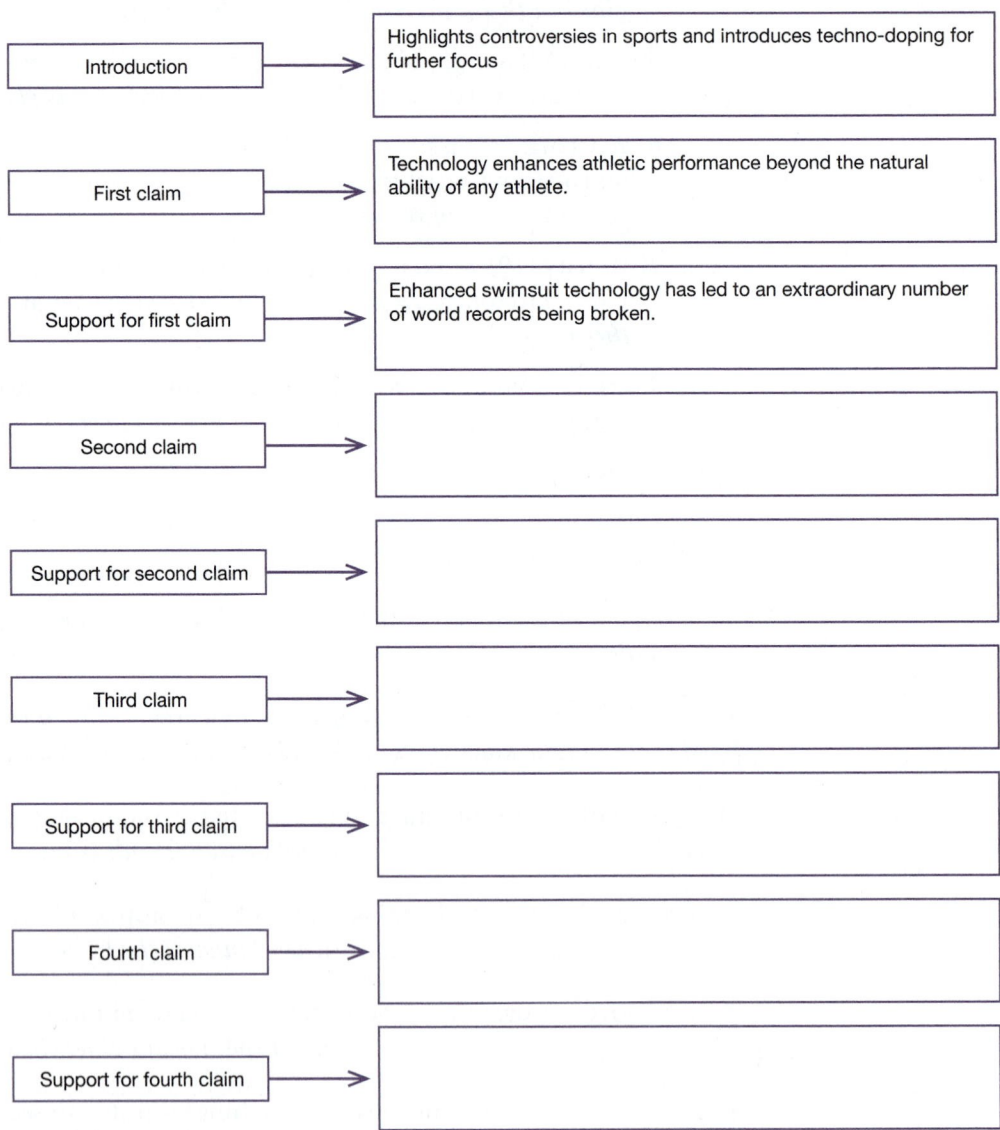

Introduction	→	Highlights controversies in sports and introduces techno-doping for further focus
First claim	→	Technology enhances athletic performance beyond the natural ability of any athlete.
Support for first claim	→	Enhanced swimsuit technology has led to an extraordinary number of world records being broken.
Second claim	→	
Support for second claim	→	
Third claim	→	
Support for third claim	→	
Fourth claim	→	
Support for fourth claim	→	

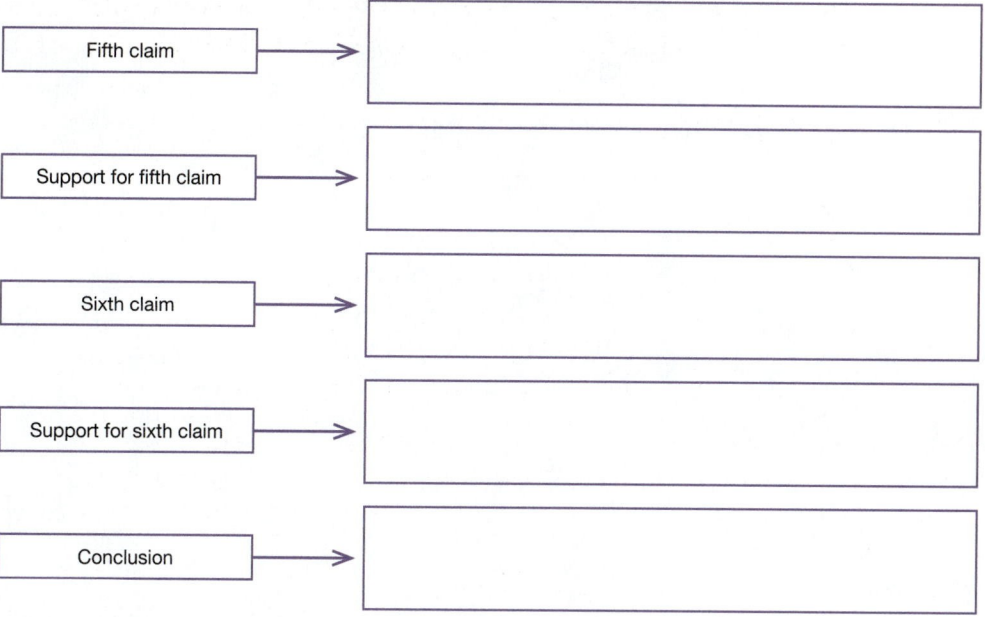

B. Now answer these questions.

1. Which statement best expresses the main idea of the whole text?

   a. Technology has led to inequality in sports at many different levels.
   b. Technology has had both positive and negative effects on the world of sports.
   c. The role of technology in sports is similar to that of doping because it allows athletes to compete above their natural ability level.
   d. Technology plays an important role in people's involvement in sports.

2. What organizational pattern did the writer use to present his ideas? What words or phrases help us recognize this pattern?

   _____

3. What is this writer's view on the role of technology? How do you know?

   _____

Focusing on Vocabulary Cards: CATEGORIZE

The name of this activity is "Categorize," and the aim is to check your knowledge of target words and to review your vocabulary cards.

Instructions

1. Form pairs or teams (Team A and Team B).

2. Team A selects fifteen vocabulary cards and puts them into three groups of five.

3. The three groups of cards are presented to Team B.

4. Team B then has to figure out how Team A has grouped the vocabulary cards and is awarded one point for each correct answer.

5. Once the scores have been noted, Team B chooses fifteen vocabulary cards for Team A, and the process is repeated.

Note: You might consider word associations, word family, pronunciation, etc., as ways of grouping the fifteen target words.

UNIT
6

Celebrity and Heroes

What Makes a Hero?

Getting Started

Discuss the questions with your classmates.

✦ What are the main characteristics of a hero?

✦ Can anybody be a hero?

✦ What kind of person is considered a hero in your home country?

Assessing Your Vocabulary Knowledge: TARGET WORDS

Look at the words in the box. These are the target words for this chapter. Use the scale to score yourself on each word.

1 I don't know this word.

2 I have seen or heard this word before, but I am not sure of the meaning.

3 I understand this word when I see it or hear it in a sentence, but I don't know how to use it in my own speaking and writing.

4 I know this word and can use it in my own speaking and writing.

TARGET WORDS

_____accelerate	_____enemy	_____native	_____restore
_____admired	_____era	_____pioneer	_____revolt
_____adventure	_____evident	_____privilege	_____soldier
_____communist	_____fame	_____profile	_____splendid
_____continent	_____hero	_____rank	_____superb
_____courage	_____horrendous	_____reformation	_____terrifying

---

KNOWLEDGE CHECK 1

Complete the sentences with words that you have scored as **1**.

1. I am not familiar with the word / term _____.

2. I have no idea what _____ means.

Fill in the first blank with a word that you have scored as **2**. Then complete the sentence.

3. I think _____ could mean _____.

Reading

The passage discusses the idea of **heroes** and looks at one author's list of the 100 greatest international heroes. As you read, pay special attention to the target vocabulary words in **bold**.

Who's a Hero?

1   What makes a **hero**? Different people will point to different characteristics—**courage**, vision, influence over important world events. In fact, we all have different ideas of what makes a **hero** and, consequently, make different choices about who our personal **heroes** are.

2   Yet there seem to be certain types of people who we are all likely to regard as **heroic**. One way of identifying these types of people is to consider the names that occur on "greatest **heroes**" lists and to try to figure out the characteristics or experiences that link these people together. H. Paul Jeffers provides one such list in his book *The 100 Greatest **Heroes**: Inspiring **Profiles** of One Hundred Men and Women Who Changed the World*. He **ranks** the people he considers the 100 greatest **heroes** of all time. So who does Jeffers consider great **heroes**, and what makes them so great?

3   One category of Jeffers's **heroes** might be called "nation builders." This includes the early American founders George Washington, Samuel Adams, and Thomas Jefferson. In Bolivia, Colombia, Ecuador, Peru, and Venezuela, Simón Bolivar is a national **hero** for leading Latin America's **revolt** for independence from Spain, and, in fact, Bolivia is named after him. On the Asian sub**continent**, the peaceful leadership of Mohandas "Mahatma" Gandhi was influential in India achieving self-rule. More recently in Eastern Europe, the **reformation** of governments from **communist** to democratic was guided by exceptional personalities, such as Václav Havel, who led the Velvet Revolution in former Czechoslovakia. In the same way, Lech Wasęa **accelerated** Poland's move toward democratic government through his influence as leader of the trade union "Solidarity."

4   The category of "war **heroes**" is also **evident** in Jeffers's list. This is not surprising as war is often **terrifying** and requires extreme **courage** in the face of **horrendous** dangers. Such **heroism** is illustrated by Audie Murphy, a **soldier** who received many decorations for battlefield **courage**, including several singlehanded attacks on **enemy** positions. One of these was the highest U.S. military award, the Medal of Honor. However, interestingly, nearly all of the other military **heroes** on the list are not battlefield **soldiers**, but rather the soldiers' political leaders and generals. For example, Winston Churchill showed **superb** leadership in Great Britain during its darkest days of World War II. Likewise, Franklin Delano Roosevelt led America through the same war. Out of the 100 **heroes** in Jeffers's book, about one-quarter are high-**ranking** military officers. Historically, Alexander the Great and Napoleon Bonaparte are considered two of the greatest generals ever, and Horatio Nelson is justifiably **admired** for his strategies in several sea battles. However, most of the military leaders in Jeffers's book come from the World War II **era**, including Generals Charles de Gaulle and Dwight Eisenhower.

5   Explorers and **adventurers** are also well represented on Jeffers's list. Christopher Columbus is popularly credited with discovering the "New World," although of course it was already discovered by the **Native** Americans living there. Richard E. Byrd gained **fame** for exploring both the Arctic and Antarctic. Perhaps one of the most **splendid** achievements of the twentieth century was the first solo flight across the Atlantic Ocean, realized by Charles

Lindbergh in 1927 and repeated by Amelia Earhart in 1932. Later in the century, space was the new frontier, and the Russian Yuri Gagarin was the first man to orbit Earth, while Neil Armstrong had the **privilege** of being the first person to walk on the moon.

6 However, any list of **heroes** must go far beyond the people named by Jeffers. Consider Nobel Peace Prize winners Wangari Maathai, whose Greenbelt Movement has planted millions of trees in Africa, and Muhammad Yunus, who **pioneered** village banks for women in Bangladesh. Both have **restored** hope in these parts of the world.

7 In the end, perhaps the best definition of **hero** is "someone with the ability to inspire," who exhibits qualities that we ourselves would like to possess.

(643 words)

The complete list is published in H. Paul Jeffers (2003). *The 100 Greatest **Heroes**: Inspiring **Profiles** of One Hundred Men and Women Who Changed the World.* New York: Kensington Publishing Corp./Citadel Press.

READING COMPREHENSION

Respond to the questions in writing. Base your responses on the reading and your own personal experiences.

1. What three types of **hero** are highlighted in the passage?

2. Do you agree that the people mentioned in the passage are **heroes**? What categories of **hero** are important but are not mentioned in the passage?

3. What characteristics do you think are most important in defining a **hero**?

4. Why do you think that many lists of **heroes** are made up mainly of men? Who are some important female **heroes**?

5. Who is your personal **hero** and why?

6. Why do you think that leaders get most of the credit for achievements, rather than the "ordinary" people who do most of the work?

Focusing on Vocabulary

WORD MEANING

A. Match the target words with their definitions. If you are unsure about a word's meaning, try to figure it out from the context by rereading the passage. Then check your dictionary.

Set 1

_____ 1. hero
_____ 2. revolt
_____ 3. communist
_____ 4. enemy
_____ 5. admired
_____ 6. adventure
_____ 7. splendid

a. someone who opposes you or wants to hurt you
b. when strong and often violent action is taken against something, particularly the government
c. excellent
d. relating to a political system where the government controls the production of all food and goods
e. a person who is admired for doing something extremely brave or remarkable
f. respected and liked because of something good you have done
g. an exciting experience in which dangerous or unusual things happen

Set 2

_____ 1. **courage**
_____ 2. **profile**
_____ 3. **continent**
_____ 4. **soldier**
_____ 5. **fame**
_____ 6. **privilege**
_____ 7. **pioneer**

a. a large mass of land surrounded by sea
b. a short description that gives important details about someone or something
c. a member of a country's army, especially someone who is not an officer
d. the state of being known by a lot of people because of your achievements
e. a special advantage, or a chance to do something that is only given to one person or a group of people
f. to lead or be part of the early development of something
g. the quality of being brave when you are facing a difficult or dangerous situation

B. Read each target word and the list below it. One word or phrase in each list is NOT a synonym for the target word. Cross it out.

1. **rank**

| categorize | order | grade | count |

2. **reformation**

| improvement | situation | reorganization | development |

3. **accelerate**

| speed up | finish | quicken | hurry |

4. **evident**

| obvious | plain | gentle | apparent |

5. **terrifying**

| frightening | scary | touching | causing panic |

6. **horrendous**

| helpful | awful | terrible | horrible |

7. **superb**

| excellent | terrific | wonderful | flexible |

8. **era**

| age | program | period | time |

9. **native**

| nasty | resident | original | local |

10. **restore**

| bring back | return | renew | assume |

WORD FAMILIES

A. The table contains word families for some of the target words in the reading. Complete the table. An **X** indicates that there is no form or that the form is not common. Sometimes more than one form may be possible. If you are unsure about a form, check your dictionary.

Verb	Noun	Adjective	Adverb
accelerate		**X**	**X**
	1. 2.	1. 2. **admired** 3.	1. 2.
X	**courage**		
X	**X**	**evident**	
X	**fame**	1. 2.	
X	**X**	**horrendous**	
pioneer			**X**
restore			**X**
	1. **revolt** 2. 3.		**X**
X	**X**	**superb**	

B. Choose the correct form of the word in **bold** in sentence **a** to complete sentence **b**. Use the word families table you just completed as a guide.

1. **a.** The invention of the microchip **accelerated** the development of computers and other digital technology.

   b. Correctly sized ski poles are used by downhill skiers to improve balance, speed, and _____.

2. **a.** He had nothing but **admiration** for his mother, who made many sacrifices to raise him.

   b. The teacher's dedication to her students was _____.

3. **a.** The soldier's **courageous** action saved the lives of many of his colleagues.

   b. The volunteers worked _____ to prevent the floodwaters from entering the town.

4. **a.** The popularity of the movie was **evident** from the long lines outside all of the movie theaters in town.

   b. The constant attention of the public was _____ too much for the actor, who locked himself in his house and refused to come out.

5. **a.** Alexander Fleming's claim to **fame** is the discovery of the antibiotic penicillin.

   b. One of the most _____ engineers in Britain is Isambard Brunel, who designed the Great Western Railway and a number of well-known steamships.

6. **a.** The **horrendous** winter conditions made the roads almost impossible to drive on.

   b. The banking failure of 2008–09 was _____ expensive, costing governments around the world many billions of dollars.

7. **a.** Pan-Am Airlines **pioneered** trans-Pacific flights, with its "Flying Clippers" taking seven days to make the five-leg, 8,000-mile trip.

   b. Robert Goddard's _____ work on rockets laid the foundation for America's *Apollo* space program, which landed men on the moon.

8. **a.** The coach hoped that a win in this weekend's game would **restore** the fans' confidence in his team.

   b. The _____ of peace in Northern Ireland has led to economic revival in the city of Belfast.

9. **a.** The political leader's move to raise taxes without consultation caused a **revolt** in his party.

   b. Galileo was a scientific _____ whose support for the theory that Earth orbits the Sun led to him spending the last nine years of his life under house arrest.

10. **a.** The sound quality of the Stradivarius violin was **superb**.

    b. Michael Phelps was _____ equipped to become one of the greatest swimmers of all time because of his ideal body shape (long thin body, long arms, big feet).

COLLOCATION

Read the common collocations in the column on the left. Give two examples of things associated with each collocation.

	Example 1	**Example 2**
1. national **hero**	_____	_____
2. great **adventure**	_____	_____
3. bitter **enemies**	_____	_____
4. economic **reform**	_____	_____

5. splendid
opportunity _____ _____

6. terrifying
experience _____ _____

7. communist
countries _____ _____

8. brave
soldier _____ _____

Expanding the Topic

A. Everyone has his or her own idea of "what makes a *hero*." The reading passage gave examples from H. Paul Jeffers's list of *heroes*. Below are eleven brief *profiles* of other people *admired* for various kinds of achievement. Complete the sentences. Use the target words from the box. You may need to change the form of the word to fit the sentence.

accelerate	era	privilege	revolt
admired	native	reformation	soldier
continent	pioneer	restored	terrifying

_____ **1.** Amerigo Vespucci was an explorer and mapmaker and is popularly believed to have given his name to the _____ of North and South America.

_____ **2.** Davy Crockett—a(n) _____, **soldier**, and politician—died at the Battle of the Alamo in Texas.

_____ **3.** Amy Johnson was an early flying **adventurer** and is _____ for being the first woman to fly solo from Britain to Australia.

_____ **4.** Pierre de Coubertin created the Olympic Games, with the first games of the modern _____ being held in Athens (1896) and Paris (1900).

_____ **5.** Sitting Bull was a(n) _____ American leader who resisted the white man's expansion onto their land.

_____ **6.** Rosa Parks sparked a _____ against the discrimination of African Americans by refusing to give up her seat on a bus in Alabama in 1955.

_____ **7.** Florence Nightingale _____ medical care for _____ and later set up a training school for nurses.

_____ **8.** Nelson Mandela led the fight against apartheid in South Africa, which _____ social justice and freedom for all citizens.

_____ **9.** Jonas Salk developed the first safe and effective vaccine against the _____ childhood disease polio.

10. John Deere developed farm machinery that allowed farmers to greatly
_____ their production of food, which helped to lower
food prices for everyone.

11. The crew of Flight 1549 was granted the _____ of
receiving the keys to New York City for successfully landing Airbus 320
on the Hudson River after it lost all power to its engines.

B. Now *rank* each person(s) for how *heroic* you feel they are: 1 = most *heroic*,
11 = least heroic. Discuss your *ranking* with a classmate. How similar are your
rankings?

Now that you have carefully considered the characteristics that make a *hero*, write a
500-word essay on a person who you believe to be a *hero* and give the reasons why
you think he or she is a *hero*.

Revisiting the Target Words

Now that you have completed this chapter, use the scale to describe your knowledge
of the target words.

1 I still don't know anything about this word.

2 I am still not sure of the meaning of this word even after studying it.

3 I understand this word when I see it or hear it in a sentence, but I don't know
how to use it in my own speaking and writing.

4 I know this word and can use it in my own speaking and writing.

TARGET WORDS			
____accelerate	____enemy	____native	____restore
____admired	____era	____pioneer	____revolt
____adventure	____evident	____privilege	____soldier
____communist	____fame	____profile	____splendid
____continent	____hero	____rank	____superb
____courage	____horrendous	____reformation	____terrifying

KNOWLEDGE CHECK 2

Select examples from words you now give a score of **3** or **4**, but didn't at the start of
the chapter, to complete the sentences.

1. I didn't know that _____ meant _____ before
reading this chapter.

2. I wasn't sure that I knew the meaning of _____, but I am now.

3. I now am confident that I know what _____ means, but I would
like more practice with how to use it in my speaking and writing.

4. I could next use _____ when I am _____.

The Appeal of Comic Book Heroes

Getting Started

Discuss the questions with your classmates.

✦ Do you read comic books? If so, which ones?

✦ Do you have a favorite comic book hero? Who is it and why?

✦ How do you think comic books might differ from one country to the next?

Assessing Your Vocabulary Knowledge: TARGET WORDS

Look at the words in the box. These are the target words for this chapter. Use the scale to score yourself on each word.

1 I don't know this word.

2 I have seen or heard this word before, but I am not sure of the meaning.

3 I understand this word when I see it or hear it in a sentence, but I don't know how to use it in my own speaking and writing.

4 I know this word and can use it in my own speaking and writing.

TARGET WORDS

_____adored	_____costume	_____harsh	_____serialized
_____boom	_____crude	_____innocent	_____sketch
_____bulging	_____deteriorate	_____mask	_____solely
_____capture	_____endowed	_____mortal	_____stark
_____cartoon	_____evil	_____naive	_____unlike
_____comic	_____fantastic	_____perpetual	_____wardrobe

KNOWLEDGE CHECK 1

Fill in the first blank with a word that you have scored as **2**. Then complete the second sentence.

1. I have seen / heard _____. I saw / heard it while I was

   _____.

Fill in the first blanks with words that you have scored as **4**. Then complete the sentences.

2. One meaning of _____ is _____.

3. I last used the word _____ while I was _____.

The passage discusses **comic** books in Japan and America and the heroes in those books. As you read, pay special attention to the target vocabulary words in **bold**.

Japanese and American Comic Book Heroes

1   To some people, the idea of reading **comic** books seems childish. To others, **comics** are nothing more than reminders of their happy childhoods. But for people who love **comic** books, they can be a **fantastic** escape from the **harsh** realities of modern life. **Comics** are able to transport readers to brightly-colored, imaginary worlds where superheroes fight with super-villains, where good can triumph over **evil**, and where heroes can save thousands of **innocent** people from the "bad guys." **Comics** are published globally, but Japanese and American versions dominate the market despite the fact—or perhaps because—they differ in a number of ways.

2   To begin, Japanese manga "books" are usually smaller in height and width but thicker than American **comics**. Manga stories are significantly longer, often hundreds of pages long compared to the typical thirty-two page format of American **comics**. Additionally, Japanese **comics** tend to be printed in black and white and often feature several long-running **serialized** stories. This is **unlike** American **comics**, which are printed in full color and only feature the headline hero.

3   The two types of **comics** are also created in very different ways. American **comics** are a group effort, beginning with the story-writing

team and the artist who produces **crude** drawings of initial ideas. When these pencil **sketches** are finalized, the outlines, dialogue, and color are added. Also, creators of **comic** superheroes sometimes sell their titles to other creative teams, who keep the superhero "alive." This is in **stark** contrast to manga creators, who are often individual authors **solely** responsible for the storylines, dialogue, and artwork. When a manga creator decides to stop, so does the hero.

4   Another difference is the appearance of the heroes. Manga heroes look smaller, younger, and more **naive** than their all-conquering American counterparts who sport **bulging** muscles and **wardrobes** of themed **costumes**. Also, manga heroes rarely look Japanese, and the stories are not typically set within a Japanese context. Conversely, American **comic** heroes, despite their **masks**, are proudly American and are **adored** for their readiness to defend U.S. cities. Importantly, in Japan a manga creator can himself or herself become a national hero, becoming almost as famous as the characters.

5   Probably the biggest difference is the readership. Up until the 1950s, American **comic** books were read by both children and adults, with popular titles such as *Superman* selling as many as half a million copies per month. The arrival of TV, however, led to a long-term decline

in sales so that now the average reader of an American **comic** book is a teenage boy with an interest in superheroes. In Japan, the contrast couldn't be greater. There manga sales are still **booming**, reaching as high as $7 billion each year largely because readers range from young boys and girls up to middle-aged men and women. A survey by the *Mainichi* newspaper estimates that 42 percent of women aged 20 to 49 read **comics**. Manga for men and boys, like the American **comics**, tend to be action-oriented, while manga for women and girls tend to be focused on relationships.

6   Though not as prevalent as the differences, some similarities between American and Japanese **comics** do exist. In terms of character design, both feature characters typically drawn with large eyes to more clearly **capture** emotions. For example, it is easy to see the similarities between the large eyes of Bambi, an early Walt Disney **cartoon** character, and the large emotional eyes of most young manga heroines. In addition, in both American and Japanese **comics**, the hero has a weakness, such as being clumsy or ill, to show that he or she is only **mortal**. (But American heroes are **endowed** with superhuman abilities as well.) Perhaps the best-known example of an American hero's weakness is that Superman's powers **deteriorate** when he comes into contact with Kryptonite. An example from Japan is the deadly illness Prince Ashitaka must fight in Hayao Miyazaki's classic anime **cartoon** *Princess Mononoke*.

7   Historical origins and box-office success are other areas of similarity. Despite there being little contact between the two countries at the time, both Japanese and American **comic** book superheroes first appeared at the start of the twentieth century. They both remained relatively obscure until sudden growths in popularity just after World War II. Both American and Japanese **comics** have had considerable crossover success into movies and computer games, which has increased the overall popularity of superheroes.

8   Their similarities and differences aside, together Japanese and American **comic** books demonstrate the world's **perpetual** desire for heroes.

(744 words)

READING COMPREHENSION

Respond to the questions in writing. Base your responses on the reading and your own personal experiences.

1. The passage describes several similarities and differences between Japanese and American **comic** books. List them.

2. Do manga writers have more or less control over their **comics** than their American counterparts?

3. Why are **comics** so much more popular in Japan than in the United States?

4. How can the popularity of **comic** superheroes be increasing if the sales of **comic** books are falling?

5. Have you seen a "**comic** hero" movie? Did you like the **comic** book version of the hero better, or the movie version? Why?

6. Comic books are less popular worldwide than they used to be, but have seen a rebirth in the form of graphic novels. What do you think might explain the growing popularity of graphic novels?

Focusing on Vocabulary

WORD MEANING

A. Read the target words. Use the paragraph number in parentheses to locate and reread the word in context. Then read the dictionary definitions and choose the one that reflects how the word is used in the reading.

_____ **1. comic** (1)
   a. amusing and making you want to laugh
   b. a type of book or magazine that tells a story using rows of pictures

_____ **2. fantastic** (1)
   a. something so large or incredible (for example, a plan or a story) that it is not likely to be possible.
   b. extremely good, attractive, enjoyable

_____ **3. harsh** (1)
   a. something that is unpleasant or uncomfortable; difficult to live in
   b. severe, cruel, or unkind in manner or treatment of someone or something

_____ **4. crude** (3)
   a. not developed to a high standard; made without any detail or with little skill
   b. offensive or rude, especially in a sexual way

_____ **5. sketch** (3)
   a. a short written or spoken description
   b. a simple, quickly made drawing that does not show much detail

_____ **6. stark** (3)
   a. very plain in appearance, with little or no color or decoration
   b. unpleasantly clear and impossible to avoid

_____ **7. bulging** (4)
   a. sticking out in a rounded shape, especially because something is very full or too tight
   b. sudden temporary increase in the amount or level of something

_____ **8. costume** (4)
   a. clothes that are typical of a particular place or period of time in the past
   b. a set of clothes worn by an actor or by someone to make the person look like something else, such as an animal or famous person

_____ **9. mask** (4)
   a. something that covers all or part of your face, to hide it or protect it
   b. a substance that you put on your face and leave there for a short time to clean the skin or make it softer

_____ **10. capture** (6)
   a. to succeed in recording, showing, or describing a situation or feeling, using words or pictures
   b. to catch and control a person or animal

_____ **11. mortal** (6)
   a. not able to live forever
   b. something very serious, that may cause the end of something

_____ **12. endowed** (6)
    a. naturally having a good feature or quality
    b. situation in which a college, hospital, etc., is given a large sum of money that provides it with an income

B. Read the target words in the box. Complete each sentence with the target word that matches the meaning of the words in parentheses. You may need to change the form of the word to fit the sentence.

adored	deteriorate	naive	solely
boom	evil	perpetual	unlike
cartoon	innocent	serialized	wardrobe

1. Scientists have unsuccessfully tried to develop a(n) "_____ (continuous, unending) motion machine," which would keep moving forever despite friction and air resistance trying to stop it.

2. Many substances _____ (become worse, weaken) when exposed to sunlight for long periods of time.

3. The king of Thailand is one of those rare leaders who is _____ (loved, admired) by all of his people.

4. _____ (different from, not alike) many musical instruments, Scottish bagpipes are meant to be played outdoors.

5. Many clothing stores start selling their summer _____ (clothes, dress) so early that snow may still be on the ground.

6. The main problem with war is that more _____ (not involved, harmless) victims are hurt than soldiers.

7. Illegal drugs are a(n) _____ (something very bad, vice) that costs the economy millions of dollars per year.

8. Because of low interest rates and inexpensive energy, the economy is _____ (increase, be very successful).

9. In the first half of the twentieth century, movies were often preceded by short, _____ (made in a series, produced in several parts) film stories, such as *Buck Rogers* and *Captain Marvel*, which usually had about a dozen parts.

10. A politician should be elected to political office based _____ (only, involving nothing else) on ability and honesty, but unfortunately, in the media era, wealth and personality also play an important part.

11. According to an estimate in 2010, *Shrek 2* was the highest-earning _____ (drawing, film made of drawings) movie of all time, making over $900 million worldwide.

12. It is _____ (inexperienced, overly trusting) to believe that every family can afford to eat healthily, as fresh fruit and vegetables can be relatively expensive.

Word Tip

A common mistake in student writing is to confuse the words *costume* and *uniform*. Both words refer to sets of clothes, but here the similarities stop. Compare the definition of **costume** that you have just studied with the definition of *uniform*.

uniform: a particular type of clothing worn by all the members of a group or organization such as the police, school children, etc.

What are some key differences? Who might wear a uniform? Who might wear a **costume**?

WORD FAMILIES

A. The table contains word families for some of the target words in the reading. An **X** indicates that there is no form or that the form is not common. Study the table. Look for spelling patterns for the verb, noun, adjective, and adverb forms of the words. List the patterns in the space below the table.

Verb	Noun	Adjective	Adverb
adore	adoration	1. **adored** 2. adoring	adoringly
deteriorate	deterioration	**X**	**X**
X	**evil**	evil	evilly
X	1. innocence 2. innocent	**innocent**	innocently
X	1. mortal 2. mortality	**mortal**	mortally
X	naivety	**naive**	naively
perpetuate	perpetuity	**perpetual**	perpetually
serialize	1. serial 2. serialaization	1. serial 2. **serialized**	serially
sketch	**sketch**	sketchy	**X**
X	**X**	sole	**solely**

verbs _____

nouns _____

adjectives _____

adverbs _____

B. Complete each sentence with the correct form of the word in parentheses. Use the word families table to help you.

1. The new mother looked _____ (**adored**) at her baby.

2. The testing of the rocket led to a _____ (**deteriorate**) of relations between the two countries.

3. Comic superheroes often battle against _____ (**evil**) scientists.

4. She smiled _____ (**innocent**) when she did not understand the joke.

5. The severe heart attack made her begin to reflect upon her _____ (**mortal**).

6. The candidate's political _____ (**naive**) was shown by his refusal to listen to his more experienced colleagues' advice.

7. Young children can be very tiring for parents because they are _____ (**perpetual**) moving around.

8. Instead of using a single drawing, comic strips typically tell a story _____ (**serialized**) through a number of pictures in order.

9. The young child much preferred _____ (**sketch**) pictures to playing sports.

10. The _____ (**solely**) purpose of many best-selling novels is to help their readers pass the time pleasantly without thinking too hard.

COLLOCATION

Combine a word from Column A with a word from Column B to form a collocation. Then match the collocation to its definition.

Column A	Column B
booming	measure
cartoon	market
capture	opportunity
crude	conditions
fantastic	a soldier
harsh	**wardrobe**
winter	characters
stark	reminder

1. _____ a very successful economy

2. _____ examples: Mickey Mouse and Winnie the Pooh

3. _____ the set of clothes you wear in cold weather

4. _____ circumstances in which it is difficult to do well

5. _____ something that makes you remember an unpleasant truth

6. _____ a great chance to do something you want to do

7. _____ an estimate of something that only gives an overall impression with little detail

8. _____ to catch a fighter

Expanding the Topic

A. Below are cartoon heroes that have appeared in comic strips, movies, and children's books. Complete the descriptions. Use the target words from the box. You may need to change the form of the word to fit the sentence. There are three extra words.

adored	comic	deteriorate	innocent	solely
bulging	costume	endowed	mask	stark
capture	crude	evil	perpetual	unlike

Hero	Description
_____ **1.** Superman	**a.** A Belgian boy newspaper reporter, he is _____ traveling around the world with his dog Snowy. He often uses clever tricks to defeat criminals.
_____ **2.** Batman	
_____ **3.** Aquaman	**b.** A magical bear-like creature who protects the forest and rides in a cat-like bus, he is _____ by Japanese children.
_____ **4.** Green Lantern	
_____ **5.** Wonder Woman	**c.** This superhero often fights against the _____ super-villain Lex Luther.
_____ **6.** The Flash	**d.** This character is able to _____ villains with the *Lasso* (rope) *of Truth*, which forces them to tell the truth.
_____ **7.** Captain Canuck	
_____ **8.** The Hulk	**e.** This hero uses a ring that shoots out energy. His _____ has a symbol on it that shows where the ring obtains its power.
_____ **9.** Tintin	
_____ **10.** Babar	**f.** This is a gentle and _____ elephant king who uses the knowledge gained during schooling in Paris to wisely rule his elephant kingdom.
_____ **11.** Totoro	
_____ **12.** Asterix	
	g. His _____ superpower is super speed.
	h. When Bruce Banner becomes angry, he turns green and develops _____ muscles.
	i. This is a _____ book superhero based in Canada.
	j. Although rather small, he is _____ with super strength after drinking a magic mixture given to him by Getafix.
	k. The _____ over his head is shaped like a night-time flying animal.
	l. _____ other superheroes, he lives in the oceans and is able to communicate with sea creatures.

B. Now try to match the descriptions to the heroes.

 Choose one of the cartoon characters from Exercise A or a character you know well and write a 500-word essay describing why you enjoy reading or watching that character's adventures.

Revisiting the Target Words

Now that you have completed this chapter, use the scale to describe your knowledge of the target words.

1 I still don't know anything about this word.

2 I am still not sure of the meaning of this word even after studying it.

3 I understand this word when I see it or hear it in a sentence, but I don't know how to use it in my own speaking and writing.

4 I know this word and can use it in my own speaking and writing.

TARGET WORDS			
____adored	____costume	____harsh	____serialized
____boom	____crude	____innocent	____sketch
____bulging	____deteriorate	____mask	____solely
____capture	____endowed	____mortal	____stark
____cartoon	____evil	____naive	____unlike
____comic	____fantastic	____perpetual	____wardrobe

KNOWLEDGE CHECK 2

Select examples from the words you now give a score of **3** or **4**, but didn't at the start of the chapter, to complete the sentences.

1. I didn't know that _____ meant _____ before reading this chapter.

2. I wasn't sure that I knew the meaning of _____, but I am now.

3. I now am confident that I know what _____ means, but I would like more practice with how to use it in my speaking and writing.

4. I now know that _____ collocates with _____.

What's Your Favorite Brand of Celebrity?

Getting Started

Discuss the questions with your classmates.

✦ Do you have a favorite brand? What is it and why do you like it?

✦ What do you think are the advantages and disadvantages of being famous?

✦ Do you think people should have to earn celebrity or should anyone be able to be famous?

Assessing Your Vocabulary Knowledge: TARGET WORDS

Look at the words in the box. These are the target words for this chapter. Use the scale to score yourself on each word.

1 I don't know this word.

2 I have seen or heard this word before, but I am not sure of the meaning.

3 I understand this word when I see it or hear it in a sentence, but I don't know how to use it in my own speaking and writing.

4 I know this word and can use it in my own speaking and writing.

TARGET WORDS

____amateur	____cable	____helicopter	____perk
____anonymity	____disturbing	____interchangeable	____plead
____attributed	____elevated	____ironically	____premium
____baffled	____fade	____liable	____substitute
____balloon	____genuine	____media	____talent
____brand	____gossip	____peculiar	____visibility

Check your progress in learning the vocabulary in this chapter.

- First, look at your scores in the table on page 202. Write the number of words for each score (1–4) in the "at the beginning" column. For example, if you scored eight words as **1** ("I don't know this word"), then write **8**.

- At the end of the chapter, score yourself again. Then compare the two sets of scores. Are you showing improvement on most of the words in the chapter?

Your score	Number of words ...		
	at the beginning:	at the end:	
		showing improvement	no improvement yet
1			
2			
3			
4			

Reading

The passage discusses the changing notion of celebrity in modern times. As you read, pay special attention to the target vocabulary words in **bold**.

Balloon Boy Brand Failure

1 On October 15, 2009, the American **media** was taken over by a breaking news story. **Cable** news networks carried the story live, and the whole country—and soon much of the world— turned its eyes to Colorado. There, an **amateur** scientist who had built an experimental weather **balloon** found that the **balloon** had broken away from its base and blown away. At about the same time, he discovered that his 6-year-old son was missing. TV news **helicopters**, emergency service workers, and the Colorado National Guard were called in to help search for the boy. Two hours later, the **balloon** landed 60 miles away with no little boy inside. Five hours later, the little boy was found hiding in the family garage. Later that evening, the boy's answer to an interview question on CNN appeared to indicate that the whole event had been a publicity stunt for the purpose of "making the family more marketable for future **media** interests." One month later, his parents **pleaded** guilty to criminal charges relating to the hoax.

2 This story is a **disturbing** comment on modern society's obsession with fame and celebrity. It appears that ordinary people are willing to do the most **peculiar** things to project themselves into the public eye. While *we* may be **baffled** by the actions of the parents in the balloon boy story and wonder, "What were

they thinking?" a marketing or public relations strategist would have an easy answer to this question. The parents, who met at acting school, were looking to achieve what marketers refer to as "high **visibility**." Marketers traditionally achieve this by creating a story about a product, advertising the product, developing events around the product, and writing news stories about the product. The **balloon** boy story follows all of these steps—only **substitute** "people" for "product."

3   We are familiar with products and even places, such as Las Vegas or Venice, being marketed as **brands**. Now, just as products and places must compete to attract the attention of potential buyers and tourists, people, too, are looking to create distinctive **brands** for themselves to separate themselves from the **anonymity** of the crowd. In other words, these people want to become highly **visible**. In the past, an otherwise ordinary person might be **elevated** to high **visibility**—or celebrity—by birth (Prince William), extraordinary talent (Venus Williams), or some heroic deed (Captain Sully Sullenberger, who landed U.S. Airways Flight 1549 on the Hudson River). However, these days, there is a new kind of celebrity.

4   This new type of celebrity occurs when ordinary people with no **genuine talent** or skill achieve fame simply through repeated exposure in the **media**. In his book titled *Celebrity*, Chris Rojek calls this *attributed* celebrity. Paris Hilton and the seemingly **interchangeable** cast members of TV reality shows are perfect examples of people who depend on **gossip** magazines and entertainment "news" programs or websites to both put them and keep them in the public eye.

5   So these days, celebrity alone no longer guarantees **visibility** because competing wannabe celebrities are vying to keep *their* places in the public eye. One way for celebrities to widen their reach is through **branding**. Thus, the already successful Richard Branson, owner of Virgin Airlines, has worked hard to successfully **brand** himself as an entrepreneur and an adventurer. David Beckham, one of the most famous human **brands** in the world, has boosted his fame by spending a lot of his time off the field endorsing products and sacrificing his privacy to the photographer's lens. By taking advantage of the worldwide popularity of soccer, his wife's early success as a pop star, and his model good looks, Beckham has boosted his earning power far beyond that of other equally **talented** players. And it is precisely this **premium** that others aspire to, because high **visibility** results in greater privilege, power, pay, and **perks**.

6   Unfortunately, for the **balloon** boy family, its quest for a family **brand** has all gone wrong. **Ironically**, not only did it not achieve the **perks** of elevated **visibility**, the parents have been judged **liable** for the cost of the rescue mission. The end of this story will, in all likelihood, be that the balloon boy and his family **fade** into obscurity.

(705 words)

READING COMPREHENSION

Respond to the questions in writing. Base your responses on the reading and your own personal experiences.

1. What publicity stunt was carried out by the balloon boy's family?

2. What were the parents' motives for what they did?

3. How is Venus Williams's celebrity different from Paris Hilton's celebrity?

4. What is the purpose of achieving high **visibility**?

5. What are your views on the new type of celebrity? Do you have a set of favorite celebrities whose activities you follow via entertainment programs, Facebook, Twitter, or magazines?

6. Name some other celebrities who have successfully **branded** themselves. Describe the key features of their **brands**.

Focusing on Vocabulary

WORD MEANING

A. Read the sentences and choose the phrase that best matches the meaning of the target word. Use context clues to determine the correct meaning. Check your dictionary if you are not sure of the answer.

1. While the total number of TV channels and **media** companies is growing, the number of owners in control of the TV, radio, and newspapers is getting smaller.

   a. places where planes take off and land
   b. forms or systems of government
   c. organizations that provide news and information for the public

2. In 1999, Bertrand Piccard and Brian Jones became the first balloonists to travel around the world in a hot air **balloon**. It took them nineteen days, twenty-one hours, and fifty-five minutes.

   a. large boat used for carrying people or goods across the sea
   b. large bag of strong, light cloth filled with gas or heated air so that it can float in the air
   c. vehicle that flies through the air and has one or more engines

3. There has been a **disturbing** rise in childhood obesity in recent decades, with 17 percent of children now considered seriously overweight.

   a. difficult to describe or explain
   b. worrying or upsetting
   c. rude and unfriendly

4. Curling is one of the most **peculiar** but fascinating sports at the Olympics. Players use brushes to help move a stone along a strip of ice.

   a. liked by a lot of people
   b. recently made, invented, or created
   c. strange, unfamiliar, or a little surprising

5. Events such as the Olympics Games in Beijing and the World Expo in Shanghai are excellent ways to raise the **visibility** of Chinese culture and technological development.

   a. something that has a bad effect on your life
   b. the process of keeping something secret
   c. the situation of being noticed by people in general

6. In cooking, yogurt can be **substituted** for sour cream, thus reducing the calorie and fat content of dishes.

   a. carefully looked at for a long time
   b. used instead of something else
   c. done over and over again

7. After being awarded the Olympic Games, the team from Rio de Janeiro boarded the airplane home with an **elevated** sense of pride in their city

   a. raised up or higher than other things
   b. not sure of where you are
   c. empty, not covered by anything

8. In the tourism business, hotel and tour guide operators look for job applicants who demonstrate **genuine** friendliness even in stressful situations.

    a. extremely bad
    b. real, rather than pretended or false
    c. working and able to be used

9. My sister has no artistic **talent**; she can't paint, draw, or sculpt. And yet she has always wanted to be an artist.

    a. strong hope or wish
    b. natural ability to do something well
    c. protection from bad things that could happen to you

10. Department stores have been gradually discontinuing many of the **perks** that were familiar to our parents, such as generous return policies and gift wrapping services.

    a. people who like you
    b. bonuses, benefits, extra things
    c. freedoms to do what you want to

11. Ironically, the women's downhill ski race was canceled because of heavy snow.

    a. done or happening without clear or sensible reasons
    b. developed in an unexpected way
    c. done or said without thinking of the possible results

12. Our hopes for a win this season **faded** when the opposing team scored its fourth goal.

    a. got attention
    b. pretended to be ill
    c. gradually disappeared

B. Read the target words and definitions. Then read the sentences. Circle the sentence in which the target word is NOT used correctly.

1. cable: a system of broadcasting television that is distributed via cables and is paid for by the person watching it

    a. The earliest **cable** projectors, such as the "magic lantern," actually showed up in the late 1600s, but presented only still images.
    b. When I was a child, all of my friends had **cable** and could watch TV programs that we weren't able to see.
    c. Our **cable** company provides a movie service, special sports channels, and Internet access.

2. amateur: doing an activity just for pleasure, not as a job

    a. The competition was open to **amateur** golfers only to ensure a more even playing field.
    b. My grandfather goes to weekend flea markets where he sometimes buys and sells antiques, but only as an **amateur** collector.
    c. Wimbledon was the last of the Grand Slam tennis tournaments to offer equal prize money to both its male and female **amateur** competitors.

3. **helicopter**: a type of aircraft with large metal blades on top that turn very quickly to make it fly

   a. In a **helicopter**, the pilot uses his or her legs for takeoff and landing and then relies on rising air to stay up in the air.
   b. The Penzance-St. Mary's route to the Isles of Scilly has been operated by **helicopter** since 1964, making it the world's longest-running scheduled **helicopter** service.
   c. The turning blades provide not only the lift that allows a **helicopter** to fly but also the control that allows it to move from side to side, make turns, and change altitude.

4. **plead**: to present an argument in a court of law for example—to argue whether or not you are guilty of a crime

   a. Paul Burrell, a former butler to Princess Diana, appeared in court to **plead** not guilty to three counts of theft.
   b. A 31-year-old local man will **plead** seven days in jail for driving without a license.
   c. Tomorrow Michael Milken, boy wonder of Wall Street, will **plead** guilty to six felonies and brace himself for the biggest fine in history.

5. **baffled**: when you cannot understand or explain something

   a. Elvis impersonator Mario Rocco was **baffled** by the theft of his suit and guitar from his car: "I can't imagine why anyone would want these things."
   b. After returning home from his travels, he developed a strange illness that left his doctors **baffled**.
   c. The football club **baffled** a signed photo of Brett Favre to raise money for new equipment.

6. **brand**: a type of product that has a particular design and is made by a particular company,

   a. That supermarket sells **brand**-name products for items such as laundry soap, paper towels, and window cleaner.
   b. The image of a **brand** or company can be hurt if it has to issue a major recall of its product, as happened with Toyota in 2010.
   c. Louis Braille invented a special **brand** of writing to help blind and partially sighted people learn to read.

7. **anonymity**: when other people do not know who you are or what your name is

   a. The government official was willing to speak to the reporter only on condition of **anonymity**.
   b. For a person coming from a small town, the **anonymity** of the city can be a little frightening.
   c. Most Americans want a society characterized by the values of integrity, **anonymity**, responsibility, fairness, and openness.

8. **attribute**: to regard as belonging to, or being caused or produced by somebody or something

   a. The popular phrase "If you can't stand the heat, get out of the kitchen" is commonly **attributed** to President Harry Truman.
   b. The light outside my window **attributed** a lot of insects, so I had to keep the window closed even though it was very hot.
   c. The easy nature of the island people has been **attributed** to the gentle breezes and easy tides of the island itself.

9. **interchangeable**: when things can be used instead of other things

    a. **Interchangeable** projects allow people from different countries, who would not otherwise meet, to get to know each other and share activities.

    b. So many towns have lost local businesses to large chain stores and restaurants that the towns themselves begin to look **interchangeable**.

    c. Eli Whitney's invention of **interchangeable** parts led the way in the development of factory assembly lines.

10. **gossip**: information that is passed from one person to another about other people's behavior and private lives, often including unkind or untrue remarks

    a. If you are looking for **gossip**, the Internet is full of celebrity sites ready to tell all about your favorite celebrities.

    b. Jobcentre Plus can provide you access to jobs, **gossip**, and guidance on getting the training you need for the job you want.

    c. I didn't enjoy my last job because there was far too much **gossip** in the office, and I found out it was sometimes about me.

11. **premium**: an additional amount of money, above a standard rate or amount

    a. If you want a hotel room with an ocean view, there is a **premium** of $100 per night compared to a room with a city view.

    b. Movie theaters are charging a $3 **premium** for tickets to 3-D movies compared to ticket prices for normal 2-D movies.

    c. The price of eating out is going up because in many places the standard **premium** for a waiter or waitress is 18 percent.

12. **liable**: legally responsible for the cost of something

    a. If you damage any of the furniture in your dormitory, you will be **liable** for the cost of repair or replacement.

    b. Scandinavian countries take a much more **liable** approach to maternity leave than the United States, with parents eligible for twelve to sixteen months of paid leave.

    c. A library is not **liable** for copyright infringement by its users if it displays a notice saying that the making of a copy may be subject to copyright law.

WORD FAMILIES

A. The table contains word families for some of the target words in the reading. Complete the table. An **X** indicates that there is no form or that the form is not common. Sometimes more than one form may be possible. If you are unsure about a form, check your dictionary.

Verb	Noun	Adjective	Adverb
X	anonymity		
		attributed	X
	X	1. baffled 2.	X
		1. 2. disturbing	
	1. 2.	interchangeable	
X			ironically
X		liable	X
X		peculiar	
substitute	1. 2.	X	X
X	visibility		

B. Read the sentences. In eight of the sentences, an incorrect form of the target word has been used. If the form of the target word is incorrect, cross it out and write the correct form. If the form is correct, put a checkmark (✔). Use the word families table to help you.

_____ **1.** One way that universities maintain quality is to give students the opportunity to **anonymity** evaluate their professors in end-of-course questionnaires.

_____ **2.** More and more people are eating like vegetarians. Observers **attributed** this trend away from eating meat to health concerns.

_____ **3.** When traveling to a foreign country for the first time, people find that even the simplest tasks, such as making a phone call, can be **baffle**.

_____ **4.** The student's work was **disturbing** similar to an essay handed in by a student from the previous year, so the teacher had to check whether it was plagiarized.

_____ **5.** The **interchangeable** of many products (for example, toothpastes, colas, ice creams) means that marketers have to work hard to convince us to buy any particular brand.

_____ **6. Ironically**, the Icelandic volcano that closed many European airports led to a tourism boom in Iceland, where the airport remained open for business.

_____ **7.** The hotel accepts no **liable** for loss or damage to items left at the hotel, although it will do its utmost to ensure the security of all belongings.

_____ **8.** One reason children are frightened by clowns is that they look a bit like human beings, but they also look **peculiarly**, and they do unusual things.

_____ **9.** Some experts think that the emotional attachments fans have with celebrities serve as a **substitute** for real social interaction with real people.

_____ **10.** The actress was **visibility** shaking as she accepted the Academy Award.

COLLOCATION

In each set of sentences, the target word is paired with different words to form different collocations. Choose the collocation that best fits the last sentence and write it in the blank. You may need to change the form of one word in the collocation to fit the sentence.

1. **a.** It's a tradition at many graduation ceremonies to **release balloons** into the sky to celebrate the students' achievement.
   b. Doctors are now able to clear a blocked blood vessel by using a small wire to insert and then **inflate a** small **balloon** inside the vessel.
   c. My friends and I used to play a game where we would blow and blow to see who could **burst a balloon** first.
   d. Many people are unaware that _____ in large numbers at special events can result in littering and harm to wildlife.

2. **a.** Many airlines, supermarkets, and stores have tried to build **brand loyalty** among their customers by developing some kind of reward card.
   b. Some **brand names**, such as Kleenex, Q-Tips, and Vaseline, have become so popular that they have replaced the original name of the product.
   c. The clothing company wanted a **brand identity** that was sexy, stylish, and had attitude to appeal to shoppers in their late teens and early twenties.
   d. The difference between simply buying the same product repeatedly and _____ is that the latter includes an emotional tie to the product.

3. **a.** My grandmother's **memories** of living through the Great Depression **were fading**, so I began recording our conversations in order to keep a family record of her life.
   b. The **light was fading**, and the snow was starting to fall, so the hikers hurried down the mountain back to the base camp.
   c. As the clock ticked closer to zero, the fans' **hope** that their team might still win **was** quickly **fading**.
   d. _____ for the peace process because neither side seemed willing to make changes to its position on land rights.

4. a. Do you think that people using reusable shopping bags are making a **genuine effort** to tackle climate change or simply making a fashion statement?

b. Although many people have expressed a **genuine concern** about how to help the community recover from the damage caused by the storm, they aren't sure what exactly they should do.

c. The success of the basketball team seems assured this year because the coach and team members have expressed a **genuine desire** to improve upon the weaknesses of last year.

d. Nurses need to be able to relate well to people of all ages and backgrounds, have strong communication and listening skills, and possess a _____ to help people.

5. a. The actor and director of the movie dismissed rumors about a major disagreement between them as **idle gossip**.

b. Before you send that e-mail packed with **juicy gossip**, double-check the name listed in your "Send to" box.

c. Beware of **office gossip**! Although being in the know sounds attractive, passing on personal information about work colleagues can get you into trouble.

d. The "news" presented in many entertainment magazines is really only _____, and some magazines have even been sued for making false statements.

6. a. After the climbers had spent thirty-six hours on the mountain in snow and freezing temperatures, a **helicopter rescue team** brought them to safety.

b. Experience the thrill of a **helicopter flight** over downtown Manhattan's Financial District, the Statue of Liberty, and many other sights that the New York City skyline has to offer.

c. The hospital's emergency center, located at the north end of the building, has a separate entrance and exit as well as a **helicopter pad**.

d. The patient was transferred to another hospital by air ambulance. The _____ took twenty minutes compared to sixty minutes by road.

7. a. The soccer team stayed at a countryside hotel to avoid the **media hype** that normally developed before an important match.

b. When a movie gets nominated for an Oscar, film companies often begin a **media campaign** to gain support for their film.

c. Studies in the U.S., U.K., and Australia all report that women's sports receive as little as 5 percent of total **media coverage** compared to 95 percent for men's sports.

d. Governments often sponsor public service _____ to encourage people to stop speeding, stop littering, or stop smoking.

8. a. Not everyone who **shows talent** at an early age will be successful. According to author Malcolm Gladwell, hard work, social context, and cultural background also make a difference.

b. If the team is going to continue to be successful in future years, the coaches must work to **develop their** young **talent** now.

c. My teachers were concerned that I would **waste my talent** if I got a job stacking shelves at a supermarket, so they encouraged me to apply for an internship instead.

d. The bosses felt that the best way to improve the company's performance was to work with current employees to _____ instead of hiring new people.

Expanding the Topic

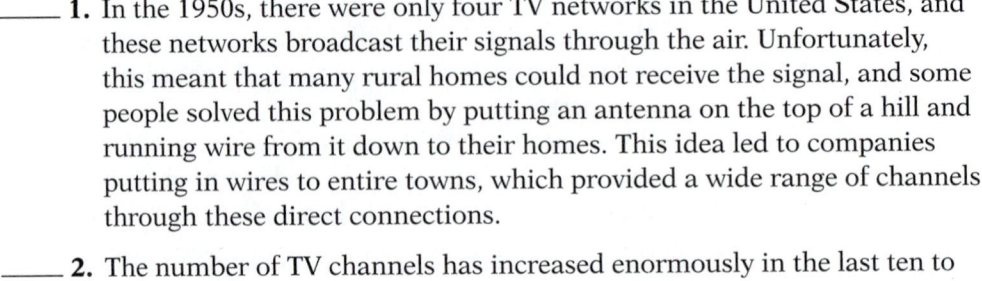

A. Match the paraphrases to the original text.

Originals

_____ **1.** In the 1950s, there were only four TV networks in the United States, and these networks broadcast their signals through the air. Unfortunately, this meant that many rural homes could not receive the signal, and some people solved this problem by putting an antenna on the top of a hill and running wire from it down to their homes. This idea led to companies putting in wires to entire towns, which provided a wide range of channels through these direct connections.

_____ **2.** The number of TV channels has increased enormously in the last ten to twenty years, with people willing to pay a **premium** to get sports and movie channels. This has resulted in many people having access to over 100 channels, the sheer number of which can be overwhelming.

_____ **3.** TV **talent** shows, though, are not new. The first **talent** shows moved from radio to TV in the 1940s. Ordinary performers were given the opportunity to act, sing, or dance, and the viewing public voted for their favorites by postcard or telephone.

_____ **4.** Unlike today's contestants, who receive recording contracts, past winners were awarded a scholarship of $2,000 and normally returned to their ordinary lives.

Paraphrases

a. The prizes for winners of early **talent** shows were extremely small in comparison to today's **perks** and prizes, and participants normally fell back into obscurity after their moment of fame.

b. The earliest TV **talent** shows began airing in the 1940s as radio programs made the switch to TV. **Amateurs** performed for a TV audience, which chose the winners through a mail or telephone vote.

c. The growth in number of TV channels now means that viewers are presented with a **baffling** assortment of programs—far more than they could ever wish to watch.

d. There were originally very few channels, but the introduction of **cable** networks, where TV companies connected directly with homes, led to a wider range of channels being available.

B. Now you try. Paraphrase the sentences. Use the target word in your paraphrase. You may need to change the form of the target word.

1. Judith Sheindlin was relatively unknown outside the legal world of family court until an article in the *Los Angeles Times* and a follow-up story on the news program *60 Minutes* brought her to the attention of TV producers who proposed that she star in the enormously popular courtroom reality show *Judge Judy*.

elevated _____

_____

2. The program deals with cases normally handled in small claims court. Viewers of the show can choose to have their cases argued on the show, provided they sign a document agreeing to accept the judgment made by Judge Judy.

plead _____

_____

3. The program has been running since 1996, and although the people involved in each case are different, if you watch too often you begin to see a pattern, and after a while the cases and the parties involved begin to all look alike.

interchangeable _____

_____

4. What prompts people to want to air their problems in front of a national TV audience? Perhaps they imagine that one appearance on TV will lead to others, and all the benefits of fame will follow.

perk _____

_____

 Write a 500-word essay in which you discuss some of the possible reasons for the increased focus on fame and celebrity in modern society.

Revisiting the Target Words

Now that you have completed this chapter, use the scale to describe your knowledge of the target words.

1 I still don't know anything about this word.

2 I am still not sure of the meaning of this word even after studying it.

3 I understand this word when I see it or hear it in a sentence, but I don't know how to use it in my own speaking and writing.

4 I know this word and can use it in my own speaking and writing.

TARGET WORDS			
___amateur	___cable	___helicopter	___perk
___anonymity	___disturbing	___interchangeable	___plead
___attributed	___elevated	___ironically	___premium
___baffled	___fade	___liable	___substitute
___balloon	___genuine	___media	___talent
___brand	___gossip	___peculiar	___visibility

KNOWLEDGE CHECK 2

Go back to the beginning of the chapter and complete the Knowledge Check 1 table.

Strategy Practice

Getting Started

Look at the three images taken from Chapters 21–23. Without looking back at the chapters, how many target words can you remember from each chapter?

Learning More about Words: USING THE WORDS

You have been introduced to meanings, the word family, and collocations for the words taught in this book. But you can only truly *learn* a word by *using* it.

Here are some short activities that give you practice in using words in different ways. Review the definitions and sample sentences for the target words and then answer the questions.

Definition and sample sentence	Questions
1. **interchangeable:** when things can be used instead of other things *Eli Whitney's invention of **interchangeable** parts led the way in the development of factory assembly lines.*	**a.** List four examples of things that are **interchangeable**. **b.** Synonyms are commonly thought of as words with **interchangeable** meanings. But are synonyms truly **interchangeable**? What are some characteristics that make synonyms different from each other?

Definition and sample sentence	Questions
2. **admire**: to respect and like someone because of something good the person has done *He **admired** Martin Luther King Jr. for leading the Civil Rights Movement.*	**a.** List five people who you **admire**. **b.** People who are **admired** have positive characteristics, e.g., bravery. List the characteristics you most admire. **c.** What characteristics would you like people to **admire** about you? Why?
3. **perpetual**: continuing all the time without changing or stopping *There is **perpetual** snow at the top of Mount Everest.*	**a.** List three things that are **perpetual**, i.e., never changing at all. **b.** ***Perpetual*** can also refer to things that only *seem* to continue forever because they are unpleasant, e.g., perpetual exams, perpetual struggle. List five different things for this meaning of *perpetual*.
4. **amateur**: used about someone who does an activity just for pleasure, not as his or her job *The golf competition was closed to professional players, to give the **amateur** players a chance.*	**a.** List two sports that remain **amateur** at all levels. **b.** What are the advantages of playing a sport as an **amateur**? As a professional? **c.** What activities besides sports can you do as an **amateur**?
5. **Now you do it**: Add a word of your own and make a set of related questions. Give the questions to a classmate to see if he or she can answer them.	

Focusing on Skills: READING

CHOOSING READING TEXTS

Making lists and brainstorming examples are great ways of practicing vocabulary. Reading is another way to use your vocabulary knowledge and has the added bonus of exposing you to *new* words. But not just any kind of reading will improve your English. In order to choose the best reading material for you, it is important to first understand the relationship between vocabulary and reading.

In our everyday lives, we read because we want to get information or pleasure from a text. In other words, we read for meaning rather than to learn new language. In order for a text to have language learning potential, it needs to both provide understanding and be challenging.

Research tells us that the 2,000 most frequent words in English normally make up about 80 percent of the words in most texts in English.

A. In the text, all of the words above the 2,000 frequency level—20 percent—have been blanked out. How much of the text can you understand?

The famous reporter Tintin has wowed fans for _____.
Traveling the world on _____ _____ with his
dog, Snowy, the _____ books contained elements of _____,
_____, even political _____. And political is exactly
what this _____ has become.

Originally published in the early 1930s, *Tintin in the Congo* follows the
_____ boy reporter to the Belgian Congo in what was seen as
"deepest, darkest" Africa—at the time a Belgian _____.
There the _____ hire a local guide, visit _____
villages, even _____ _____. So far, so normal
for an _____. But it's the language and imagery used in the
_____ that has caused _____ in those critical of it.

The guide looks like a _____—with a black
_____, large eyes, and _____, _____
red _____. And the views _____ are
_____ and _____. The Belgian writer and
_____ Hergé later said he _____ writing it—a style
that reflected the _____ _____ of the time.

But that's not Bienvenu Mbutu's _____ of it. He's a Congolese
national living in Belgium, and he's asking the courts to _____
the book, although he says he would be satisfied if it was sold with a warning
about the content.

....

You probably understand the gist of the story, but missed out on a lot of detail.
That's the experience of knowing only the 2,000 most frequent words in English.

B. Now look at the text. With all of the words at the 3,000 and 4,000 frequency levels (the words studied in this book) added, your understanding increases significantly. Only five words remain blank, or "unknown."*

The famous reporter Tintin has wowed fans for decades. Traveling the world
on wild **adventures** with his dog, Snowy, the **comic** books contained elements
of **fantasy**, **mystery**, even political thrillers. And political is exactly what this
_____ has become.

Originally published in the early 1930s, *Tintin in the Congo* follows the **courageous** boy reporter to the Belgian Congo in what was seen as "deepest, darkest" Africa—at the time a Belgian **colony**. There the **adventurers** hire a local guide, visit remote villages, even encounter _____. So far, so normal for an **explorer**. But it's the language and imagery used in the **comic** that has caused outrage in those critical of it.

The guide looks like a _____—with a black _____, large eyes, and _____, red **lips**. And the views **adopted** are racist and **colonialist**. The Belgian writer and illustrator Hergé later said he regretted writing it—a style that reflected the **intolerant outlook** of the time.

But that's not Bienvenu Mbutu's **perception** of it. He's a Congolese national living in Belgium, and he's asking the courts to **ban** the book, although he says he would be satisfied if it was sold with a warning about the content.

....

*episode, wildlife, golliwog, complexion, plump

Research tells us that in order for a text to both provide understanding and be challenging, the most favorable balance is 98 percent known vocabulary to 2 percent unknown vocabulary. In other words, if you know 98 percent of the words in a text (only one word in fifty is unknown), you'll understand enough to find it interesting and useful, while still being challenged by the 2 percent of new words. This balance also allows you to further develop understanding of words you have previously studied.

You can determine if a text is at the right level simply by reading a page or two and noting how many unknown words you see. Happy reading!

Focusing on Vocabulary Cards: STEPPING STONES

The aim of this activity is to use your knowledge of target words to successfully get across a grid before your opponent does.

Instructions

1. Form pairs or teams (Team A and Team B).
2. Each team selects twenty-five vocabulary cards and arranges them into a 5x5 grid. The cards should be placed in such a way that the side of the card with the pronunciation, word family, and collocation information is not visible to the opposing team.

3. Team A points to a card in the first column of Team B's grid. A member of Team B picks up the card and, without letting Team A see the target word information written on the reverse of the card, asks Team A a question about one feature of the target word that had been hidden from view.

Example:

Team A points to a card.

Team B picks up the card and reads the word on it: *courage*.

Team B then asks, *What part of speech is the word "courage"?* or any other question related to the information on the card.

4. Team A responds, and Team B checks the card to confirm the answer.

5a. If correct, Team A points to another card and steps 3 and 4 are repeated. Only cards that are adjacent to (touching) correct answer cards and in the next column to the right (or "moving forward") can be selected, as shown here.

X	adjacent card			
correctly answered card	adjacent card			
X	adjacent card			
X	X			
X	X			

5b. If Team A is incorrect, the card is returned to the grid, face up, and is out of play.

6. It's now Team B's turn. Team B points to a card on Team A's grid, and steps 3 through 5 are repeated.

7. The first team to get across the grid, as shown here, wins.

Step 1			Step 4	Step 5
	Step 2	Step 3		

UNIT
7

Environment

Eco Fashion

Getting Started

Discuss the questions with your classmates.

✦ How frequently do you go shopping for clothes?

✦ What do you consider important when buying clothes—for example, price? style? the material the clothes are made of?

✦ What do you do with your old clothes?

Assessing Your Vocabulary Knowledge: TARGET WORDS

Look at the words in the box. These are the target words for this chapter. Use the scale to score yourself on each word.

1 I don't know this word.

2 I have seen or heard this word before, but I am not sure of the meaning.

3 I understand this word when I see it or hear it in a sentence, but I don't know how to use it in my own speaking and writing.

4 I know this word and can use it in my own speaking and writing.

TARGET WORDS			
_____autumn	_____fabric	_____novel	_____surrounding
_____conscience	_____federation	_____recycle	_____sustainable
_____discard	_____fiber	_____secondhand	_____textile
_____ease	_____grave	_____sew	_____trend
_____expenditure	_____lease	_____soil	_____triple
_____extraordinary	_____mend	_____stained	_____turnover

KNOWLEDGE CHECK 1

Complete the sentences with words that you have scored as **1**.

1. I am not familiar with the word/term _____.

2. I have no idea what _____ means.

Fill in the first blank with a word that you have scored as **2**. Then complete the sentence.

3. I think _____ could mean _____.

Reading

The passage is about fast fashion and the consequences for the environment and people in less developed countries. As you read, pay special attention to the target vocabulary words in **bold**.

Fashion Victim or Environmental Victory?

1   You are on your way home and you make a quick visit to the mall to see if there is anything **novel** or interesting in any of your favorite stores. Chances are there will be if you shop at any of the retail chains that use the *fast fashion* model of business. There's no longer any need to wait for a change of season (for example, from **autumn** to winter) to see a new collection of clothes, because fashion retailers are introducing new lines of clothing on a monthly, or even weekly, basis.

2   Fast fashion retailers make it possible for fashion-conscious shoppers to stay current without breaking the bank by offering up low-priced clothes that follow the latest **trends**. Over the past ten years, falling prices have led to **extraordinary** growth in **expenditures** on clothing. In Britain alone, shoppers spend over $37 billion per year on clothes, and the fast / discount fashion sector makes up one-fifth of this market.

3   In fact, there's so much shopping going on that our closets can't keep up, and people in developed countries are now **discarding** clothes at higher rates than ever before. There's no thought of **mending** a hole or **sewing** on a new button when a new shirt can be bought for six or seven dollars. When a dress gets **stained**, why pay to dry-clean it when we can buy a new one instead? According to the Environmental Protection Agency, the average American throws away more than 68 pounds of clothing and **textiles** per year. So what happens to all of the clothes we throw away?

4   Clothing and **textiles** are the fastest growing waste product in Britain with 63 percent of unwanted clothes ending up in landfills and only 16 percent being **recycled**. This has serious consequences for the environment because many of today's clothes are made from synthetic **fibers**, which do not break down naturally. This can create problems as water cannot flow into the **soil**, and chemicals from the **fabrics** release poisons into the **surrounding** air and water.

5   There are other options for our unwanted clothing. Many of us **ease** our **conscience** about all this waste by donating our unwanted clothing to charities. However, even charities cannot keep up with the **turnover** of clothing and end up selling the excess for **recycling** or export. Since 1989, U.S. exports of used clothing and other worn **textiles** have more than **tripled** and now exceed 7 billion pounds per year. Many of these clothes get a new **lease** on life when they end up in the flourishing markets for **secondhand** clothes in Africa and Eastern Europe. Clothing that is in good condition is highly sought after and provides consumers there with the opportunity to be smartly dressed.

6   However, this virtuous circle of developed countries providing clothes for those in poorer countries is only **sustainable** if the clothing is well-made and durable. Unfortunately, a major reason fast fashion clothes are so cheap is because of a decrease in the quality of materials and manufacturing. This leaves less reason for developing countries to buy the poorly made clothing, and so will eventually lead to a fall in demand for Western castoffs.

7   So we need to take a closer look at the economic and ecological impact of fast fashion. Both government bodies and the fashion **federations** are calling for eco approaches to

fashion. For example, the British government used the occasion of London Fashion Week to launch its **sustainable** clothing action plan. The plan encourages everyone to consider the impact of a fashion item, from the cradle (its design) to the **grave** (its disposal).

(598 words)

READING COMPREHENSION

Respond to the questions in writing. Base your responses on the reading and your own personal experiences.

1. According to the text, why is fast fashion so successful?

2. How much money is spent on clothing in Britain each year?

3. Why is throwing away old clothes a growing environmental issue?

4. What is meant by a *virtuous circle*? What is the opposite of a *virtuous circle*?

5. Would you consider wearing **secondhand** clothes? If so why? If not, why not?

6. What measures do you think were included in the British government's "**sustainable** clothing action plan"?

Focusing on Vocabulary

WORD MEANING

A. Match the target words with their definitions. If you are unsure about a word's meaning, try to figure it out from the context by rereading the passage. Then check your dictionary.

Set 1

_____ **1. autumn**
_____ **2. trend**
_____ **3. expenditure**
_____ **4. sew**
_____ **5. textile**
_____ **6. recycle**
_____ **7. fiber**

a. the total amount of money that a government, organization, or person spends during a particular period of time

b. to use a needle and thread to make or repair clothes or to fasten something on to them

c. a current style; something in vogue

d. a mass of threads used to make rope, cloth, etc.

e. to put used objects or materials through a special process so that they can be used again

f. the season between summer and winter when leaves change color and the weather becomes cooler

g. any type of woven cloth that is made in large quantities, used especially by people in the business of making clothes

Set 2

_____ 1. fabric
_____ 2. conscience
_____ 3. turnover
_____ 4. triple
_____ 5. lease
_____ 6. sustainable
_____ 7. grave

a. the number of times a particular stock of goods is sold and restocked during a given period of time
b. able to continue without causing damage to the environment
c. cloth used for making clothes, curtains, etc.
d. if something has "a new lease on life," it is changed or repaired so that it can continue
e. to increase by three times as much, or to make something do this
f. the place in the ground where a dead body is buried
g. the part of your mind that tells you whether what you are doing is morally right or wrong

B. Read each target word and the list below it. One word or phrase in each list is NOT a synonym for the target word. Cross it out.

1. **novel**

fresh	new	original	traditional

2. **extraordinary**

amazing	astonishing	average	unexpected

3. **discard**

cast off	get rid of	throw away	unload into

4. **mend**

arrange	fix	patch up	repair

5. **stained**

blemished	marked	pristine	tainted

6. **soil**

dirt	ditch	earth	mud

7. **surrounding**

encircling	enfolding	enriching	enveloping

8. **ease**

alleviate	amend	lessen	relieve

9. **secondhand**

manual	nearly new	pre-owned	used

10. **federation**

alliance	apprenticeship	association	partnership

WORD FAMILIES

A. The table contains word families for some of the target words in the reading. Complete the table. An **X** indicates that there is no form or that the form is not common. Sometimes more than one form may be possible. If you are unsure about a form, check your dictionary.

Verb	Noun	Adjective	Adverb
X	conscience		
discard	X		X
X	X	1. 2. **extraordinary**	
	1. 2. 3. **federation**	1. 2.	
	lease		X
recycle		1. 2.	X
sew			X
		1. 2. **surrounding**	X
		sustainable	
	trend		

B. Choose the correct form of the word in **bold** in sentence **a** to complete sentence **b**. Use the word families table you just completed as a guide.

1. **a.** I'd park my car in the handicapped parking space, but my **conscience** would bother me.

   b. She _____ asked the others where they wanted to go before giving her suggestion.

2. **a.** You should **discard** any old cleaning materials.

   b. The committee _____ his idea saying that it was unworkable.

3. **a.** The actor had **extraordinary** power over her audience in the theater.

   b. Miles Davis was a jazz trumpeter _____.

4. **a.** The British **Federation** of Film Societies supports all aspects of the film industry in Great Britain.

   b. _____ is a type of government with a strong central authority.

5. **a.** The operation gave her a new **lease** on life.

   b. The newly renovated building was already _____ when we went to view it.

6. **a.** The new governor pledged to improve the state's **recycling** and waste disposal systems.

   b. Fleece is a human-made fabric created from _____ plastic bottles.

7. **a.** The army surgeon attempted to **sew** up the wound on the soldier's leg.

   b. _____ was a popular pastime for ladies during the Victorian era.

8. **a.** The SWAT team decided to **surround** the bank in an effort to stop the robbers from getting away.

   b. Being back in her hometown relaxed her she realized as she walked through familiar _____.

9. **a.** Governments around the world are looking for more **sustainable** sources of energy.

   b. Diane was able to _____ the quick pace of the marathon thanks to all of her road training over the winter.

10. **a.** A combination of formal and informal garments worn at the same time is the latest **trend** in fashion.

    b. He thought he was so _____ wearing those leather trousers.

Word Tip

Compound nouns are fixed expressions that are made up of more than one word. They can be two or more words written separately—for example, *credit card*—or they can be joined by a hyphen—for example, *sister-in-law*. Or they can be one word—for example, ***turnover***.

Compound nouns can be a source of confusion for students in their writing because there are no hard and fast rules about when to separate, hyphenate, or join together. Also, writing conventions change over time. If you are in any doubt, check your dictionary.

Read the common collocations in the column on the left. Give two examples of things associated with each collocation.

	Example 1	Example 2
1. autumn tints	_____	_____
2. ease the tension	_____	_____
3. cut **expenditures**	_____	_____
4. fiber optics	_____	_____
5. grave digger	_____	_____
6. novel idea	_____	_____
7. soil erosion	_____	_____
8. stained glass	_____	_____

Expanding the Topic

Complete the passage on the following pages. Use the target words from the box. You may need to change the form of the word to fit the sentence. There are two extra words.

autumn	fabric	secondhand	triple
ease	mend	textile	turnover

Fast Fashion in the U.K.

1   Students were once the pioneers of edgy, eclectic fashion. New customized pieces were mixed with (**1**) _____ classics. Nothing was off-limits in terms of style; in fact, the crazier the better. But these days university campuses are full of fashion clones. Where has all the experimental fashion gone?

2   Student budgets are tight and leave little room for luxury. The success of chain stores, such as Primark and H&M, has led to the rise of "fast fashion." Clothes are being produced more cheaply than ever and are regarded as disposable rather than as a long-term wardrobe investment. These days there is genuinely no reason to wear an outfit twice or to bother with (**2**) _____ the holes in old favorites.

3   Now it's easier than ever to look like the celebrities of the moment, with retailers churning out more-or-less exact replicas of their outfits. As soon as designers send a garment down the catwalk, chain stores are copying them for a fraction of the price.

4   The rise of chain stores and their incredibly rapid stock (**3**) _____ has also meant that smaller businesses have struggled to compete. Independent boutiques in particular have been hard hit by the threat of larger retailers because nobody wants to pay $95 for a pair of jeans when that is (**4**) _____ the price of a pair of jeans at Primark. The truth is, students are going to opt for whatever seems to be the biggest bargain, and are increasingly turning their backs on designer brands—hardly surprising given the amount of student debt.

5   Thrift stores were once loved by students for their unique vintage clothing; nowadays they are more like the **grave**yards of cheap supermarket garments. Genuine bargains are lost beneath piles of human-made (**5**) _____ and unwanted cast-offs that the stores simply can't sell. "Fur coats, brooches, and patterned dresses have made way for cheap, badly made, mass-produced exports," said one student we interviewed.

6   It's not all doom and gloom; vintage stores appear to be bucking the **trend** and doing well, thanks to the rise of vintage fashion. Often tucked away on back streets, they can be heaven for a fashion lover with unique pieces from across the decades. The Internet also offers alternative retailers a platform, and clothes can be customized or professionally altered. And though more expensive, dressmakers will often make outfits from scratch if you provide the (**6**) _____.

7   Alternatives to the mainstream do exist, students just have to look harder to find them. Being a poor student shouldn't mean you have to sacrifice style.

Adapted from http://www.independent.co.uk/student/student-life/fashion/fast-fashion-1517291.html.

Read this statement: "The fashion industry's need to produce new **trends** every season is morally and environmentally un**sustainable**." Do you agree or disagree with the statement? Write a 500-word essay explaining why.

Revisiting the Target Words

Now that you have completed this chapter, use the scale to describe your knowledge of the target words.

1 I still don't know anything about this word.

2 I am still not sure of the meaning of this word even after studying it.

3 I understand this word when I see it or hear it in a sentence, but I don't know how to use it in my own speaking and writing.

4 I know this word and can use it in my own speaking and writing.

TARGET WORDS

____autumn	____fabric	____novel	____surrounding
____conscience	____federation	____recycle	____sustainable
____discard	____fiber	____secondhand	____textile
____ease	____grave	____sew	____trend
____expenditure	____lease	____soil	____triple
____extraordinary	____mend	____stained	____turnover

KNOWLEDGE CHECK 2

Select examples from the words you now give a score of **3** or **4**, but didn't at the start of the chapter, to complete the sentences.

1. I didn't know that _____ meant _____ before reading this chapter.

2. I wasn't sure that I knew the meaning of _____, but I am now.

3. I now am confident that I know what _____ means, but I would like more practice with how to use it in my speaking and writing.

4. I could next use _____ when I am _____.

Hunting the Hunters

Getting Started

Discuss the questions with your classmates.

✦ How many dangerous animals can you think of? List them.

✦ How would you react if you saw a shark?

✦ Do you agree with hunting? If so why? If not, why not?

Assessing Your Vocabulary Knowledge: TARGET WORDS

Look at the words in the box. These are the target words for this chapter. Use the scale to score yourself on each word.

1 I don't know this word.

2 I have seen or heard this word before, but I am not sure of the meaning.

3 I understand this word when I see it or hear it in a sentence, but I don't know how to use it in my own speaking and writing.

4 I know this word and can use it in my own speaking and writing.

TARGET WORDS			
affection	diver	lion	seldom
aggressive	fin	menace	soup
campaign	fragile	nuisance	species
catastrophic	headline	ocean	vicious
crop	intimidate	poaching	wolf
decline	jungle	pose	zone

KNOWLEDGE CHECK 1

Fill in the first blank with a word that you have scored as **2**. Then complete the second sentence.

1. I have seen / heard _____. I saw / heard it while I was

    _____.

Fill in the first blanks with words that you have scored as **4**. Then complete the sentences.

2. One meaning of _____ is _____.

3. I last used the word _____ while I was _____.

Reading

The passage is about the food chain and other complex relationships within natural ecosystems. As you read, pay special attention to the target vocabulary words in **bold**.

Pray for the Predators

1   The financial cost of protecting endangered **species** is enormous. Since 1985, the World Wildlife Fund, a charity largely funded by public donations, has invested over $1 billion in endangered **species**. In 2007, U.S. federal and state spending on wildlife protection was around $1.65 billion. What's more, wildlife protection **campaigns** frequently feature predator **species**, such as sharks, tigers, **wolves**, and **lions**, in their **headlines** even though these animals **pose** a direct threat to human lives and incomes. So why protect them when they are so costly?

2   Fishermen, **divers**, and surfers might indeed question the need to protect sharks. After all, in 2008 the International Shark Attack File (ISAF) reported that there were nearly sixty cases of attacks on humans. However, sharks do far more than **intimidate** swimmers. As apex predators—**species** at the top of the food chain—they perform a key role in maintaining the **fragile** balance of the **ocean** ecosystems. For instance, coral reefs with lots of sharks have greater numbers of and a better variety of other fish **species**, particularly those that eat coral-killing algae. Also, where shark numbers have been severely reduced, the negative effects on **ocean** ecosystems are apparent. For example, the number of large sharks off the east coast of the United States has **declined**

by more than 50 percent and, as a result, there are now ten times as many cownose rays. These rays eat shellfish, such as scallops and clams, which has severely damaged the U.S. scallop industry. The fishing industry has also been affected; the drop in shellfish has led to a **decline** in water quality, which leaves coastal **zones** struggling to support large numbers of young fish.

3   On land, the image of apex predators as **vicious** killers is also hard to ignore. Their apparently **aggressive** behavior means that they are **seldom** looked upon with much **affection**, especially in areas where life for local people is already very difficult. Take Tanzania for instance, where more than 300 people have been killed by **lions** since 1990. However, the relationship between these predators and land-based ecosystems has been found to be just as connected as sharks are to **ocean** environments. Justin Brashares, a researcher at the University of California, has found that the falling number of **lions** in sub-Saharan Africa is the most likely cause of the sudden increase in baboons. The growing baboon population is more than just a **nuisance**. The baboon presence in the area now threatens **crop** production on an unprecedented scale.

4   It's even more difficult to convince people of the value of apex predators when conservation projects might result in these animals becoming more of a **menace**. In forest conservation areas in Nepal for example, tiger attacks have jumped to around seven per year. Studies showing that the effects of not protecting apex predators are worse than the effects of protecting them are not limited to far-off Indian **jungles** or Africa grasslands. In the United States, the reintroduction of **wolves** was fiercely criticized by farmers at the time it was first authorized. However, the growing population has controlled elk numbers, which, in turn, has led to tree regeneration. Other related effects include an increased variety of **species**, reduced erosion,

and improved forest fire recovery rates. Coincidentally, **wolves** also attack coyotes, which are responsible for twenty-two times more livestock deaths than **wolves** and cost farmers and ranchers $7 million a year.

5   Although apex predators may be costly in terms of lives and money, the overall returns on the conservation investment appear to outweigh individual losses. So if ever you are tempted to try **soup** made from shark **fins**, or if you see a TV program showing the death of a big cat from **poaching**, consider the **catastrophic** effect these activities have up and down the food chain—from the smallest organisms at the bottom, to the number one predator at the top: us.

(637 words)

READING COMPREHENSION

Respond to the questions in writing. Base your responses on the reading and your own personal experiences.

1. What is an apex predator?

2. Outline the effects on the ecosystem when the number of apex predators changes. Create one outline for an **ocean**-based ecosystem and one for a land-based ecosystem.

3. Why is the portrayal of apex predators as **vicious** a problem for organizations trying to save them?

4. Go back to the introduction. Why do you think wildlife protection **campaigns** feature **lions**, **wolves**, and sharks instead of other **species** in the food chain?

5. Is the author of the text largely in favor of or against the protection of apex predators? How do you know?

6. Do you think it is worth protecting **species** of animals that are endangered? Why or why not?

Focusing on Vocabulary

WORD MEANING

A. Read the target words. Use the paragraph number in parentheses to locate and reread the word in context. Then read the dictionary definitions and choose the one that reflects how the word is used in the reading.

_____ 1. **campaign** (1)
   a. marketing materials and public actions that are intended to persuade people to buy, use, or support a product, service, or cause
   b. to promote your candidacy as you run for a political office

_____ 2. **wolf** (1)
   a. someone or something that is bad and causes all the problems in a situation
   b. a wild animal that looks like a large dog and lives and hunts in groups

_____ 3. **headline** (1)
   a. to be the main band at a concert
   b. the title of a news story or key point of campaign material

_____ 4. **pose** (1)
   a. to sit or stand in a particular position in order to be photographed or painted
   b. to exist in a way that may cause a problem, danger, or difficulty

_____ **5. diver** (2)

    a. someone who swims or works under water using special equipment to help with breathing

    b. someone who jumps into the water head and arms first

_____ **6. ocean** (2)

    a. a very large area of water on Earth's surface

    b. a lot of something, especially a liquid

_____ **7. crop** (3)

    a. the part under a bird's throat where food is stored

    b. a plant or plant product such as wheat or apples that is grown by farmers and used as food

_____ **8. menace** (4)

    a. something that is dangerous

    b. a person with a threatening quality, feeling, or way of behaving

_____ **9. jungle** (4)

    a. a thick tropical forest with many large plants growing very close together

    b. something that is very untidy, complicated, or confusing

_____ **10. soup** (5)

    a. to have problems (be in the soup)

    b. cooked liquid food, often containing small pieces of meat, fish, or vegetables

_____ **11. fin** (5)

    a. one of the thin body parts that aquatic animals such as fish use to swim

    b. part of a plane that sticks up at the back and helps the plane fly smoothly

_____ **12. poaching** (5)

    a. gently cooking food, especially fish, in a small amount of water or milk

    b. illegally catching or shooting animals, birds, or fish, especially on private land without permission

B. Read the target words in the box. Complete each sentence with the target word that matches the meaning of the words in parentheses. You may need to change the form of the word to fit the sentence.

affection	decline	lion	species
aggressive	fragile	nuisance	vicious
catastrophic	intimidate	seldom	zone

1. Most duck _____ are meat eaters, but geese eat plants on land,
                   (types, kinds)
    and swans are able to use their long necks to get to water plants.

2. All of the kids in the class were _____ by the school bully.
                               (frighten, scare)

3. My grandmother's glass vases were extremely _____.
                                    (delicate, easily broken)

4. The movie was spoiled by three teenage boys at the back of the theater who

    were talking and generally making a(n) _____ of themselves.
                                     (annoyance, bother)

5. Because of new anti-smoking measures, the numbers of young people who

smoke is steadily _____.
(fall, reduce)

6. Even two months after the event, it was still difficult to travel within the

earthquake _____.
(area, region)

7. Jimmy hated delivering the mail to the Simpson family because of their huge

_____ dog.
(mean, fierce)

8. Police say that _____ behavior while driving causes more
(forceful, violent)

accidents than anything else.

9. I _____ have time to go to the movies these days because work
(hardly ever, rarely)

is taking up so much of my time.

10. Zac wished his pet lizard showed a little more _____.
(fondness, love)

11. The chances of being killed by a mountain _____ are minimal.
(cat, large animal)

You have a greater chance of dying from a bee sting.

12. Last night's blackout was caused by a(n) _____ failure in the
(disastrous, terrible)

local power grid.

WORD FAMILIES

A. The table contains word families for some of the target words in the reading. An
X indicates that there is no form or that the form is not common. Study the table.
Look for spelling patterns for the noun, adjective, and adverb forms of the words.
List the patterns in the space on the next page.

Verb	Noun	Adjective	Adverb
X	**affection**	affectionate	affectionately
X	aggression	**aggressive**	aggressively
campaign	1. **campaign** 2. campaigner	campaign	**X**
X	catastrophe	**catastrophic**	catastrophically
decline	decline	**X**	**X**
dive	1. dive 2. **diver**	diving	**X**
headline	1. **headline** 2. headliner	headline	**X**
intimidate	intimidation	1. intimidated 2. intimidating	**X**
poach	1. poacher 2. **poaching**	poached	**X**
X	viciousness	**vicious**	viciously

nouns _____

adjectives _____

adverbs _____

B. Complete each sentence with the correct form of the word in parentheses. Use the word families table to help you.

1. Lionesses are well known for being _____ (**affection**) mothers.

2. Wolves show their teeth and growl as signs of _____ (**aggressive**).

3. Greenpeace _____ (**campaign**) boarded the whaling ship and displayed a huge banner.

4. Dinner last night was an absolute _____ (**catastrophic**).

5. Last year the number of complaints _____ (**decline**) sharply as a result of the new customer service approach.

6. My dream is to move to Tobago and open a small _____ (**diver**) school.

7. Usain Bolt's performance in the 100 and 200 meter finals grabbed all of the _____ (**headline**).

8. She refused to be _____ (**intimidate**) by the mean-looking neighborhood.

9. _____ (**poaching**) regularly shoot at wildlife wardens in many of Africa's big game reserves.

10. The _____ (**vicious**) and negativity of some political campaigns has begun to put off voters.

COLLOCATION

Combine a word from Column A with a word from Column B to form a collocation. Then match the collocation to its definition.

Column A	Column B
drop in the	**nuisance**
heart of a	**jungle**
lone	kitchen
menace	**lion**
soup	**ocean**
urban	out
public	to society
zone	**wolf**

1. _____ to stop paying attention because you are bored or tired

2. _____ someone who has committed many crimes or is very dangerous

3. _____ someone who does things that annoy a lot of people

4. _____ narrow and / or crowded city streets, alleys, subways, and inner-city neighborhoods

5. _____ a very small amount of something compared to what is needed or wanted

6. _____ brave

7. _____ someone who prefers to be by himself or herself

8. _____ a place where people with no money and no home can get free food

Expanding the Topic

An important part of developing your vocabulary involves forming and supporting opinions about the topic you are studying. Read the statements and indicate whether you agree (**A**) or disagree (**D**). Then discuss your opinions and reasoning with a partner.

_____ **1.** Farmers should be allowed to kill apex predators if the predators threaten animals and **crops**.

_____ **2.** There should be an international ban and severe punishment for those who continue to serve shark **fin soup**.

_____ **3.** Richer, more developed economies have a responsibility to fund the protection of **fragile ocean** ecosystems around the world.

_____ **4.** Humans **pose** a greater threat to sharks than sharks do to us.

     5. Because we **seldom** hear about attacks on humans and livestock, apex predators should be reintroduced into areas where they had previously been found, for example, the **wolf** in the United States or the cheetah in India.

     6. It is wrong for the U.S. government to spend so much money on the protection of endangered **species** when so many of its citizens lack basic health insurance.

Identify and research another food chain or ecosystem relationship. Write a 500-word essay that outlines the relationships between the **species** in that ecosystem.

Revisiting the Target Words

Now that you have completed this chapter, use the scale to describe your knowledge of the target words.

1 I still don't know anything about this word.

2 I am still not sure of the meaning of this word even after studying it.

3 I understand this word when I see it or hear it in a sentence, but I don't know how to use it in my own speaking and writing.

4 I know this word and can use it in my own speaking and writing.

TARGET WORDS			
____affection	____diver	____lion	____seldom
____aggressive	____fin	____menace	____soup
____campaign	____fragile	____nuisance	____species
____catastrophic	____headline	____ocean	____vicious
____crop	____intimidate	____poaching	____wolf
____decline	____jungle	____pose	____zone

KNOWLEDGE CHECK 2

Select examples from the words you now give a score of **3** or **4**, but didn't at the start of the chapter, to complete the sentences.

1. I didn't know that _____ meant _____ before reading this chapter.

2. I wasn't sure that I knew the meaning of _____, but I am now.

3. I now am confident that I know what _____ means, but I would like more practice with how to use it in my speaking and writing.

4. I now know that _____ collocates with _____.

High-Tech Trash

Getting Started

Discuss the questions with your classmates.

✦ How often do you replace your cell phone and other similar computer equipment?

✦ What happens to your old gadgets?

✦ Do you think it's right for some countries to export their trash? Explain your reasons.

Assessing Your Vocabulary Knowledge: TARGET WORDS

Look at the words in the box. These are the target words for this chapter. Use the scale to score yourself on each word.

1 I don't know this word.

2 I have seen or heard this word before, but I am not sure of the meaning.

3 I understand this word when I see it or hear it in a sentence, but I don't know how to use it in my own speaking and writing.

4 I know this word and can use it in my own speaking and writing.

TARGET WORDS			
____accountability	____dent	____invention	____shore
____bypass	____disposal	____mount	____substance
____cancer	____dreadful	____overseas	____tide
____curb	____grind	____penalty	____token
____currency	____hardware	____scope	____warehouse
____delete	____hazardous	____sheer	____weave

Check your progress in learning the vocabulary in this chapter.

- First, look at your scores in the table on page 238. Write the number of words for each score (1–4) in the "at the beginning" column. For example, if you scored eight words as **1** ("I don't know this word"), then write **8**.

- At the end of the chapter, score yourself again. Then compare the two sets of scores. Are you showing improvement on most of the words in the chapter?

Your score	Number of words ...		
	at the beginning:	at the end:	
		showing improvement	no improvement yet
1			
2			
3			
4			

Reading

The passage looks at the consequences of consumerism and technology on the environment. As you read, pay special attention to the target vocabulary words in **bold**.

Waste-Age

1   On a computer, it is easy to **delete** software and files by sending them to the recycling bin. Text messages, TV programs, music, and photographs can also simply be **deleted**. If they couldn't, our tech products would fill up and **grind** to a halt. However, the situation isn't quite so straightforward when it comes to getting rid of the **hardware** itself.

2   The rate of demand for technological **invention** has resulted in annual sales of technological consumer goods (TCGs) growing year after year. In 2008, for example, global sales of TCGs increased by 14 percent to $694 billion. Some of this growth is due to new users buying TCGs in developing economies, but the vast majority is the result of users in developed economies replacing existing equipment. The resulting problem is **disposal** of the old equipment. In the United States, 80 percent of TVs and 70 percent of computers end up in landfills, and nearly 200 million old PCs are being kept in **warehouse** facilities. According to the U.S. Environmental Protection Agency, another 40 million PCs could join them in the next few years. Unfortunately, the challenge doesn't end there.

3   According to the United Nations Environmental Program, the **sheer** volume of discarded technological consumer goods, also called "e-waste," could be as high as 50 million tons per year worldwide. Not only that, but

e-waste contains toxins, such as lead, cadmium, and PVC. An increasing problem is that some e-waste is now being **disposed** of in countries not equipped to deal with it. It is estimated that California alone shipped about 10,000 tons of e-waste **overseas** in 2006, and 40 percent of that was sent to developing countries such as Malaysia, India, Ghana, and Brazil. Ineffective waste **disposal** in these areas has led to higher levels of environmental pollution and **dreadful** medical conditions, such as **cancer** in adults and birth defects in babies.

4   However, there are several possible solutions to **curb** this growing **tide** of e-waste washing up on the **shores** of developing countries. First of all, there needs to be more consumer awareness and use of specialist recycling companies in developed economies. At present, only a **token** 20 percent of e-waste is **disposed** of in this way.

5   A second solution could lie with greater global regulatory and legislative power. In the early 1990s, a campaign was **mounted** to stop trade in e-waste, and in 1995 an international ban on **hazardous** waste being shipped to developing countries was signed. The European Union has subsequently **woven** this agreement into its legal framework. Unfortunately, the United States has yet to sign up, and illegal trade in e-waste by companies wanting to **bypass** expensive waste treatment processes or earn much-needed foreign **currency** continues to grow.

6   An alternative to these solutions is to shift the burden from consumers and governments to manufacturers and retailers of high-tech goods. Since they are the ones profiting from technology sales, they should be part of the solution. For example, more companies now collect and recycle old technology and are looking at ways to make their equipment "greener." For example, equipment could be made with fewer harmful **substances**, making it easier and cheaper to recycle. It could also be made of more recycled components. Finally, green equipment could be designed to have a greater **scope** of possibilities in terms of updating, therefore minimizing the need for replacement.

7   Perhaps we are now turning the corner in e-waste management as stronger laws and **penalties** and growing corporate **accountability** are all starting to have an impact. However, without us actively seeking ways to rethink our development and use technology to protect the planet against further environmental damage, these measures will only make a small **dent** in an ever-growing pile of waste.

(628 words)

Adapted from http://ngm.nationalgeographic.com/ 2008/01/high-tech-trash/carroll-text.

READING COMPREHENSION

Respond to the questions in writing. Base your responses on the reading and your own personal experiences.

1. Currently how is the United States tackling the problem of increasing TCG sales and the resultant waste?

2. Why is **disposal** of old computer **hardware** such a big problem?

3. In addition to the growing number of domestic users creating e-waste, why are some less developed countries facing an additional e-waste burden?

4. In your own words, summarize the three ways to solve the problem of e-waste outlined in the reading.

5. Which of the three ways to solve the problem of e-waste do you think is most likely to have the biggest impact? Explain your reasons.

6. What e-waste **disposal** facilities are available in your area? Can you think of any other small-scale solutions that could be introduced in your neighborhood?

Focusing on Vocabulary

WORD MEANING

A. Read the sentences and choose the phrase that best matches the meaning of the target word. Use context clues to determine the correct meaning. Check your dictionary if you are not sure of the answer.

1. The lack of available credit meant the global banking system **ground** to a halt.

   a. sped up
   b. stopped gradually
   c. fell over

2. Marketers say that computer **hardware** needs to be replaced every three years in order to keep up with advances in computer programming.

   a. computer programs and games
   b. people who write computer programs
   c. machinery and equipment

3. They were shocked by the **sheer** amount of work their boss expected them to get through in the next few days.

   a. very heavy, large
   b. very unusual, rare
   c. very boring, uninteresting

4. Many species of birds migrate **overseas** to find food during the winter.

   a. when birds or animals travel regularly from one part of the world to another
   b. to or in a foreign country
   c. to go around searching for food or other supplies

5. Lance Armstrong has won the Tour de France seven times despite having had **cancer**.

   a. a very serious back problem that affects cyclists and other athletes
   b. a very serious emotional problem in which concentrating for long periods of time is difficult
   c. a very serious disease in which cells in the body start to grow in a way that is not normal

6. In an effort to save the firm money, the executives were required to **curb** their expenses, especially when traveling.

   a. make something become larger in size, number, or amount
   b. control or limit something in order to prevent it from having a harmful effect
   c. find the total number or total amount of something by adding

7. The best time for inexperienced surfers is close to low **tide** since the waves are much smaller.

   a. continuous movement of water in a river, lake, or sea
   b. regular rising and falling of the level of the sea
   c. waves in the sea or on a lake that are white at the top

8. There were only a **token** number of the groom's friends and family at the wedding; most of the guests were members of the bride's family.

    a. small and not very important
    b. much more than is reasonable or necessary
    c. not unusually big or small

9. The value of one **currency** compared to another is called the exchange rate.

    a. arrangement with a store that allows you to buy something and pay for it later
    b. system or type of money that a country uses
    c. amount of money that you borrow from a bank

10. Mercury is a strange **substance** because it is the only metal that is liquid at room temperature.

    a. result produced by burning something
    b. thing that you use instead of the one that you usually use
    c. particular type of solid, liquid, or gas

11. The **scope** of the investigation was limited because so much evidence had been destroyed in the fire.

    a. right to use official power to make legal decisions
    b. range of things that a subject, activity, book, etc., deals with
    c. official decision made in a court of law

12. Failing my last assignment has really put a **dent** in my confidence.

    a. something that helps someone feel better and more positive
    b. something that helps something increase, improve, or become successful
    c. reduction in the amount of something

B. Read the target words and definitions. Then read the sentences. Circle the sentence in which the target word is NOT used correctly.

1. **delete:** to remove something that has been written down or stored in a computer

    a. I accidentally **deleted** my assignment when I tried to print it out.
    b. Congress decided to **delete** the final clause of the legislation.
    c. He couldn't **delete** the grass stains from his shorts no matter how many times he washed them.

2. **invention:** a new and clever idea or product

    a. Necessity is the mother of **invention**.
    b. The new version of the Ford GT is an amazing **invention**.
    c. Many **inventions** have contributed to the modern computer—for example, scientists built machines that could do basic mathematical equations as early as the seventeenth century.

3. **warehouse:** a large building for storing a large quantity of goods

    a. Most major museums have a **warehouse** where they store the items in their collection that they don't have room to exhibit.
    b. The company had a computerized system that made it possible to know exactly how much merchandise was in the **warehouse** at any one time.
    c. **Warehouses** offer great advertising opportunities for companies because sporting events bring in tens of thousands of fans.

4. **disposal:** when you get rid of something, especially something that is difficult to get rid of

    a. The safe **disposal** of nuclear waste is a very complex problem.
    b. The **disposal** of signatures for our petition took two weeks.
    c. In 2005, the **disposal** of household waste in landfills in the United States totaled 133 million tons.

5. **dreadful:** extremely unpleasant

    a. Tiger Woods shot a **dreadful** score in the first round, which made him co-leader after eighteen holes.
    b. I had a **dreadful** headache after babysitting the kids next door.
    c. The Lakers have had a **dreadful** start to the new season, losing two out of three games.

6. **shore:** the land along the edge of a large area of water such as an ocean or lake

    a. Niagara Falls, two very large **shores** on the border between Canada and the United States, are popular with tourists and are used to produce electricity.
    b. On the **shores** of the sub-Antarctic islands, tons of waste—mainly plastics—wash up every year.
    c. According to the Jamaican tourist board, about 2 million tourists visit Jamaica's **shores** each year.

7. **mount:** to plan, organize, and begin an event or a course of action

    a. The army unit was preparing to **mount** an early morning attack on the rebel base.
    b. Bob Geldof and Midge Ure **mounted** the world's biggest names in rock to raise money for millions starving in Africa.
    c. The New York Metropolitan Museum of Art plans to **mount** an exhibition of rare Greek temple artifacts later this year.

8. **hazardous:** dangerous, especially to people's health or safety

    a. France is the most **hazardous** overseas tourist destination in the world, receiving more foreign tourists per year than any other country.
    b. Ship breaking, or demolition, is one of the most **hazardous** and dangerous jobs in the world, according to the International Labor Organization.
    c. Basketball is the most **hazardous** sport in the United States, with more than 529,000 estimated injuries in 2006.

9. **weave:** to put many different ideas, subjects, stories, etc., together and connect them smoothly

    a. The popularity of the Harry Potter books comes from J. K. Rowling's ability to effortlessly **weave** new characters and plot twists together.
    b. Many bands **weave** together because of personality clashes between the musicians.
    c. Social networking websites are able to **weave** communities closer together.

10. **bypass:** to avoid obeying a rule, system, or someone in an official position

    a. Heavy job losses are an unfortunate **bypass** of the current economic environment.
    b. The aid workers **bypassed** the official government channels in an attempt to get the food and clothing to those in need as soon as possible.
    c. They have installed new software on our computers, which makes it impossible to **bypass** the company's Internet security settings.

11. **penalty:** a punishment for breaking a law, rule, or legal agreement

   a. More than 60 percent of the world's population lives in countries that still have the death **penalty**.

   b. Mobile broadband users face stiff **penalties** for exceeding their download limits.

   c. The government is offering special tax **penalties** for those wanting to start up their own businesses.

12. **accountability:** the state of being responsible for the effects of your actions and willing to explain or be criticized for them

   a. A frequent criticism of large multinational corporations is that they lack sufficient **accountability**.

   b. There have been several high-profile meetings to improve California's waste management and social **accountability** measures.

   c. Proof of professional **accountability** qualifications and a college degree are the minimum standards required by accounting firms when recruiting new staff.

WORD FAMILIES

A. The table contains word families for some of the target words in the reading. Complete the table. An **X** indicates that there is no form or that the form is not common. Sometimes more than one form may be possible. If you are unsure about a form, check your dictionary.

Verb	Noun	Adjective	Adverb
	accountability		X
delete			X
	disposal	1. 2.	X
		1. 2. dreadful	
X		hazardous	
	invention		
	penalty		X
X	tide		X
	1. warehouse 2.	X	X
weave			X

B. Read the sentences. In eight of the sentences, an incorrect form of the target word has been used. If the form of the target word is incorrect, cross it out and write the correct form. If the form is correct, put a checkmark (✔). Use the word families table to help you.

_____ **1.** Social **accountability** is an important part of many companies' social responsibility measures.

_____ **2.** The news editor insisted on the **delete** of the section discussing Tom Cruise and his height issues.

_____ **3.** Towns and cities must give careful consideration to the **dispose** of items such as batteries, computers, TVs, and cell phones.

_____ **4.** Sue and Nick wrote in their blog that the journey to Lake Titicaca was **dreadful**.

_____ **5.** Laborers working in the gold mines of the Congo face untold **hazardous** in their effort to strike it rich.

_____ **6.** It is widely believed that Leonardo da Vinci **invention** the first submarine and helicopter, but this isn't actually true.

_____ **7.** Governments should make stricter laws that **penalty** companies that make no effort to use greener technology.

_____ **8.** Countries with long shorelines are able to consider **tide** energy as a renewable, green energy source.

_____ **9.** The accountant was concerned about the cost of **warehouse** large stocks of products during the economic downturn.

_____ **10.** James Cameron has a rare ability to **woven** live action and computer generated effects to create extremely successful blockbuster movies.

COLLOCATION

In each set of sentences, the target word is paired with different words to form different collocations. Choose the collocation that best fits the last sentence and write it in the blank. You may need to change the form of one word in the collocation to fit the sentence.

1. a. Poor weather forced the tour group to **curb its activities**.
   b. City traders have **curbed their excesses** in response to the public outcry.
   c. The Federal Reserve has made several recommendations to **curb the growth** in unsecured loans.
   d. My dad has insisted that retirement is in no way going to

   _____ .

2. a. Many investors buy and sell **foreign currency** as a way of making money.
   b. The **local currency** of South Korea is called the won.
   c. A **strong currency** is one that lenders are willing to accept as payment, other than their own.
   d. Some communities in the United States have created their own

   _____ to bring the community together and boost their economies.

3. **a.** Green **computer hardware** is computer equipment that has been built from recycled materials and that uses a fraction of the electricity normal equipment uses.

   b. Helicopters and heavily armored vehicles are the most effective **military hardware** in the current conflict.

   c. Huge out-of-town DIY stores, which sell tools and paint at discount prices, are largely responsible for the dramatic decline in local **hardware stores**.

   d. I ran out of screws while fixing the shelving unit, so I drove down to the _____ to see if they had any.

4. **a.** The athlete hired a new coach once he had decided to **mount a challenge** for the Olympic gold medal.

   b. After the ship ran aground in the storm, the coast guard **mounted a rescue**.

   c. The director was looking for financial backing to **mount a** modern **production** of *Hamlet* during the festival.

   d. The opposition party thought the prime minister's poor health provided them with a good opportunity to _____ to his leadership.

5. **a.** The Far East and Pacific regions received over $600 million in **overseas aid** from the United States in 2008.

   b. More than 670,000 **overseas students** attended an American college or university in 2008.

   c. The 2008, **overseas travel** statistics show that 31 million U.S. citizens traveled abroad.

   d. The largest numbers of _____ currently in the United States are from India and China.

6. **a.** The police are **broadening the scope of** their investigation.

   b. Britney severely **limited the scope of** the biography being written about her.

   c. Teaching ESL to immigrants **falls within the scope of** adult literacy.

   d. The city council hopes to _____ services for young people during the summer vacation.

7. **a.** Jane was overwhelmed by the **sheer luxury** of their five-star, beachfront apartment in Hawaii.

   b. Sue's dad thought her attempt to sail across the Atlantic Ocean was **sheer madness**.

   c. While on safari in Namibia, Sam and Charlie were stunned by the **sheer number** of elephants drinking at the waterhole.

   d. Many industry experts have been taken aback by the _____ of people who now use Amazon's Kindle as their main source of reading material.

8. **a.** It is estimated that 8 percent of persons aged 12 years and over have been involved in some form of illicit **substance abuse** in the past month.

   b. Marion Jones-Thompson, the former world champion track and field athlete, agreed to return her gold medals after she was found to have taken a **banned substance** during the Sydney Olympics in 2000.

   c. Botulinum is the most lethal naturally occurring **toxic substance** known to humankind, and yet it is used as an effective medication.

   d. Sports stars around the world have to be very careful when they catch a cold or flu because some of the most common remedies appear on the international _____ list.

Expanding the Topic

A. Each of the boxes has associations that belong to one of the target words. Match each box of associations to a target word. Then explain the meaning links.

coast	distant	off	rocky	waves

cell	charity	hospital	smoking	treatment

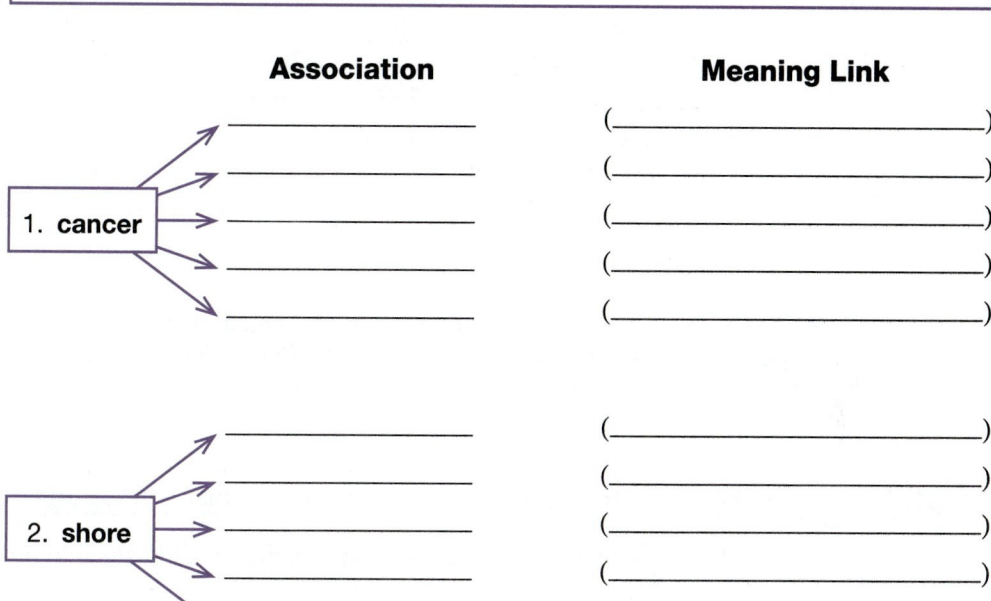

Association   **Meaning Link**

1. **cancer**

2. **shore**

B. Now add your own associations to the target words. Then explain the meaning links.

Association   **Meaning Link**

1. **bypass**

2. **dent**

	Association	Meaning Link

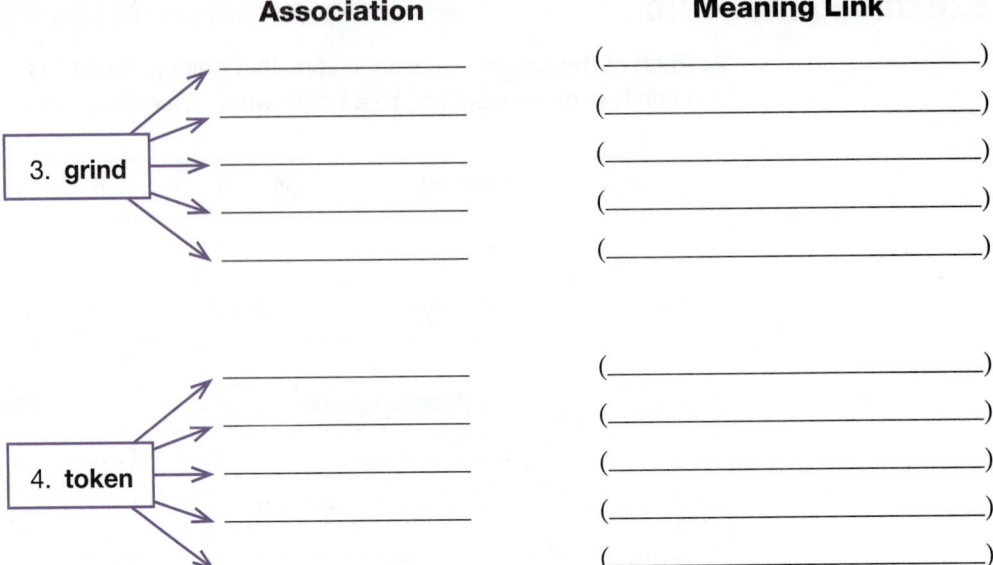

3. grind

4. token

 Read this statement: "The burden of e-waste **disposal** and recycling should be borne by consumers." Do you agree or disagree with the statement? Write a 500-word essay explaining why.

Revisiting the Target Words

Now that you have completed this chapter, use the scale to describe your knowledge of the target words.

1 I still don't know anything about this word.

2 I am still not sure of the meaning of this word even after studying it.

3 I understand this word when I see it or hear it in a sentence, but I don't know how to use it in my own speaking and writing.

4 I know this word and can use it in my own speaking and writing.

> **TARGET WORDS**
>
> | | | | |
> |---|---|---|---|
> | ____accountability | ____dent | ____invention | ____shore |
> | ____bypass | ____disposal | ____mount | ____substance |
> | ____cancer | ____dreadful | ____overseas | ____tide |
> | ____curb | ____grind | ____penalty | ____token |
> | ____currency | ____hardware | ____scope | ____warehouse |
> | ____delete | ____hazardous | ____sheer | ____weave |

KNOWLEDGE CHECK 2

Go back to the beginning of the chapter and complete the Knowledge Check 1 table.

Strategy Practice

Getting Started

Look at the three images taken from Chapters 25–27. Without looking back at the chapters, how many target words can you remember from each chapter?

Learning More about Words: MULTIPLE MEANINGS

You've almost reached the end of this book. As you continue reading and studying, you will come across many of the words studied in this book in a variety of new contexts. However, when you meet a "known" word in a new context, you may be surprised to find that you do not fully know it after all. This is because many words in English have more than one meaning. Verbs like *fix* with fifteen meanings and *beat* with thirty-one meanings are good examples of this.

We have primarily focused on ensuring that you learn the most frequent meaning of each of the words studied. Since you are certain to come across the other meanings of the words in this book, it is important to be aware that the different meanings of a word may have different patterns of use. For example, they may partner with different collocations.

Look at the collocations of ***mounting***, a target word from Chapter 18:

> **Example:**
> **mounting** (gradually increasing)
> mounting numbers   mounting evidence
> mounting criticism   mounting pressure

Compare these with the collocations for ***mount***, a target word from Chapter 27:

> **Example:**
> **mount** (to plan, organize, and begin an event or course of action)
> mount a campaign   mount a rescue
> mount an attack   mount a challenge

Another target word with several collocations is **novel** from Chapter 25:

Example:
novel (not like anything known before, unusual and interesting)
novel idea novel approach
novel method novel way

A. Now find four collocations for **novel** in Chapter 19 and write them in the blanks.

novel (a long written story)

1. _____ novel 3. _____ novel

2. _____ novel 4. _____ novel

Different meanings of a word may also have different word families. For example, the word *grave* can mean "the place in the ground where a dead body is buried" (Chapter 25). The word family for this meaning is as follows:

Verb	Noun	Adjective	Adverb
X	grave	X	X

But *grave* can also be an adjective meaning "very bad or serious." Here is the word family for this meaning:

Verb	Noun	Adjective	Adverb
X	X	grave	X

Another example is *currency*. It can mean "the state of being up-to-date or happening now" and is part of the word family for *current*:

Verb	Noun	Adjective	Adverb
X	currency	current	currently

B. In Chapter 27, you learned that **currency** can also mean "the system or type of money that a country uses." Are there any other word family members for this meaning?

Verb	Noun	Adjective	Adverb
	currency		

SPOKEN VERSUS WRITTEN ENGLISH

Words can have more than one meaning, but of course English also has more than one way to express the same meaning. Which words we choose to express an idea may be different depending on whether we are speaking or writing. Spoken English typically contains words that are more common and colloquial than those found in written English. A good case of this is *phrasal verbs*. Although they are very frequent in spoken discourse, they occur much less frequently in written texts. An example is *discard ↔ throw away*. The table shows the occurrence per million words:

	discard	throw away
written English	15	213
spoken English	13	529

We see that *discard* is used about the same amount in written and spoken English, but that *throw away* is much more common in spoken English than written English.

Match the words from this unit with their phrasal verb synonyms.

_____ 1. mend	a. cross out
_____ 2. bypass	b. fall off
_____ 3. curb	c. get rid of
_____ 4. dispose	d. patch up
_____ 5. decline	e. hold back
_____ 6. delete	f. go around

Focusing on Vocabulary Cards: THE BIG QUIZ

As you have seen throughout this book, word knowledge involves several elements as illustrated in the "word wheel."

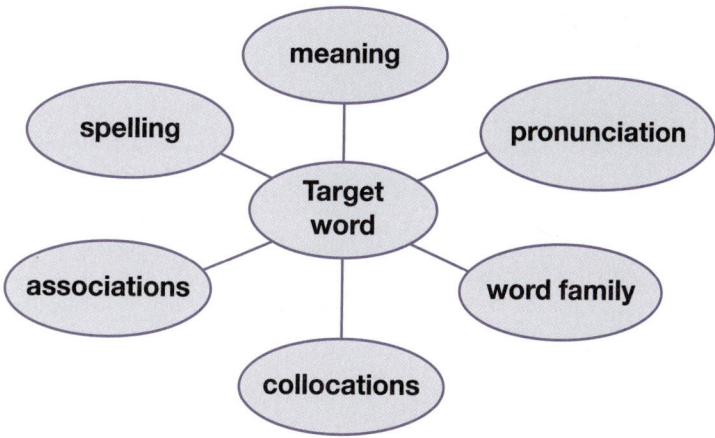

The aim of this quiz is to review your target word knowledge. You will need your entire collection of vocabulary cards. Read the instructions on the next page.

Instructions

1. Form pairs or teams (Team A and Team B).

2. On the classroom whiteboard (or piece of paper) draw a blank word wheel.

3. Team A selects a vocabulary card and reads the target word to Team B.

4. Without using its vocabulary cards, Team B completes the word wheel for the target word by giving examples, definitions, etc. Team B is awarded two points for each correct answer.

5. If Team B is unsure about any of its answers, it can opt to consult its vocabulary cards to find the answer. In this case, only one point can be awarded for correct answers.

6. Once the scores have been noted, Team B chooses a target word for Team A and the process is repeated.

7. The team with the most points at the end of the quiz is the winner.

Index of Target Words

The following is a list of target words and the chapter in which each word is introduced.

peculiar   23
peer   2
penalty   27
perceive   13
perception   6
perfume   14
perk   23
perpetual   22
persist   11
personality   6
philosophy   1
pioneer   21
planet   3
plead   23
poaching   26
poisonous   14
pollution   3
portable   9
portrait   13
portrayal   6
pose   26
possess   5
powder   14
premium   23
presence   5
preserve   3
primary   5
priority   3
privacy   18
privilege   21
professor   10
profile   21
prominent   6
prompt   7
prosperity   3
protest   19
provisional   7
prune   7
publicize   19
pursue   3

Q

questionnaire   18

R

rank   21
rapidly   13
receiver   19
recipe   14
recollect   15
recycle   25
refined   6
reformation   21
refrigerator   9
rehearse   7
relevant   3
relieve   10
remedy   15
reproduce   13
resolve   11
restaurant   1
restore   21
retail   18

review   1
revival   6
revolt   21
reward   13
rhythm   5
rip   18
rose   6
routine   14
ruin   19
rural   3

S

sacrifice   18
salvation   19
scan   9
scandal   17
scope   27
secondhand   25
seep   6
seldom   26
sensitive   18
sequential   15
sergeant   19
serialized   22
sew   25
shadow   14
sheer   27
shelf   10
shore   27
shrink   18
silence   18
silk   17
simultaneous   6
sketch   22
sneak   15
sniff   6
software   9
soil   25
soldier   21
solely   22
sophisticated   19
soup   26
spark   9
species   26
speculate   7
splendid   21
spoil   3
spontaneously   6
squeeze   11
stained   25
stark   22
starvation   5
steak   1
steal   19
sting   11
strict   14
strive   2
stumble   19
substance   27
substitute   23
summon   15
superb   21
superior   13

surgeon   13
surrounding   25
sustainable   25
sweat   13
symbolically   5

T

tablet   9
tackle   3
talent   23
temper   7
tension   2
terrifying   21
textile   25
therapy   1
thorny   19
thrill   1
throat   5
thus   2
tide   27
token   27
tolerate   11
tongue   5
tragic   15
translate   7
trek   9
trend   25
trial   19
trim   7
triple   25
trivial   2
tuck   13
turnover   25

U

uniquely   5
unlike   22
unprecedented   17

V

vastly   3
verbal   5
verify   18
viable   9
vice   3
vicious   26
vigorous   18
virus   19
visibility   23
vital   18

W

wander   15
wardrobe   22
warehouse   27
wax   14
weave   27
wobbly   6
wolf   26
wool   17
worthwhile   2

Z

zone   26